John G. Gunnell

John Gunnell has compelled political theorists to rethink their relation to political science, the history of political thought, the philosophy of social science, and political reality. His thinking has been shaped by encounters with Heidegger and Plato, Wittgenstein and Austin, the Berkeley School and émigrés such as Strauss and Arendt. His writings have challenged the idealist assumptions behind the idea of a Great Tradition of Political Thought and the philosophical claims about mind and language. Gunnell has engaged and challenged colleagues in political theory, political science, and the philosophy of social science on a range of issues from political action, time, pluralism, ideology, concepts, conventions, "the political," and democracy to the roles of philosophy, science, literary theory, cognitive science, mind, and history on the enterprise of theorizing today.

The book focuses on his work in three key areas:

- Political theory and political science: Gunnell's work has often focused on the historical emergence of the study of political theory as a subdiscipline of political science, and its critical relation to and alienation from political science from the postwar era. His argument has been consistent: political theory self-identified as an interpretative social science and mode of historical reflection is an invention of political science. Political theory divorced from political science weakens both activities in their ties to, concerns with and relevance to political society and the contemporary university.
- Interpretation and action: Gunnell has been particularly interested in the nature of concepts and how they change. These investigations begin with analysis of theory and theorizing as they are constituted and practiced in historiography, the philosophy of social sciences, the philosophy of science, political science, and metatheory. He engages with thinkers whose positions inform and oppose his own and explores concepts such as: democracy, justice, time, pluralism, science, liberalism, and action.
- Theorists, philosophers, and political life: Gunnell's work has developed through a series of encounters with theorists and philosophers. He has rejected attempts to present politics as a stable and essential set of phenomena. There are common themes that guide conversations with the German émigrés, ordinary language philosophers, and theorists from the history of political thought. This book includes works that focus on Max Weber, Leo Strauss, and Eric Voegelin, Gilbert Ryle, J.L. Austin, and Ludwig Wittgenstein.

Christopher C. Robinson is an Associate Professor of Political Science at Clarkson University in Potsdam, New York. He has published in the fields of contemporary political theory, the philosophy of language, and environmental political thought.

Routledge Innovators in Political Theory

Edited by Terrell Carver, University of Bristol and
Samuel A. Chambers, Johns Hopkins University

Routledge Innovators in Political Theory focuses on leading contemporary thinkers in political theory, highlighting the major innovations in their thought that have reshaped the field. Each volume collects both published and unpublished texts, and combines them with an interview with the thinker. The editorial introduction articulates the innovator's key contributions in relation to political theory, and contextualises the writer's work. Volumes in the series will be required reading for both students and scholars of 21st century politics.

For more info please visit: www.routledge.com/series/RIPT
Recent series titles include:

4. Chantal Mouffe
Hegemony, radical democracy, and the political
Edited by James Martin

5. Ernesto Laclau
Post-Marxism, populism, and critique
Edited by David Howarth

6. George Kateb
Dignity, morality, individuality
Edited by John Seery

7. Hanna Fenichel Pitkin
Politics, justice, action
Edited by Dean Mathiowetz

8. Richard E. Flathman
Situated concepts, virtuosity liberalism and opalescent individuality
Edited by P. E Digeser

9. John G. Gunnell
History, discourses and disciplines
Edited by Christopher C. Robinson

John G. Gunnell
History, discourses and disciplines

Edited by
Christopher C. Robinson

Routledge
Taylor & Francis Group
LONDON AND NEW YORK

First published 2017
by Routledge
2 Park Square, Milton Park, Abingdon, Oxon OX14 4RN

and by Routledge
605 Third Avenue, New York, NY 10017

First issued in paperback 2021

Routledge is an imprint of the Taylor & Francis Group, an informa business

Publisher's Note
The publisher has gone to great lengths to ensure the quality of this reprint but
points out that some imperfections in the original copies may be apparent.

British Library Cataloguing in Publication Data
A catalogue record for this book is available from the British Library

Library of Congress Cataloging in Publication Data
A catalog record for this book has been requested

ISBN 13: 978-1-03-209751-0 (pbk)
ISBN 13: 978-1-138-91072-0 (hbk)

Typeset in Times New Roman
by Taylor & Francis Books

For Dede and Sunhee

Contents

Table

Acknowledgements

We are grateful to the following publishers and journals for permission to reprint the chapters in this collection:

Cambridge University Press for Chapter 1 "Deduction, Explanation, and Social Scientific Inquiry," *American Political Science Review*, 63, 4, pp. 1233–1246, 1969. Chapter 3 "American Political Science, Liberalism, and the Invention of Political Theory," *American Political Science Review*, 82, 1, pp. 199–220, 1988. Chapter 5 "Interpretation and the History of Political Theory: Apology and Epistemology," *American Political Science Review*, 76, 2, pp. 317–327, 1982.

The University of Massachusetts Press for Chapter 2 "The Alienation of Political Theory" in *Between Philosophy and Politics: The Alienation of Political Theory* (Amherst), 1986, pp. 10–42.

Sage Publications for Chapter 4 "Political Theory and the Theory of Action," *Political Research Quarterly (formerly Western Political Quarterly)*, 34, 3, pp. 341–358, 1981. Chapter 9 "Reading Max Weber: Leo Strauss and Eric Voegelin," *European Journal of Political Theory*, 3, 2, pp. 151–166, 2004.

Palgrave Macmillan for Chapter 6 "Interpretation and the Autonomy of Concepts" in *Political Theory and Social Science: Cutting Against the Grain* (New York), 2011, pp. 9–31. Chapter 7 "Why There Cannot Be a Theory of Politics," *Polity*, 29, 4, pp. 519–537, 1997. Chapter 10 "Leaving Everything as It Is: Political Inquiry After Wittgenstein," *Contemporary Political Theory*, 12, 2, pp. 80–101, 2013.

Rowman and Littlefield for Chapter 8 "Speaking Politically" in *The Orders of Discourse: Philosophy, Social Science, and Politics* (Lanham, MD), 1998, pp. 195–221.

Every effort has been made to contact copyright holders for their permission to reprint material in this book. The publishers would be grateful to hear from any copyright holder who is not here acknowledged and will undertake to rectify any errors or omissions in future editions of this book.

Introduction

Because of the critical nature of his work on the discipline of political theory, John Gunnell's influence on political theorists is difficult to describe, much less measure. A number of political theorists trained in the 1970s have mentioned that his scholarship was an influence on their writing and their very reason for pursuing a career in political theory. The work they often hold up for special praise is *Political Philosophy and Time* (1968), his first book. This was based on his doctoral dissertation and represents what must be described as his most romantic work. Ghita Ionescu, for example, regarded Gunnell's study of Plato and the emergence of a new temporal order wherein humans, for the first time, questioned their relation to the larger cosmic order, as a work that signaled – along with works by Brian Barry and John Rawls – a new maturity in political thought.[1] This is typical of the praise for that study.

But Gunnell's reputation in political theory is not as a Plato scholar, though he is one. Rather, his reputation is based largely on his writings in political and social inquiry, historiography, the genealogy of theory generally and political theory in particular, and the philosophy of science and social science. These studies form the basis of larger claims by Gunnell pertaining to the relations of political theory to political science and the relation of these modes of inquiry to political reality. His writings engage critically the work of his contemporaries in order to examine the status of various elitist claims to special insight, epistemic authority, and privileged knowledge and to expose any category errors such as those that take the form of mistaking a second-order mode of inquiry, like political science, for a first-order mode, like natural science, or those that manifest the mistaken belief that one is talking about politics when really talking about a philosophical or social scientific model of political reality.[2]

There are many theorists working today who admire Gunnell's deep and thoughtful studies of various philosophical and historical traditions, but there is also a fair share of detractors.[3] John Gunnell does not belong to any school of thought within contemporary political theory. He tends to position himself as an anthropologist and historian of the field. The critical tenor of his writings resists the formation of any school around his work. In this respect, his writings about political theory tend to perform the same role as those that his favorite philosopher, Ludwig Wittgenstein, played in philosophy (or that Thomas Kuhn played in the philosophy of science or Peter Winch played in the philosophy of social science). The purpose was to break up any icy formations of dogmatism in the discourse and return theorizing to the rough ground of the study of political and social life.

One focus of inquiry and critical engagement has been with the "Berkeley School" of political theory, associated most closely with Sheldon Wolin and John Schaar, and with concepts of "vocation," "the Great Tradition of Political Thought," and "the political." This engagement has an autobiographical dimension. Gunnell attended Berkeley where he received his MA and doctorate after his undergraduate education at Tufts University and a stint in the Navy. While in graduate school, Gunnell had an opportunity to work for a year in Sacramento as a Ford Foundation intern with the California Assembly, where he was given the amazing responsibility (for anyone, but especially a political theorist) to work on a revision of the state constitution. He managed to shorten the document by almost half. After Berkeley, Gunnell became an Assistant Professor at the State University of New York at Albany, and rose through the ranks to achieve a Distinguished Professorship. After retiring from teaching, Gunnell has continued his research and writing on the philosophy of Wittgenstein and a range of issues in the philosophy of social science.

Political theory and political science

The first piece included here, "Deduction, Explanation, and Social Scientific Inquiry," was published in 1969 in the same volume of the *American Political Science Review* as David Easton's "The New Revolution in Political Science" and Wolin's "Political Theory as a Vocation." I would argue that Gunnell's article was the most controversial of the three, and it would appear that the journal editors at the time saw it similarly. Indeed, they agreed to publish this study of the (unreflective and distorted) use of philosophy of science in political theory and political science only if it was accompanied by three opposing responses. What was so radical and challenging about the argument that it required formal responses? The thesis contended that political scientists, in their search for scientific identity and intellectual authority, had blinded themselves to a number of relevant developments in the philosophy of science and philosophy of social science. But, at the same time, and paradoxically, "certain doctrines originating in the philosophy of science" had been "uncritically insinuated into … social science as informing categoricals." This had encouraged the assumption that an account of scientific investigation propounded not by scientists but by philosophers of science "is an appropriate model for understanding and prescribing the role of the social scientist." Thus, first of all, if political scientists want to be like natural scientists, then, contends Gunnell, they have gone to the wrong place for this self-image.

Second, formulations such as the deductive model of the logic of social scientific inquiry borrowed from the philosophy of science distort the nature of social scientific inquiry. Further, this borrowing itself undermines any effort to establish political and social inquiry as autonomous modes of investigation. The study and criticism of unreflective borrowing, by both political theorists and political scientists, from various fields of philosophy, as well as of misunderstandings about the relationship between the practice of political inquiry and meta-theoretical and para-philosophical claims about inquiry, would become a central area of intellectual endeavor for Gunnell. This work culminated in his *The Orders of Discourse* (1998) and *Political Theory and Social Science* (2011).

Tensions between political theory and mainstream political science led many political theorists to explore intellectual and disciplinary terrain outside of political science departments.[4] For Gunnell, the correct response to the increasing distance between political theory from its original disciplinary home was (and is) to continually insert theory as a critical voice into political science, and he believed this was for the good of both activities. No other theorist in the behavioral and postbehavioral eras has published more in mainstream political science journals.[5] His account of the inextricably linked histories of political theory and political science, along with origins of estrangement between the two in the period from 1940 to 1950, is included here. Studies in the emergence of political theory as an increasingly estranged sub-discipline of political science led to *The Descent of Political Theory* (1993).

"The Alienation of Political Theory" is the first chapter of *Between Philosophy and Politics* (1986). This analysis is a comprehensive articulation of an argument Gunnell began in 1968,[6] and it synthesized a range of arguments pertaining to the idea of the tradition, the nature of science, and the epistemological grounds of political judgment, which he had been rehearsing and honing over two decades. It focuses on political theory's attempt to ground a new identity in a variety of arguments derived from philosophy, or often from secondary and tertiary images of philosophy. This study is largely a historical analysis of the evolving distinction between political science and political theory. He claimed that as political theorists turned to philosophy for a vocabulary to distinguish what they did from the work of behavioralists in political science, they became entangled in decontextualized meta-theoretical conversations, which did not allow theory "to come to grips with its actual relationship to politics."

"American Political Science, Liberalism, and the Invention of Political Theory," is an article best viewed as a study of how and why émigré thinkers – such as Leo Strauss, Hannah Arendt, Hans Morgenthau, Arnold Brecht, members of the Frankfurt School – challenged both the scientism that had developed in American political science and the image of the history of political theory that characterized the work of individuals such as William Dunning, Charles Merriam, and George Sabine. These German thinkers, whose intellectual and political background was rooted in the Weimar Republic, questioned the resilience of liberalism in the face of totalitarianism, criticized the scientific ethic, and offered various versions of the tradition of western political thought as story of decline, in contrast to the image of progress that had previously dominated the field. In the end, they succeeded in forging a new identity for political theory as a practice that was not only separate from American political science but in opposition to it. This is the historical backdrop for an accurate understanding of the rise of behavioralism, which was less a revolution than a counter-revolution and response to this emerging vision of political theory.

Much of the Gunnell corpus has been taken up with conceptual and historical issues involved in the relationship between political theory and political science. But there is an array of other work focused on individuals such as Strauss, Kuhn, Winch, and Wittgenstein as well as on issues such as pluralism, the role of the intellectual in relation to political life, historiography, ordinary language philosophy, and the theory of action, which need to be confronted in an analysis of Gunnell's thought. Taken together, they compose a thick, detailed description of the philosophical traditions and figures that were representative of the post-behavioral era. Gunnell has claimed, however, that this period was marked by an evasion of politics and a lack of serious consideration of the nature of political phenomena. His attention to these issues should not be considered a recent development in his work or as something of passing concern. It was an incipient feature of his early work in the philosophy of science, and it has been even more pronounced in recent years.

Interpretation and action

The theory of action, developed in chapter four of this volume, is a rich and pervasive dimension of Gunnell's theoretical work, and it illuminates his move toward conceiving social inquiry as a comprehensive set of second- and occasionally third-order practices and discourses such as political theory. The central insight that inaugurates this undertaking of theorizing social action is that anti-positivistic "interpretative" or "phenomenological" approaches to social inquiry had not, any more than behavioral political science, really advanced a substantive detailed theoretical account of human action. They had instead adopted epistemological images as modes of inquiry and as the basis of claims about the symmetry or asymmetry between social and natural science. In effect, social scientific problems had been exchanged for philosophizations of the character of social scientific problems. Theory as a claim about the nature and content of social reality was displaced by a view of theory, similar to the positivist account of theory, as a framework for explaining facts. Political theorists began to talk about inquiry as scientific or interpretive, positivist or anti-positivist, quantitative or qualitative, and so on. The theory of action, however, was, for Gunnell, a general account of social phenomena, whether these phenomena were instantiated in the form of politics or other particular social practices. The lack of such a theory was a dimension of what Gunnell saw as the distance between politics and political inquiry throughout the 1970s and 1980s. That is, for Gunnell, the theory of action was conceived as a way to break from "the metatheoretical search for a solution to metatheoretically generated issues," issues that originated in academic philosophy and turned political theory into an epistemological enterprise. His purpose was to show what a turn to "substantive theoretical issues" looks like, even if someone did not agree with his particular theory or some element of it. Gunnell criticized the positivist/empiricist view of theory as "models" for organizing and describing facts and instead urged a view of theories as incommensurable fact-creating and incommensurable claims about the nature and behavior of social reality.[7]

The theory of action made explicit the linguistic vein in Gunnell's thought, and so it is not surprising that the concept of speech-acts is central to this work and that, over time, this concern with action, which avoided dichotomies such as agency and structure, evolved into a more general focus on what he referred to as "conventional objects." It was in part disagreements with philosophers like Donald Davidson and John Searle that prompted Gunnell to emphasize the idea of conventionality in order to circumvent the problem of choosing between social ontologies based on either the individual or collective nature of action. The conventionality of social reality was also a firm challenge to various other ontologizations, such as the Arendtian conception of "the social" and "the political," which were reified abstractions from political or social life. These conceptions may have rhetorical force when politics is defended against those who would subjugate it, say, to economics. However, what is lost in the process is the conventional, and thus malleable or even ephemeral nature of politics as a particular historical and cultural form of social phenomenon.[8] For Gunnell, the response to political theory's alienated condition was not only to imply the possibility of an unalienated way of theorizing politics, but also to deconstruct the "myths" that gave rise to and continued to perpetuate the estrangement. These included the myth of a tradition of political thought – as an ongoing conversation – from Plato to Marx; the myth that social inquiry involves a choice between competing epistemologies, which leads to a failure to recognize that, in both natural science and social science, epistemologies as well as methods are grounded in and entailed by theories; the myth that epistemology reveals the logic of thought and lends the possessor of this logic the authority to judge what counts as knowledge among the faculties of the university, including science, and for political actors as well; and the myth of "the political" as something essential and universal, even if viewed as in danger of existential erasure, and the accompanying belief that there can be a theory of politics any more than of any other particular conventional social construction.[9]

Criticizing the myth of the tradition required a detailed examination of the philosophical presuppositions in the historical approaches of, on the one hand, Merriam, Sabine, and others who saw the history of political thought as a triumphal narrative showing the progress of political science and democracy, and, on the other hand, the work of those such as Easton, Strauss, Wolin, and Arendt who saw the tradition in terms of a declination of political theory. But it also required a critical analysis of the "new historians" associated with the Cambridge School, including J.G.A. Pocock, Quentin Skinner, and John Dunn.[10] Gunnell's analysis of what he referred to as the myth of the tradition contained some of the same kinds of criticisms the Cambridge historians had directed toward past research in the field, such as the imposition of normative philosophical claims in constructing a holistic image of the history of political theory. Gunnell, however, was not sanguine about what they claimed was their truly "historical method" or even their claim to have relinquished the idea of the "great tradition." "Interpretation and the History of Political Theory: Apology and Epistemology" is a focused encounter with the epistemological claims advanced by the new historians. Subsequent exchanges between Gunnell, Pocock, and Skinner were, however, productive enough to reveal some of the common ground that they shared.

How we go about reading a text, or theorizing politics, involves concepts and, more specifically, issues such as the relationship between concepts and words and between different kinds of concepts. "Interpretation and the Autonomy of Concepts" is a continuation and refinement of a previous extended discussion in *The Orders of Discourse*. It critically evaluates the work of Hanna Pitkin and W.B. Gallie as well as approaches to conceptual history in the work of Reinhart Koselleck, Melvin Richter, and Skinner. This is a rich and intricate argument that eschews claims about any cognitive foundation of concepts and instead stresses their grammatical character and the parallel autonomy of language and world. Gunnell examines three kinds of concepts – theoretical, modal, and analytical – and observes that insensitivity to, and conflations of, these types leads to ontologizations of politics and claims about the cognitive basis of interpretation and understanding. This argument is developed further in Gunnell's latest book, *Social Inquiry after Wittgenstein and Kuhn* (2014).

Theorists, philosophers, and political life

The final section of the volume is composed of articles that will give the reader a sense of what unalienated political theory might look like, while also emphasizing two main thrusts in Gunnell's research: a further turn toward Wittgenstein that entailed a close reading, from the perspective social inquiry, of the *Tractatus Logico-Philosophicus*, *The Blue and Brown Books*, and the *Philosophical Investigations*, as well as a pronounced turn away from the idea of political theory as a special kind of intellectual activity and toward a broader category of second-order social scientific activities, which Gunnell generalizes as "social inquiry." The final essay in this volume, "Leaving Everything as It Is: Political Inquiry after Wittgenstein," maps out this move from political theory and toward an image of social inquiry that is manifest in the philosophical work of Wittgenstein.

"Why There Cannot Be a Theory of Politics" involves the transformation of the theory of action into a more generalized claim about the conventional nature of social reality. Gunnell writes that "Politics is a historical form of convention" that is part of a larger landscape of human practices and conventional objects. Theories are claims about the nature of reality, and, for Gunnell, social reality is irreducibly conventional. "We can theorize about conventions but not about their particular manifestations, just as we can have theories of atomic structure but not of particular chunks of matter." With conventions we have hit rock bottom. There is nothing unitary or essential beneath, and attempts to say something essential about politics is often simply an attempt to evade the phantom of relativism and to seek a claim to epistemic authority, a transcendental epic vantage outside of politics, at the price of distracting attention from the actual life of politics. Gunnell has had a great deal to say about the fear of relativism (e.g. *The Orders of Discourse* and *Political Theory and Social Science*), which he sees as a distinctly meta-practical anxiety, which practices such as philosophy and social inquiry tend to displace onto their subject matter.

The central issue in "Speaking Politically," the concluding chapter of *The Orders of Discourse*, is how we should go about addressing the relationship of theory to practice and the structural constraints that keep a political scientist or a theorist from playing an authoritative role in politics. The argument here pertains to the difference between first and second-order practices. Political theory is a second-order practice – a meta-practice that speaks about political practices. It is typically a denizen of the university. When Jeffrey Isaac wondered aloud about the "strange silence of political theory" in the wake of the events of 1989,[11] Gunnell responded suggesting that what would have been truly strange is if theorists had been able to say something predictive or explanatory about the collapse of the Berlin Wall and the Soviet empire. When literary theorists and political scientists conceive of themselves as "connected critics" or "organic intellectuals," they often miss the significant difference between knowing about something and knowing how to do something. If theorists and social scientists did know something about democratization and wanted to achieve it, then their home turf, the university campus, should be an embodiment of that knowledge. The fact that the university has often been overtaken by anti-democratic corporatization speaks volumes about the "authority" of meta-practitioners and their capacity for participating in the practices they study.

The problem of theory's relation to practice and the very idea of epistemological solutions to practical problems that arose in the context of the Weimar conversation, animates "Reading Max Weber: Leo Strauss and Eric Voegelin." Gunnell's scholarship on the works of émigré political theorists is substantial and goes back to his encounter with Voegelin's work in *Political Philosophy and Time*. Gunnell examines the criticisms of Weber's dichotomization of the vocations of science and politics by Strauss and Voegelin. These criticisms are important, because Strauss and Voegelin were close enough to the historical context that Weber was addressing to grasp the political need to insulate science from ideologues posing as scientists. The arguments of Strauss and Voegelin, however, were instead directed at what they saw as the philosophical weakness of the protections offered by Weber.

The final essay in the volume is "Leaving Everything as It Is: Political Inquiry after Wittgenstein." This essay opens with a consideration of the limitations of what has been, for decades, the most comprehensive treatment of the philosophy of Wittgenstein by a political theorist, Hanna Pitkin's *Wittgenstein and Justice* (1972). Gunnell observes that Pitkin did not really address Wittgenstein's use of the term "justice," which usually involved matters of interpretation and was something of an ethical reflection on what we, philosophers and social scientists, owe to our subject matter, which is fairness and generosity. Pitkin, instead, deployed Wittgenstein's remarks on language and meaning to provide theorists with some new tools for conceptual analysis. This was very much in the spirit of philosophical and methodological eclecticism that suffused the post-behavioral era in political theory and political science. Gunnell, by contrast, sees in Wittgenstein's remarks on justice a way out of self-absorbed third-order reflection on the identities of theory and empirical social science and toward scrutiny of their *"practical* and *cognitive* relationship to their subject matter."

This reflection brings us back to the issue of theory and practice at the center of Strauss's and Voegelin's reading of Weber. The problem is one endemic to epistemic or cognitive authority as the impetus for the emergence of second-order practices from their subject matter; Strauss and Voegelin, like critics of Wittgenstein from the right as well as those like Herbert Marcuse from the left, feared the loss of universal standards of thought and judgment and were wary of any acknowledgement of the conventional basis of both critical reflection on social practices and the practices themselves. They worried that relativism would unleash instability in philosophy, culture, and society. Of course particular claims to universality would inevitably be undermined, and we who are engaged in second-order inquiries are left not with regulative ideals, but with an ethical regard for our subject, which was described by Wittgenstein in terms of interpretive justice achieved through perspicuous representation. This work of description does not prevent us from making judgments about events and objects constitutive of social reality. It only deprives us of the false senses of certainty and authority that attend judgments bolstered by epistemic claims to transcendent or transcendental truths. This Wittgensteinian position on how we tend to forget that meta-practices originate from self-reflection within the first-order practices that they are designed to study, and on how we need to "return to the rough ground" of social conventions and away from delusions of epistemological privilege, really captures the unifying theme of John Gunnell's work. It is an unfailingly democratic stance but not in the sense that it evinces an argument about the way the political world should be organized. Rather, it is democratic because it opposes elitist claims to privileged knowledge and grounds for judgment predicated on foundational assertions about the nature of reality and truth, including recent cognitive arguments about human nature. Gunnell does not impose a barrier on academic voices weighing in on political issues, but instead urges the kind of critical reflection that, on the one hand, steers away from specious claims to intellectual authority, such as those of moralism and scientism, and, on the other hand, guards against the failure to distinguish politics from philosophical constructions of politics.

Notes

1 Ghita Ionescu, "What Is Political Thought Thinking of Now? Reading Notes 1964–1980", *Government and Opposition* 15 (1980): 405–426.
2 See the various responses to Gunnell's work in John S. Nelson, ed., *Tradition, Interpretation and Science: Political Theory in the American Academy* (Albany: State University of New York Press, 1986).
3 See, for example, Sheldon Wolin's response to Gunnell's *Political Theory: Tradition and Interpretation*, wherein Wolin accuses Gunnell of apostasy against the vocation of political theory; Sheldon S. Wolin, "History and Theory: Methodism *Recidivivus*," in Nelson, *Tradition, Interpretation and Science*, pp. 43–68.
4 See, for example, George Kateb, "The Condition of Political Theory," *American Behavioral Scientist* 21 (Sept./Oct., 1977): 135–159.
5 Between 1969 and 2006 Gunnell published six articles in the *American Political Science Review.*
6 John G. Gunnell, "Social Science and Political Reality: The Problem of Explanation," *Social Research* 35 (Spring, 1968): 159–201.
7 John G. Gunnell, *Philosophy, Science, and Political Inquiry* (Morristown, NJ: General Learning Press, 1975), Ch. 6.
8 See John G. Gunnell, *Between Philosophy and Politics: The Alienation of Political Theory* (Amherst, MA: University of Massachusetts Press, 1986), Ch. 6; and *The Orders of Discourse: Philosophy, Social Science and Politics* (New York: Rowman & Littlefield, 1998), Ch. 2.
9 John G. Gunnell, *Between Philosophy and Politics*, p. 1.
10 John G. Gunnell, *Political Theory: Tradition and Interpretation* (Cambridge, MA: Winthrop Publishers, 1979).
11 Jeffrey Isaac, "The Strange Silence of Political Theory," *Political Theory* 23.4 (November 1995): 636–688.

Part I
Political theory and political science

1   Deduction, explanation, and social scientific inquiry (1969)

I. Introduction

The purpose here is to explore certain aspects of the philosophy of science which have serious implications both for the practice of social and political science and for understanding that practice. The current relationship between social science and the philosophy of science (or the philosophy of the social sciences) is a curious one. Despite the emergence of a considerable body of literature in philosophy which is pertinent to the methodological problems of social science, there has been a lack of ostensive ties between the two areas. A justified concern with the independence of social scientific research has contributed to a tendency toward isolation which is unfortunate in view of the proliferation of philosophical problems which necessarily attends the rapid expansion of any empirical discipline. Although in the literature of contemporary social science there are frequent references to certain works in the philosophy of science and to philosophical issues relating to methodology, these are most often in the context of bald pronouncements and shibboleths relating to the nature of science, its goals, and the character of its reasoning. But what is most disturbing about the fact that social scientists have little direct and thorough acquaintance with the philosophy of science is not merely that there has been a failure to carefully examine the many logical and epistemological assumptions which are implicit in social scientific inquiry, since this task might normally and properly be considered to be within the province of the philosopher of science. It is more significant that this unfamiliarity has, paradoxically, obscured the extent to which certain doctrines originating in the philosophy of science have been uncritically insinuated into the enterprise of social science as informing categoricals.

Much of the theoretical literature in political and social science, as well as attempts to explicate the epistemic features of social scientific investigation, rest on a belief that the activity of the natural scientist is an appropriate model for understanding and prescribing the role of the social scientist. Although it may be granted that social and natural science must be distinguished in terms of such characteristics as technique and subject matter, this is often understood as explaining certain inherent or temporary limitations of social science. Generally it has been assumed that with regard to the logic of explanation, social science must be fundamentally symmetrical with natural science if it is to count as science. Although there are a number of common features that would support the idea of symmetry, such as a mutual empirical orientation and concern for systematic explanation and description, and although philosophy, science, and everyday life may be analytically as well as existentially differentiated as modes of thought and activity, this view is misconceived to the extent that it tends to postulate a hierarchy of epistemological structures with impermeable boundaries and fails to take account of some of the more generic aspects of explanation. As a consequence of this misconception, social scientists have been reluctant to move beyond the realm of natural science when seeking a model of inquiry even when the requirements of explanation in the two spheres seem hopelessly disparate. The result has been principally either an imperious attempt at assimilation or an assignment of social science to some inferior position within the general class of activities understood as science. Both positions are seriously defective, and a more adequate formulation is possible only by breaking down some of the alleged constraints which are assumed to be endemic to scientific inquiry.

A conception of social scientific explanation can be elaborated which will not only support the case for logical asymmetry between the natural and social sciences and at the same time preserve the characteristics essential to any mode of empirical inquiry but will better illuminate what most social scientists in fact do in producing explanations as well as what sort of explanations are required by the character of the phenomena with which they are concerned.[1] But the problem of supporting the contention that natural science is inadequate as a paradigm governing the conception of methodology in the social sciences is complicated by the fact that what is often construed by social scientists as natural science is actually an ideal typification of the logic of science which is the invention of certain philosophers of science. This philosophical reconstruction has been accepted in one form or another by many social scientists, especially those concerned with the problems of theory construction, as an adequate representation of the character of all scientific explanation and as a prescriptive norm for inquiry. What the social scientist accepts as his model is, then, itself a model and one that, although popularly received for many years, has recently been severely criticized within the philosophy of science itself not only as a reconstruction of the logic of scientific explanation in general but even natural science in particular.

A thorough critical analysis of this model, the so-called deductive model, is a necessary prologue to any further evaluation of the thesis of logical symmetry between explanation in the natural and social sciences as well as an explication of the substantive character of social scientific explanation, and such an analysis is the principal, although limited, concern of this chapter. Consideration of the deductive model also provides a vehicle for examining certain more general problems about explanation and the relationship between social science and the philosophy of science. Since social scientists, and especially political scientists, have been influenced, either directly or indirectly, by the deductive model and other aspects of the philosophy of logical empiricism from which it emanates, there is not only the obvious question whether social scientists have correctly understood this construct and this school of thought but the question of the validity of logical empiricism, even if correctly understood, as an approach to the philosophy of science (and social science). Finally, and possibly most important, there is the problem of the extent to which the philosophy of science may be understood as an enterprise charged with establishing a theory of science which can serve as an authoritative guide for substantive empirical inquiry and a norm for the evaluation of particular explanations.

II. The deductive model

The persistent, pervasive, and yet largely unexamined assumptions that the logic of any enterprise claiming the title of science must be symmetrical with that of natural science and that there is universality in the logic of empirical inquiry, as well as the conception of the logic of explanation in natural science accepted by most social scientists, have for the most part been derived either explicitly or implicitly from certain formulations in the philosophy of science. In seeking to emulate natural science, "the model taken for imitation has been the artifact of the philosopher of science rather than the actual practice of scientists."[2] This formulation, the deductive model, has become the basis of the modern "textbook" view of science. Although in many instances it is difficult to judge whether social scientists have drawn their model of inquiry directly from the philosophy of science or whether they have merely unreflectively accepted some popular version of that model, the latter hypothesis seems more tenable in view of the numerous and basically unexplicated statements in the literature of social science to the effect that "the task of science is the reasoned interpretation of experience through the discovery of valid generalizations and the application of such generalizations to particular events."[3] The precise meaning of such assertions is seldom unpacked; they are inserted as ritualistic formulae. But whether the conception of natural science which is entertained is once or twice removed from that activity, it is clear that social scientists have rarely attempted either to defend in any rigorous manner the idea that there must be symmetry in the logic of inquiry or to systematically support the notion of the exemplary character of natural science. Yet, more specifically, there has been a failure both to justify the deductive model as a proper reconstruction of the logic of natural science and to demonstrate its applicability to empirical science as a whole, including social science.

The argument to be advanced here is that the deductive model is deficient in most relevant respects. It presents an incorrect, or at least otiose, reconstruction of the logic of natural science, and there has been no adequate demonstration that it is applicable either as a norm for social scientific inquiry or as an explication of social scientific explanation. But unfortunately this argument can be set against social scientists only indirectly, since they themselves have not developed a defense of the deductive model. The battle must be joined on the ground of the philosophy of science, and this would be entirely the proper ground for such a discussion if the question were merely one of developing a general structural description of social scientific explanation, that is, if it were not for the extraordinary fact that much of theory construction in the social sciences takes the philosophers' deductive model as a standard, however poorly approximated and understood. This assertion may invite the charge of setting up a straw man since the defense of the deductive model in principle as well as its applicability to social scientific explanation has been conducted essentially by philosophers of science while there is little in the way of explicit advocacy by social scientists.[4] But although a separate treatment would be required to thoroughly support the intellectual history of the influence of the deductive model and logical empiricism on social science, it is assumed that this influence is not a matter of serious dispute and that it can be readily recognized in a variety of works dealing with methodological problems of social and political science as well as popular treatises on theory construction and specific empirical studies.

Some of the most prestigious theoretical literature in political science contains numerous phrases such as "scientific method," "scientific enterprise," "scientific credo," "the rigorous logic and rules of science," "scientific reasoning," and "scientific rules of procedure," but little concrete elaboration is presented. Despite professions of faith in the unity of science and an enumeration of attributes often associated with natural science such as "systematization," "quantification," and the search for "regularities," there is a singular absence of argument which would support the assumption of the logical equivalence of social and natural science, and there are few explicit references to either the philosophy of science or the actual practice of natural scientists which would give tangible meaning to these vague assertions about the defining characteristics of scientific activity.[5] When David Easton, in *The Political System*, challenged political science to become truly scientific, it was far from clear what he meant in substantive terms. Notwithstanding the plea for the development of an empirically grounded "causal theory," which in his view was the only indication of "the attainment of reliable knowledge," and despite his later pronouncements about the "gargantuan strides" which have been taken during the intervening period toward the goal of a social science that would compare favorably with the natural sciences, the meaning of "science" in the sense of a logic of inquiry has remained nebulous.[6] Neither in 1953 nor in the 1960s has Easton either defended the accuracy of his conception of natural science or detailed the philosophical view on which this conception is based. Yet it was assumed that the character of this anticipated theory would be "deductive" and that although a theoretic framework which "might reach the stage of maturity associated with theory in physics" where "from a few basic premises, empirically derived, it has proved possible to formulate deductively a whole body of intermediate theory and from this in turn, to predict the occurrence of empirical events," might be a long way off, such a "theoretical system" was to be the goal and standard of inquiry in political science.[7]

For political scientists, the meaning of "science" is seldom interpreted beyond such formal, and essentially empty, equations of explanation and "generalization" and statements to the effect that explanation can be understood as "simply the subsuming of a particular event or class of events ... under a more general law or hypothesis," or "deriving it from some more general proposition that describes a regular sequence which we believe to hold true in the world of politics."[8] It is from the philosophy of science, and from a rather well-defined group of scholars within that discipline, that political and social scientists have ultimately derived their views about explanation and the requirements of scientific logic. The works of such philosophers as Carl Hempel and Ernest Nagel[9] have become philosophical primers for social scientists and are continually cited as presumably unimpeachable authority to support statements about the purpose and function of science, the symmetry of natural and social science, and the logic of scientific explanation. The indefeasibility of this philosophical perspective and the incorrigibility of its representation of science is taken for granted, and it is assumed that from this body of literature can be extracted the fundamental principles which must govern and give direction to empirical inquiry in political science.[10]

As Eugene Meehan has recently noted, the deductive model has become "an albatross around the neck of the social scientist"[11] in the sense that it provides a set of demands which are not only impossible to realize but often irrelevant to the requirements of explanation in social science. But the answer to the problem is not to substitute a "systems paradigm" for the deductive model as Meehan has suggested; these constructs are not logically comparable. Before embarking on any extended criticism of the deductive model, it is necessary to precisely determine its character and to understand its present status in the philosophy of science. Meehan, perpetuating a common misconception in social science, tends to view the deductive model as if it were essentially a procedural recommendation for scientific inquiry; but the model, as presented by most of its proponents, was never conceived either as a methodological norm in the sense of how to go about the task of explanation or as a reconstruction of the process of explanation. Meehan also maintains that this model has been "rarely criticized" in the literature of the philosophy of science, but, on the contrary, every indication is that at present the weight of argument is against the deductive model, and that the revolt against the model as well as other aspects of logical empiricism "has now lasted long enough to produce something of a counterrevolution."[12] Even the defenders of the deductive model recognize that the "global nature of the attack gives the current controversy its special interest."[13] Yet the fact that the impact of the debate has scarcely been felt in the social sciences is only a symptom of the cultural lag in the relationship between these two disciplines.

As the term "deductive model" is used here, it refers to a quite specific formulation which in its essential characteristics is embraced and advocated by a number of philosophers but most prominently associated with the work of Hempel. The Hempelian thesis of deductive nomological explanation is most fundamentally an argument for the "methodological unity of all empirical science"[14] since it attempts to reduce the criteria of scientific explanation to one universal logical pattern. It asserts that "all scientific explanation," as opposed to the manifold everyday senses of "explain" and other specialized meanings of the term, "involves, explicitly or by implication, a subsumption of its subject matter under general regularities; that it seeks to provide a systematic understanding of empirical phenomena by showing that they fit into a nomic nexus."[15] More specifically, it is argued that an event or phenomenon that is to be explained, or strictly speaking, the statement describing the phenomenon or event (the *explanandum*), must be deducible from premises (the *explanans*) which are assumed to be true and contain, in addition to certain statements of fact or initial or antecedent conditions, at least one general law expressing empirical regularities. Empirical laws are in turn explained in the same manner by deductive subsumption under more inclusive laws or comprehensive theories which consist of a deductively joined system of axioms and theorems. The proponents of the model are unequivocal in their assertion that "science looks for laws, because without them neither explanation nor prediction is possible" and that the sense in which the term "deduction" is to be taken is the strict one of following the rule of *modus ponens* of formal logic, that is, that laws function as the "premises of a deductive argument" and "the conclusion may be deduced from the premises because the premises logically imply the conclusion. And the premises logically imply the conclusion because the corresponding conditional, if the premises are true then the conclusion is true, is a tautology."[16] Explanation is viewed principally as answering "why" questions, and explanation and prediction, although differing pragmatically, are construed as possessing the same logical form in the sense that any explained event could, in principle, have been predicted in advance. There are certain aspects of the deductive model about which there is less than complete agreement among its exponents, such as whether the relationship between explanation and prediction is actually one of logical symmetry and whether an explanation in terms of statistical and probabilistic laws is strictly deductive. There are also a number of other features of the model, and logical empiricism in general, which are significantly related to issues of social scientific inquiry, such as the problems of hypothesis confirmation and especially the questions of theoretical reductionism and the relation between theoretical and observation terms and their cognitive status. But these problems are less relevant to the particular focus of this discussion.[17]

What must be clearly understood is that the deductive model is expressly "not intended to reflect the manner in which working scientists actually formulate their explanatory accounts."[18] Although it is offered as an explication of the "logical structure and rationale of various ways in which empirical science answers explanation-seeking why-questions," it is a "philosophical thesis" and not an empirical claim.[19] It is sometimes argued that a defect of the model is that it accepts physical mechanics as the paradigm of scientific explanation and thus judges all other forms of explanation accordingly, but the reverse is the case. From the point of view of May Brodbeck and others who accept and defend this concept of explanation, "physics is an advanced and 'model' science precisely because it does provide deductive explanation and prediction of its phenomena."[20] But to argue that the model is prescriptive rather than descriptive may be to attempt too general a characterization, since on the one hand its exponents do not primarily intend it as a norm for scientists to follow and on the other hand it does provide a conceptual framework in terms of which one can view and categorize particular explanations.

The model principally provides a set of formal logical criteria which are timeless and placeless and state what any explanation must include to truly count as a scientific explanation, that is, "a *philosophic* demand is being put upon explanation – a demand that the cohesion of its components should not depend upon the background of the person who asks for the explanation, nor upon the context in which it is given, but upon the relations which are, so to speak, intrinsic to explanation."[21] And the essence of the demand is simply that what is to be explained must be strictly deducible from a law to count as a fully adequate explanation. Whether the content of explanations in any branch of science in fact does, or conceivably can, coincide with this meta-scientific reconstruction is considered irrelevant as far as judging the validity of the model, and there is "no claim whatever concerning the extent to which scientific explanations can actually be achieved for the phenomena studied in different branches of scientific inquiry."[22] In other words, there is no necessary coincidence between science and scientific explanation.

III. Logical empiricism and contextualism

In addition to clarifying the content of the deductive model, it is necessary to understand the philosophical position which supports it. Logical empiricism as an approach to the philosophy of science has been concerned with developing formal representations or reconstructions of the logical structure of scientific explanation and with a meta-logical analysis of the language applied to science. In this view there is a very strict correlation between the philosophy of science and formal logic. Although the object of analysis is science, and despite the claim of providing reconstructions of scientific logic, neither the history nor the current practice of any branch of science is considered pivotal, and references to specific scientific theories are seldom invoked to support conclusions about the character of scientific explanation. Although the aim is not to provide a guideline for empirical research, the import of this reconstructed logic is clearly nominative or legislative, in the sense that it is considered to stand above and outside any particular scientific context and to serve as an authoritative guide for judging or evaluating the explanatory adequacy of any particular scientific assertion. Recent work in the philosophy of science has severely challenged many of the specific formulations of logical empiricism such as the deductive model, but most of these criticisms are intelligible only in terms of a fundamental change in the conception of the philosophy of science itself. This recent literature is marked by its empirical orientation, that is, its attention to actual scientific practice and especially the history of science. The attitude is non-legislative, and the role of the philosophy of science is understood as principally one of explication; the stress is on the diversity rather than the unity of science and on the autonomy of science rather than its dependence on formal logic and philosophy.

Philosophers such as Stephen Toulmin and Michael Scriven, who may be described as embracing a descriptive or contextualist approach to the philosophy of science, attack the deductive model on many grounds, but the basis of the attack is centered around the charge that the model does not actually reflect the character of scientific explanation. From their standpoint, the philosophy of science is principally an endeavor which describes and renders scientific practice intelligible rather than attempting to construct formal and definitive representations of scientific explanation and provide trans-contextual logical standards by which to judge any aspect of scientific explanation. What is involved in the conflict between these approaches is "a disagreement about the nature of philosophic method,"[23] and this difference in perspective can be clearly discerned in the attitude of the adherents of these respective positions toward the notion of logic. For the deductivist, "logic" is defined in the narrow and specific sense of the formal logician, and a sharp distinction is drawn between the "context of discovery" or theory formulation and the "context of justification," with the logic of science restricted to the latter.[24] The opponents of the deductive model use the term "logic" in its more generic sense to encompass the various modes of inquiry and inference actually followed by scientists and stress the distinction between "working logic" and "idealized logic" or "logic-in-use" and "reconstructed logic."[25] It is the reluctance of the reconstructionists to grant any autonomy to "working logic" and the non-justificatory aspects of explanation, or in fact to recognize it as logic at all, which leads them to ignore many aspects of scientific inquiry and to characterize all explanations which do not approach the deductive ideal as "imperfect," "incomplete," "elliptical," "partial," or, worst of all, merely "explanation sketches" which is the phrase understood as best describing most explanations in history and social science. In this view, "perfect knowledge is the ideal, actualized only in certain branches of physical science. Elsewhere, as in biology, economics, sociology, psychology, and the social sciences generally, knowledge is conspicuously 'imperfect'."[26]

The opponents of the deductive model reject this rationalistic approach and the attempt to postulate an extra-scientific standard of completeness of explanations and perfect knowledge. They argue that the notion of complete explanation in any absolute sense is misconceived and that completeness and perfection are contextually relative rather than depending on some universal standard such as the idea that explanations are "imperfect" if they do not make it possible "to compute (predict or postdict) the state of a system, either an individual or a group, at any moment from its state at one moment."[27] The contextualist holds that "where the standards for judging the soundness, validity, cogency or strength of arguments are in practice field-dependent, logical theorists restrict these notions and attempt to define them in field-invariant terms."[28] For the contextualist, "explanations are practical, context bound affairs" and the "completeness or correctness of an explanation is a notion without meaning except in a given context."[29] To neglect substantive "context criteria" and require that a complete scientific explanation involves laws, that it be logically symmetrical with a predictive statement, and that it be limited to answering "why" questions is to impose standards which are at once too restrictive in the sense that they exclude much of what scientific practice finds perfectly acceptable and too inclusive in the sense that they admit assertions which in many instances would not count as relevant explanations.[30] Mere deduction may be wrong, trivial or no explanation at all, and thus "it is an illusion to suppose that scientific explanation is anything as simple as deductive subsumption under a true generalization."[31] While the deductivist holds that explanations which do not conform to the model are inadequate *a priori*, the contextualist maintains that there is a "family of explanations" and "a diversity of types" and that "the simple fact must be faced that certain evidence is adequate to guarantee certain explanations without the benefit of deduction from laws."[32]

The criticism of the deductive model, however, reaches deeper than merely asserting a certain relativity and autonomy with regard to the logic of explanation and renouncing a legislative role for the philosophy of science, for it is further maintained that there can be no deductive demonstration in empirical inquiry in the sense in which Hempel and others employ the term "deduction," since there is a necessary "divergence between the categories of practical argument-criticism and those of formal logic."[33] Toulmin argues that many of the current problems in logic and the philosophy of science have arisen from a historical tendency to make the analytic syllogism and the categories of formal logic a paradigm for all arguments. Contrary to what certain defenders of the deductive model maintain,[34] the opponents do not wish to claim that there is no such thing as "deduction" in science but rather that the term should apply to detective work as well as physics and that there is no reason why the notion of deductive inference and the meaning of concepts such as "valid" and "certain" should be interpreted in terms of formal logic or why formal logic should be a standard for judging the infinite variety of substantive scientific arguments. The seemingly irredeemable difference between the certainty of formal logic and the contingent character of scientific assertions has sometimes led to a view such as that of Reichenbach that all scientific explanation is inductive and probabilistic, but such a formulation accepts the logician's preference for certainty and fails to recognize that terms like "probable" and "certain" are modals whose substantive meaning is contextually determined.

For Toulmin, and contextualists in general, the structure of analytical arguments, and the very notion of deduction implied there, are inapplicable for judging substantial arguments whether in science, ethics, or jurisprudence, but it is precisely this standard which the strict deductivist has attempted to apply to scientific explanation. Many difficulties "spring from the misapplication of these categories to arguments of other sorts," and this approach tends to obscure the fact that the most important distinction is not between deductive and inductive reasoning but between analytical and substantial arguments or between demonstrative inference and ampliative or non-demonstrative inference.[35] The philosopher of science who embraces the contextualist perspective does not reject formal logic but only its application as a criterion for evaluating and explicating actual forms of justification in various fields of empirical inquiry. What the contextualist will accept as the logic of explanation in any field, the strict deductivist dismisses as the "psychological and pragmatic aspects of explanation" and demands a "non-pragmatic conception of scientific explanation."[36] But for the contextualist, explanation itself is a "pragmatic notion." The contextualist approach is, again, "largely an empirical one" and assumes that the "meaning of terms and concepts or logical problems can only be thoroughly understood if we include a meticulous examination of the circumstances in which they occur, rather than relying on a relatively rapidly extracted formulation of their apparent internal logical features."[37]

IV. The inadequacy of deductivism

Once this difference in perspective is understood the basis for much of the controversy over the logic of explanation becomes clear, and it should be equally clear that the conflict between these positions cannot be reconciled. An understanding of these two approaches to the philosophy of science makes it evident why the arguments on both sides tend to pass one another by, yet there are grounds for choosing between them, and such a choice is necessary if there is to be any clarity in philosophical discussions of social scientific explanation and any meaningful critical analysis of the claims of social scientists regarding the adequacy of substantive explanations. The choice in the first instance must be essentially between the reconstructionist and contextualist approaches, yet even if the reconstructionist position were to be accepted, the particular philosophical criteria advocated by the deductivist seems questionable. The basic assumptions which inform reconstructionism as well as its particular offspring, in this case the deductive model and the implications of this model as a standard for judging social scientific practice, are unacceptable.

Philosophers such as Hempel maintain that deductive-nomological explanation, or what has been termed the "covering laws," obviously do not encompass all the contexts in which one speaks of explanation. They are quick to point out that the concern is with explicating the concept of scientific explanation rather than explanation in its more generic sense, in somewhat the same way that there are meta-mathematical formulations of mathematical proof which do not apply to all the fields in which one might speak of proof.[38] But the problem facing the deductive model is its justification as the standard or ideal for the critical appraisal of scientific explanation and as a form for exhibiting its underlying "logical structure and rationale." To approach scientific explanation from the standpoint of an ideal type may be defensible, but it is more problematical when this idealization is admittedly not primarily extracted from an examination of the activity which it seeks to judge and illuminate. It would seem that we could not ask more of an argument in any particular field than that it "achieve whatever sort of cogency or well-foundedness can relevantly be asked for in that field."[39] But even if an idealization is constructed in view of some non-empirically grounded external philosophical criterion, such a procedure is not necessarily defective if the criterion can be adequately justified, that is, if it can be demonstrated that deductiveness should, or must, be the standard of the logic of scientific explanation. Hempel admits that such a conclusion is not "susceptible to strict 'proof'" and that "its soundness has to be judged by the light it can shed on the rationale and force of explanatory accounts offered in different branches of empirical science."[40] But this would seem to land him in something of a contradiction. He emphasizes that the validity of the model is independent of explanations actually formulated by scientists in various branches of empirical inquiry and yet maintains "that the logic of *all* scientific explanations is basically of the covering-law variety"[41] and further that the viability of the covering-law model must essentially be justified pragmatically. The peculiar and circular chain of reasoning would seem to be that only explanations subsumable under the covering-law model can be classified as scientific, and consequently, by definition, the logic of scientific explanation is of this type and thus the model necessarily illuminates "scientific" explanations.

It is apparent that few, if any, actual explanations in natural science, let alone social science, do conform to this schema, and thus the saving clause which enables the deductive model to perform a descriptive or typological function is the notion of explanatory incompleteness. This allows almost any branch of empirical inquiry and most of history and social science a certain claim to scientificness as long as it is willing to pay the price of humility and accept the stigma of incompleteness and imperfection. But the important difference between the social sciences and the physical sciences is not that one has and one does not have complete explanations, but that one has more quantitative laws than the other ... But they confer no benefit on the explanation that cannot be obtained in other ways, and in particular they do not convey the blessing of deduced truth since they are usually only approximations.[42]

Hempel and other deductivists have been singularly unsuccessful in providing examples from physics or any other science which conform to the deductive model. Even the laws of physics produce no automatic deductions or explanations; they require judgment in their application, and judgment necessitates substantive criteria.[43] The idea of "exact deduction" in science is a myth because the laws of science are not exact.[44] To claim that scientific inference is purely "a logical question" in the sense of formal logic is to fail to recognize that explanation is primarily an epistemological concept.[45]

The justification for the deductive model is in fact not "pragmatic" at all. It relies instead on the submerged informing assumption that the norm of acceptable argument is analytic or demonstrative argument, but it is unreasonable, and misleading, "to treat this type of argument as a paradigm and to demand that arguments in other fields should conform to its standard regardless, or to build up from a study of the simplest forms of argument alone a set of categories intended for application to arguments of all sorts."[46] It is not merely that the identification of the logic of science with analytic or demonstrative argument presents a very truncated view of both logic and science, but that the judgment of all justification by the ideal of analyticity neither provides a relevant standard for judging empirical or substantial arguments nor illuminates in any significant manner the underlying logical structure of most aspects of scientific explanation. The deductivist denies the charge that he equates deduction with either analytic or syllogistic reasoning.[47] But whatever label is applied, the argument is that "geometry is the prototype of all scientific theories" and that "in philosophy and elsewhere an appeal either to a definition or to a logical truth is conclusive" and "conclusive in a way that appeal to contingent truth is not" and that "any other kind of explanation of individual facts cannot possess this conclusiveness. Either the explanation is deductive or else it does not justify what it is said to explain."[48]

It is often maintained that the deductive model is epistemologically neutral, and although this is not entirely true since it does preclude certain substantive explanatory accounts, it is precisely this formal or empty character which vitiates its adequacy as an explanatory norm. What the model demands is that the cogency of an explanation depend on a particular logical form, but this severing of logic and epistemology and the attempt to find an Archimedean point from which to view and judge all scientific explanation is untenable. "Not deducibility, but intelligibility constitutes the basic feature of the logic of explanation,"[49] and to understand and criticize the explanations produced in any science is at once to become acquainted with that science both in its present form and its historical development and with what characterizes its claims to know. The point is not that existential explanations in social science and history are by their very nature partial, incomplete, sketchy, or in some other way fundamentally unsound (although in any particular instance and judged by the contextual field-dependent criteria of a specific science they may be) but rather that they are qualitatively different and autonomous kinds of explanation. To reject the deductive model and argue for the contextual evaluation of explanations does not constitute, as Brodbeck and others insist, an abandonment of critical judgment and philosophical questions about explanation or the acceptance of a precept that would read "every man his own explainer." Nor does it entail the approval of "ordinary usage" as a paradigm of explanation or make all criticism finally dependent on subjective psychological tests.[50]

The request for an explanation presupposes that *something* is understood, and a complete answer is one that relates the object of inquiry to the realm of understanding in some comprehensible and appropriate way. What this way is varies from subject matter to subject matter just as what makes something better than something else varies from the field of automobiles to the solution of chess problems; but the logical function of explanation, as of evaluation, is the same in each field. And what counts as complete will vary from context to context within a field; but the logical category of complete explanation can still be characterized in the perfectly general way just given, that is, the logical function of "complete" as applied to "explanation" can be described.[51]

What will count as an adequate explanation or what will constitute valid inferences in any scientific or other context in which there are recognized rules and forms of judgment and criticism has a "systematic" aspect. It is against a background of accepted laws, theories, and regulative principles, that is, a substantive scientific paradigm, that the intelligibility of any explanation is judged.[52] Generalizations, laws, and theories function as rules, "inference tickets," or "warrants," or justifying grounds in terms of which explanatory inferences are drawn, not as premises in a deductive argument.[53] To see this as the logical function of laws and theories is not to confuse "experience and the logical methods by which we think about the experience"[54] as long as the distinction between the logical function a justifying statement plays and the substantive meaning of that statement are distinguished. But the more important point is that much of scientific explanation does not involve laws. The statements justifying inferences or serving the logical function of principles of inference cannot be restricted to laws without either radically curtailing what might be called science or arbitrarily assigning a large part of the results of inquiry in both the natural and social sciences to the status of imperfectness or incompleteness. To maintain that "insofar as an individual fact justifies the inference to one or more facts, laws are always implicitly invoked" since "otherwise, the justification remains a mystery,"[55] is not only to take a very narrow view of scientific reasoning but to distort scientific practice. Yet such a narrow view is precisely what the deductive model requires by its insistence that laws which can constitute the premises of a formal deductive argument must be present, either overtly or in some suppressed form, before any assertion may be accepted as a fully adequate explanation.

This demand becomes particularly pernicious in its effects on social science which, attempting to be "scientific," begins with this model, or at least hearsay about it, and seeks to formulate procedures and goals of inquiry accordingly while uncritically accepting the philosophers' evaluation of its present claims to knowledge as imperfect. What has happened in social science, unlike natural science in which the philosophy of science and reconstructed logic have had little or no impact or as in history where, despite a longstanding debate about the Hempelian model in the philosophy of history,[56] there has been only a minor influence on historiography, is that there has been a peculiar synthesis of the language of the philosophy of science and the language of substantive inquiry which has resulted in a rather bizarre corpus of theoretical literature. In a sense the idea of a science of society modeled after natural science has been an ideology from the very beginning of social science, and the acceptance of the deductive model is part of the continuing tradition of that ideology. The result has been an overriding concern with developing generalizations and a proliferation of pseudo-laws which are little more than abstracted summaries of empirical findings which carry no explanatory value in any commonly accepted sense of the term "explain."[57] The theorist in the social sciences tends merely to take Hempel and others at face value without careful regard for what constitutes, or must constitute, explanation in his particular field, and finds it sufficient to state that "the higher the level of generality in ordering ... facts and clarifying their relations, the broader will be the range of explanation and understanding."[58] Social scientists find little in the deductive model except the precept ordering them to generalize, but explanation in terms of a "'mere empirical generalization' is very rarely explanatory, and it is only because laws usually involve more than this ... that they carry explanatory force."[59] But raising the question of "more than this" is what social scientists have avoided by their allegiance to the formalistic standard of the deductive model.

The idea derived from the deductive model which most seriously infects the social scientific enterprise is the attenuated picture of the model which enters the literature of social science as the dictum that all suitable explanation involves the subsumption of phenomena under general laws, or, given the imperfect nature or at best temporary theoretical impurity of social science, at least generalizations. But the acceptance of this dictum, the equation of explanation and generalization, has been *a priori*, that is, it has not evolved from a consideration of what constitutes social scientific phenomena and consequently what in any substantive sense would constitute an adequate explanation, and thus it has been able to provide neither a tenable description nor a viable prescriptive ideal. As Abraham Kaplan points out, any such offering of reconstructed logic must be treated as a "hypothesis."[60] But to accept without question the general demand for laws and generalizations as the prerequisites of explanation often leads in practice only to truisms which add nothing to the explanation of individual phenomena.[61] The problem is not so much to "stop trying to imitate physics" but rather "only what a particular reconstruction claims physics to be,"[62] and the first lesson that social science might learn from natural science, if it penetrated beyond the ideological screen of the deductive model, is the value of devotion to the autonomy of inquiry and a passionate concern with the substance of explanation rather than a fixation on the form of explanation. Social science might well remember that some of the most important advances in science have been achieved not by solving problems but by abandoning them, and this might well be the case in regard to the social scientist's attempt at explanation through conformance with the deductive model.

The deductive model is only one more attempt to find the scientific method. The model's more strenuous advocates go so far as to identify the acceptance of the deductive model with the acceptance of science itself and, like Brodbeck, classify those who dissent as humanists, members of the literary tradition, and intuitionists.[63] But this dichotomizing technique is too facile to be convincing, and the contemporary logical empiricist must be reminded, as the logical positivist before him, that "often what presents itself to us as obscurantism is only a departure from the particular reconstruction that we have come to identify with reason itself."[64] The deductivist's definition of science is especially misleading, because it subverts what Kaplan has termed the "autonomy of inquiry"[65] not only by creating a hierarchy of sciences but by attempting to subject empirical inquiry, which is always contingent, to the rule of noncontingent *a priori* extra-scientific principles and ideas of certainty and conclusiveness which belong to formal logic. There would seem to be little justification for social science, or any other science, seeking its standards and concepts of explanation from philosophers and logicians. This is not to say that science does not involve "philosophic" and even metaphysical presuppositions or that philosophy is irrelevant for science. It also does not mean that there are no similarities between certain modes of scientific and philosophic explanation. One of the disabilities of the deductive model is that it implies a strict separation between science and other forms of explanation which may not adequately represent scientific practice and which, if accepted, may block fruitful avenues of inquiry. Finally, to deny that philosophy and formal logic can provide the criteria of what will count as explanation in empirical science is not to deny that there are philosophical and logical problems in science or that science is amenable to logical or philosophical analysis either in the sense of illuminating the structure of scientific reasoning or clarifying, and even dissolving, certain "scientific" problems, dilemmas, or confusions which have their origin in the language of science.

V. Conclusion: the meaning of "explanation"

The social scientists' fascination with the deductive model, or at least the mandates which spring from it, is closely allied to the search for what Toulmin has termed "portmanteau characterizations of science, finding in some one requirement (such as predictive success) the unique test of a scientific hypothesis."[66] But this attempt to discover some final standard by which to define and judge scientific assertions is ultimately regressive since some exception or counter-example can always be suggested where prediction, the presence of laws, or deductive relationships between statements is not the criterion. Any analysis of scientific inquiry must include not only classificatory criteria which serve to differentiate it from other activities but also standards of "appraisal."[67] Yet it is a mistake to assume that there is some ultimate criterion and form of appraisal for scientific assertions which is based on or implied by the purpose or function of science. Appraisal in science does not carry with it any such universal criterion, nor does it entail any unitary logical standard. There is appraisal in ethics, politics, and in the various branches of science, but both the criteria and logic of appraisal differ from field to field and from context to context within a field. There is no reason to believe that in not accepting some purpose such as prediction as the ultimate standard for judging a scientific assertion or in rejecting deduction from general laws as the hallmark of adequate explanation that one is somehow placing himself outside the realm of scientific activity. One must not be misled by the fact that scientists have purposes and science has functions and assume that there is a given purpose or function for science which governs its logic and serves as a final standard of justification and appraisal. The meaning of "science" at any time or place is determined by the paradigm which informs scientific activity and reasoning and which specifies the conception of reality and the phenomena to be investigated, designates problems for investigation, and determines the criteria of acceptable explanation and inference.[68] But the specific content of paradigms is in principle infinitely variable both in time and space.

Science has not one aim but many, and its development has passed through many contrasted stages. It is therefore fruitless to look for a single, all-purpose "scientific method": the growth and evolution of scientific ideas depends on no one method, and will always call for a broad range of different inquiries. Science as a whole – the activity, its aim, its methods, and ideas – evolves by variation and selection.[69]

Faced with the dilemmas arising out of attempts to state the governing value and defining characteristics of science, there has been a tendency to move toward positing some more general and seemingly more neutral formulation of the purpose of scientific activity. Probably the leading candidate in this regard is the idea "that the goal of inquiry is explanation,"[70] but such a notion seems to complicate the problem rather than solve it. Such a definition is at once too broad and too narrow, for, on the one hand, the search for explanation encompasses a greater range of activities than science and, on the other hand, it would seem much too restrictive to limit science to merely a search for explanation. It would seem that "if the goal of some branch of science does not consist in explaining, it can scarcely be criticized on the count of *failing* to do so."[71] A great deal of scientific activity is concerned with what might be termed "positing" and "substantiating" which cannot easily be accommodated within the notion of explanation.[72] It might well be argued that although science includes more than explanation, this is nevertheless its central aim, but then the problem becomes one of distinguishing *scientific* explanation, and inevitably one is driven back to seeking the essence, purpose, or function of science and to such postures as the equation of science and a search for causes. But, as with prediction, it would appear that "neither the search for causes, nor causal explanation, is *primary* in any likely sense that may be assigned to this vague term."[73] In the end, attempts to isolate and define scientific explanation seem to result in a regressive process of conceptual reduplication.

These comments should suffice to demonstrate that there is something fundamentally wrong with this entire line of argument. There is, however, a sense in which science and explanation are related, or, better, there is a manner in which one can speak cogently about the relationship between these concepts. But this involves conceiving of explanation neither as a goal of science nor as a product, but rather as a kind of activity of which scientific explanation is one type. This idea might be expressed by saying that in this sense of "explanation" it would be as odd to say that explanation is the goal or function of science as it would be to say that playing games is the goal or function of card games. To engage in science is, in part, to engage in a particular kind of explaining activity, and "explaining" must be understood in terms of "systemic explanation" or a "generic form of explanation of which scientific explanation is only a species," and the various fields of science, such as social science and natural science, are sub-species.[74] This idea of explanation may be described as a "search for understanding" or intelligibility and it encompasses many modes of thought including logic, philosophy, science, and everyday life; "explaining, in short, is a particular way of using a form of argument; it has no logical form peculiar to it."[75] What the particular logical structure of explanation will consist of in any of these areas will differ, but "the only ultimate element in the logic of explanation is understanding itself, and that comes in many ways."[76] There are certainly aspects of scientific explanation which distinguish it from other species of explanation, but to state precisely what the boundaries are is an empirical problem and a problem to which there is no final solution. Most important, it is necessary to guard against the presumption that the logic of explanation in any particular field such as formal logic can claim trans-contextual validity or that a model, and therefore corrigible picture, of the logical structure of some sub-field, such as natural science, can be universalized into an authoritative paradigm for all sub-fields.

At first it may appear that the introduction of concepts such as "understanding" and "intelligibility" merely confuses rather than clarifies the issue, since to seek their meaning is to again embark on a regressive journey. It is obvious that what one person or community may accept as intelligibility will be rejected by another and that what will constitute scientific understanding in one historical period may be viewed as inadequate at a later time. But this is precisely the point. Explanation, and in fact most of the central concepts relating to the epistemic and logical structure of science, must be construed as carrying a certain universal force with regard to their characteristic use or meaning but varying contextually with regard to their specific and substantive meaning, that is, with regard to their sense and reference and criteria of application. To speak of intelligibility and understanding as the characteristic logical force of explanatory assertions and as the differentiating criteria of explanatory activity is not to lapse into some sort of obscurantism. Explanation (or intelligibility) is not merely a psychological matter, for what will count as explanation as well as what requires explanation is pragmatically determined against a framework of ideas about reality, theories, and rules which together constitute a paradigm or conceptual scheme for interpreting and organizing experience. This is true whether we are speaking of philosophy, science, religion, or everyday life. What will constitute the standards of adequate understanding in any field at any time is similarly contextually determined; "what is required for understanding differs with the type of explanation," and "the epistemic features, usually in the background of explanations, emerge when we shift from one to another kind of explanation within science."[77] "Scientific explanation" can be defined as "a topically unified communication, the content of which imparts understanding of some scientific phenomenon" and understanding is, roughly, organized knowledge, that is, knowledge of the relations between various facts and/or laws. These relations are of many kinds – deductive, inductive, analogical, etc. ... It is for the most part a perfectly objective matter to test understanding, just as it is to test knowledge, and it is absurd to identify it with a subjective feeling, as have some critics of this kind of view.[78]

To throw off the burden of the deductive model and the approach to the philosophy of science and explanation advocated by logical empiricism implies first of all a re-examination, although not necessarily a rejection, of the idea that there is logical symmetry between explanations in the natural and social sciences; it allows an investigation of the actual logical and epistemological foundations of these two enterprises rather than merely accepting popular philosophical reconstructions. What is required is that social scientists undertake a consideration of what counts, or should count, as adequate explanation, and this in turn means the formulation of a substantive view of social and political phenomena which must provide the criteria for such judgment. It is precisely such an undertaking which has been prevented, or avoided, by adherence to the deductive model. Yet to reject the deductive model and support an approach to the philosophy of science which recognizes the relativity and autonomy of explanations in various branches of science immediately engenders the charge of subjectivity and the abdication of objective standards of appraisal which would allow everything from astrology to cooking to claim the title of science. What Hempel and other deductivists are searching for is a standard of explanation which clearly distinguishes scientific assertions and which is "objective in the sense that its implications and evidential support do not depend essentially on the individuals who happen to apply or to test them."[79] But to charge the advocates of the contextualist approach with abandoning the ideals of objectivity and intersubjectivity is to completely miss the point of their argument.

The reconstructionist and contextualist approaches to the philosophy of science are not comparable in the sense that the contextualist thesis is basically descriptive and explanatory rather than normative. It is not an argument for subjectivity and the abandonment of objective criteria since it assumes in any particular context that perfectly objective or inter-subjective standards may obtain, and it is not an argument advocating relativity but rather a recognition that appraisal in science is, and must be, relative to a context. The choice is not between logical positivism and subjectivism. To reject a legislative role for the philosophy of science and advocate the autonomy of scientific inquiry is not to suggest that evaluations of scientific explanations are impossible. Those who see the contextualist approach as "the current threat of subjectivism" assume that the philosophy of science must be responsible for developing standards of evaluation for empirical science, but to accuse the contextualist of advocating subjectivism because he fails to develop universal standards of appraisal and criteria for what will count as science to replace the deductive model would be like suggesting that an anthropologist must be an ethical relativist if he recognizes a diversity of moral systems and fails to establish universal moral norms for judging the values of particular societies. The analogy with morality is not strained, for one recent critic of the contextualist position sees this approach as a threat to "the moral import of science: its dynamic articulation of the impulse to responsible belief, and its suggestion of the hope of an increased rationality and responsibility in all realms of conduct and thought."[80] He suggests that this was the real meaning of the positivist doctrine of "the unity of science,"[81] and it may well have been. But moral dogmata have often been obstacles to the advancement of science.

Notes

1 For some preliminary arguments supporting this position, see John G. Gunnell, "Social Science and Political Reality: The Problem of Explanation," *Social Research*, 35 (Spring, 1968).
2 Norton E. Long, Foreword to Eugene J. Meehan, *Explanation in Social Science* (Homewood. IL: Dorsey Press, 1968), p. v.
3 Harry Eckstein and David Apter, *Comparative Politics* (Glencoe. IL: Free Press, 1963), p. v.
4 See, for example, Richard S. Rudner, *Philosophy of Social Science* (Englewood Cliffs, NJ: Prentice-Hall, 1966).
5 David Easton, *A Framework for Political Analysis* (Englewood Cliffs, NJ: Prentice-Hall, 1965), pp. 316–317; *The Political System* (New York: Knopf, 1953), p. 25.
6 Easton, *System*, pp. 52–59; *Framework*, p. 3.
7 Easton, *System*, p. 58; *Framework*, p. 7.
8 Robert Dahl, "Cause and Effect in the Study of Politics," in Daniel Lerner (ed.), *Cause and Effect* (New York: Free Press, 1963), pp. 75, 77–78.
9 For the most comprehensive statement of Hempel's position see his *Aspects of Scientific Explanation* (New York: Free Press, 1965). Ernest Nagel's most popular work is *The Structure of Science* (New York: Harcourt, Brace and World, 1961).
10 See, for example, Eugene Meehan, *The Theory and Method of Political Analysis* (Homewood. IL: Dorsey Press, 1965), pp. v, vi, 3, 8, 9.
11 Meehan, *Explanation*, p. 3.
12 Ibid., p. 2; Edward MacKinnon, "Epistemological Problems in the Philosophy of Science, I," *Review of Metaphysics*, XXII (Sept., 1968), p. 113.

13 May Brodbeck, "Explanation, Prediction, and 'Imperfect' Knowledge," in Brodbeck (ed.), *Readings in The Philosophy of the Social Sciences* (New York: Macmillan, 1968), p. 364; cf. M. B. Hesse, "A New Look at Scientific Explanation," *Review of Metaphysics*, XVII (Spring, 1953).
14 Hempel, "Explanation in Science and History," in Robert G. Colodny (ed.), *Frontiers of Science and Philosophy* (Pittsburgh, PA: University of Pittsburgh Press, 1962), p. 32.
15 Hempel, *Aspects,* p. 488.
16 Brodbeck, "Introduction," in Brodbeck (ed.), *Readings,* pp. 7, 9.
17 For a discussion of some of these problems and their relation to assumptions about theory construction in social science, see John G. Gunnell, "The Idea of The Conceptual Framework: A Philosophical Critique," *Journal of Comparative Administration,* I (August, 1969). In order to scotch any misunderstanding from the outset, it must be emphasized that in this context the "deductive model" is not to be understood as equivalent to the rather loose and variable characterization of scientific reasoning often referred to as the hypothetico-deductive method or, roughly, the idea that explanation is a process of formulating hypotheses which are tentatively confirmed or disconfirmed by observational tests. Although there are often numerous similarities between the deductive model and specific formulations of the H-D method [*e.g.*, R. B. Braithwaite, *Scientific Explanation* (Cambridge: Cambridge University Press, 1953)] such as the tendency to view the logic of science as essentially deductive in character and although many of the criticisms relating to the accuracy and sufficiency of the H-D account such as those most prominently associated with the work of N. R. Hanson and his concern with the "logic of discovery" are pertinent to a consideration of the deductive model, it is probably generally accepted that science utilizes a form of inference which in its broad outlines resembles this representation. Neither should the deductive model be equated with Karl Popper's ideas on the deductive testing of theories and the attending thesis of falsifiability. Although Popper maintains that the logic of science is entirely deductive in character in the sense that the principle of *modus tollens* is the only rule of inference available to science, his concern is essentially with the criteria for the rejection and corroboration of empirical hypotheses and choosing between hypotheses [*The Logic of Discovery* (New York: Science Editions, 1961), pp. 41, 75–76]. Whatever labels may be attached to Popper's position, his focus is on "providing some sort of justification for a mode of non-demonstrative inference," and it might well be argued that in this sense his approach "is not properly characterized as *deductivism*" [Wesley C. Salmon, "The Foundations of Scientific Inference," in Robert G. Colodny (ed.), *Mind and Cosmos* (Pittsburgh, PA: University of Pittsburgh Press, 1966), pp. 160–161]. While the deductive model stresses the subsumption of phenomena under general laws, Popper stresses the development of theories and conjectures which can survive the severest possible tests or attempts at falsification, and the difference in distribution of emphasis is significant. Finally, Popper's views, especially those concerning the relation between theory and observation language, have provided the foundations for some of the most damaging criticism of traditional logical empiricism.
18 Hempel, "Explanation in Science and History," p. 15.
19 Hempel, "Explanatory Incompleteness," in Brodbeck (ed.), *Readings,* p. 399.
20 Bradbeck, "Explanation, Prediction, and 'Imperfect' Knowledge," p. 369.
21 Rudolph H. Weingartner, "The Quarrel About Historical Explanation," in Brodbeck (ed.), *Readings,* p. 355.
22 Hempel, "Explanation and Prediction by Covering Laws," in Bernard Baumrin (ed.), *Philosophy of Science: The Delaware Seminar* (New York: Interscience Publishers, 1963), Vol. I., p. 116.

23 Weingartner, "Quarrel," p. 350; Also see Dudley Shapere, "Meaning and Scientific Change," in Robert G. Colodny (ed.), *Mind and Cosmos* (Pittsburgh, PA: University of Pittsburgh Press, 1966), pp. 41–50.
24 Rudner, *Philosophy of Social Science*, pp. 4–5.
25 See Stephen Toulmin, *The Uses of Argument* (Cambridge: Cambridge University Press, 1958), Ch. IV and Abraham Kaplan, *The Conduct of Inquiry* (San Francisco, CA: Chandler, 1964), Ch. 1.
26 These distinctions are set forth by Hempel in many of his writings. See *Aspects*. Brodbeck, "Explanation, Prediction, and 'Imperfect' Knowledge," p. 375. Also Gustav Bergmann, "Imperfect Knowledge," in Brodbeck (ed.), *Readings*.
27 Brodbeck, "Explanation, Prediction, and 'Imperfect' Knowledge," pp. 375, 371–372.
28 Toulmin, *Uses of Argument*, p. 147.
29 Michael Scriven, "Truisms as the Grounds for Historical Explanation," in Patrick Gardiner (ed.), *Theories of History* (Glencoe, IL: Free Press, 1959), p. 450.
30 Ibid., pp. 468–469; Scriven, "Explanations, Predictions, and Laws," in Herbert Feigl and Grover Maxwell (eds), *Minnesota Studies in the Philosophy of Science* (Minneapolis: University of Minnesota Press, 1962), Vol. III, pp. 173–190, 196, 202.
31 Scriven, "Explanations, Predictions, and Laws," p. 225.
32 Scriven, "Truisms as the Grounds for Historical Explanation," pp. 452, 456.
33 Toulmin, *Uses of Argument*, p. 146.
34 Brodbeck, "Explanation, Prediction, and 'Imperfect' Knowledge," p. 371.
35 Toulmin, *Uses of Argument*, p. 146. Also Scriven, "Definitions, Explanations, and Theories," in Feigl, Scriven, and Maxwell (eds), *Minnesota Studies in the Philosophy of Science* (Minneapolis: University of Minnesota Press, 1958), Vol. II, pp. 192–193; Max Black, "The Justification of Induction," in Sidney Morgenbesser (ed.), *Philosophy of Science Today* (New York: Basic Books, 1967).
36 Hempel, "Explanatory Incompleteness," p. 400 and "Explanation and Prediction by Covering Laws," p. 130.
37 Scriven, "Truisms as the Grounds for Historical Explanation," p. 452 and "Definitions, Explanations, and Theories," p. 100.
38 Hempel, "Explanatory Incompleteness," p. 399.
39 Toulmin, *Uses of Argument*, p. 45.
40 Hempel, "Explanatory Incompleteness," p. 411.
41 Ibid., emphasis added.
42 Scriven, "Explanations, Predictions, and Laws," p. 211.
43 Scriven, "Truisms as the Grounds for Historical Explanation," pp. 459, 460, 462.
44 Scriven, "Definitions, Explanations, and Theories," p. 193. See also Scriven, "The Limits of Physical Explanation," in Bernard Baumrin (ed.), *Philosophy of Science: The Delaware Seminar* (New York: Interscience, 1963), Vol. 2.
45 Brodbeck, "Explanation, Prediction, and 'Imperfect' Knowledge," pp. 369, 374; John Yolton, "Explanation," *British Journal for the Philosophy of Science*, 10 (1959), p. 105.
46 Toulmin, *Uses of Argument*, p. 144.
47 Scriven, "Truisms as the Grounds for Historical Explanation," p. 462; Toulmin, *The Philosophy of Science* (London: Hutchinson, 1953) pp. 25, 33, 40, 102; Hempel, "Explanation and Prediction by Covering Laws," p. 120; Brodbeck, "Explanation, Prediction, and 'Imperfect' Knowledge," pp. 370, 371, 373.
48 Bergmann, *Philosophy of Science* (Madison: University of Wisconsin Press, 1958), p. 31; Brodbeck, "Explanation, Prediction, and 'Imperfect' Knowledge," pp. 370, 385.
49 Yolton, "Explanation," p. 207.
50 Brodbeck, "Explanation, Prediction, and 'Imperfect' Knowledge," pp. 365–368.
51 Scriven, "Explanations, Predictions, and Laws," p. 202.
52 Theodore Mischel, "Pragmatic Aspects of Explanation," *Philosophy of Science*, 33 (1966).

53 Toulmin, *Philosophy of Science*, pp. 93–94, 103–104; *Uses of Arguments*, 101, 114, 121–122, 220; Gilbert Ryle, *The Concept of Mind* (New York: Barnes and Noble, 1949), pp. 120–125; Scriven, "Truisms as the Grounds for Historical Explanation," pp. 445–451; Wilfrid Sellars, "The Language of Theories," in Herbert Feigl and Grover Maxwell (eds), *Current Issues in The Philosophy of Science* (New York: Holt Rinehart and Winston, 1901), esp. p. 71.
54 Brodbeck, "Explanation, Prediction, and 'Imperfect' Knowledge," p. 384.
55 Ibid., p. 383.
56 For representative discussions see Gardiner (ed.), *Theories of History*.
57 See, for example, Bernard Berelson and Gary A. Steiner, *Human Behavior: An Inventory of Scientific Findings* (New York: Harcourt, Brace and World, 1964).
58 Easton, *System*, p. 4.
59 Scriven, "Explanations, Predictions, and Laws," p. 212.
60 Kaplan, *Conduct of Inquiry*, p. 10.
61 A. R. Louch, *Explanation and Human Action* (Berkeley: University of California Press, 1966) pp. 38–40.
62 Kaplan, *Conduct of Inquiry*, p. 11.
63 Brodbeck, "Introduction," p. 2.
64 Kaplan, *Conduct of Inquiry*, p. 346.
65 Ibid., p. 3.
66 Toulmin, *Foresight and Understanding* (Bloomington: Indiana University Press, 1961), p. 15.
67 Ibid., p. 14.
68 See Thomas Kuhn, *The Structure of Scientific Revolutions* (Chicago, IL: University of Chicago Press, 1962).
69 Toulmin, *Foresight and Understanding*, p. 17.
70 Meehan, *Explanation*, p. 1.
71 Ibid., p. 21.
72 Israel Scheffler, *The Autonomy of Inquiry* (New York: Knopf, 1963), pp. 53–55.
73 Ibid., p. 54.
74 Yolton, "Explanation," p. 194.
75 Toulmin, *Foresight and Understanding*, p. 99.
76 Scriven, "Explanations, Predictions, and Laws," p. 213.
77 Yolton, "Explanation," pp. 200–201.
78 Scriven, "Explanations, Predictions, and Laws," p. 225; "Truisms as the Grounds for Historical Explanation," p. 452.
79 Hempel, "Explanation and Prediction by Governing Laws," p. 130.
80 Israel Scheffler, *Science and Subjectivity* (Indianapolis, IN: Bobbs-Merrill, 1967), p. 4.
81 Ibid., p. 5.

2   The alienation of political theory (1986)

More than thirty years ago, Alfred Cobban (1953) charged that the Western tradition of political theory, a tradition concerned with ethical issues, had ceased to develop and had entered a period of decline. Cobban's argument was only one of many claims about the decline of political theory that appeared in the 1950s, and the idea of political theory as it is understood today was in large measure invented during the course of these discussions. Cobban, like many of the period, argued that the immediate cause of the retreat from questions of what "ought to be" was the impact of the "modes of thought" characteristic of science and history, that is, value freedom and relativism, but he believed that the underlying source of the problem was the circumstance in which political theory had become "disengaged from political facts" and "practice" and had "become instead an academic discipline" (rep. 1969: 298–99).

Cobban's analysis of political theory was perceptive, but it also involved a fundamental mistake that was made by almost all those engaged in these debates about the decline of political theory. It was the assumption that the canon of classic texts that had become part of the curriculum of political studies in the university represented an actual historical tradition whose latest phase was academic political theory, including the study of those texts. Arguments about decline begged the fundamental issue. There was no doubt that there was an academic tradition of political theory, but the notion that it was the decline of a greater tradition reaching from Plato to recent years was a pervasive myth. It is difficult to be sure just how literally someone like Cobban intended this connection, but it is clear that the idea of the historical integrity of the tradition gained increasing importance during the next decade.

Although Cobban did not correctly understand the genesis of the situation, he recognized the dilemma of political theory as an academic discipline. And, even as an academic discipline, it was by the 1950s becoming increasingly alienated from direct engagement with issues in political practice and from contact with political facts. The question of the extent to which political theory had concerned itself with ethical issues was more moot, for many during this period would claim that it was precisely an excessive emphasis on such matters that was the problem. The behavioralist account of the decline of political theory also recognized a detachment of political theory from political reality. This account, which began to develop during this period, was also historically questionable, and its diagnosis and recommendations were significantly different from those of individuals such as Cobban. It claimed that science offered a way of re-engaging political facts and creating an identity for political theory.

Even if the self-image of political theory in the past had, in retrospect, not always been very plausible, its failure, beginning in the 1950s, to face up to what it was and might be was nothing short of prodigious. And in seeking an identity it increasingly lost its intellectual autonomy. Although certain elements, under siege within the discipline of political science, would by the 1970s achieve a large measure of professional independence as an interdisciplinary field, political theory increasingly became little more than variations on metatheoretical themes in philosophy and philosophical history. By the 1980s, not only was political theory thoroughly estranged from its object, politics, but its components, both inside and outside political science, had become dispersed and even incapable of meaningful debate.

The alienation of political theory had its immediate origins in the controversy that arose in the midst of the behavioral revolution in political science. Although it is difficult, and artificial, to make a sharp distinction between the pre- and post-1950 eras, the division is a somewhat indigenous one, and the continuities as well as the transformations are worth noting. It is most important to understand the nature of the behavioral revolution and its relationship to the earlier history of political science, because this information is not readily accessible in the rhetoric of either the revolutionaries or the counterrevolutionaries.

It would be a mistake to impose too programmatic and schematic an image on these events associated with the behavioral revolution. The participants were far from fully able to articulate the circumstances in which they were involved, and the various positions were more diverse and complex than they often seem in retrospect. But, despite many appearances to the contrary, the behavioral revolution was a conservative revolution. This is not to say that it did not fundamentally change the character of political science or that it did not institute new research programs, but it was fought in defense of old ideals and traditional, if unrealized, goals in both politics and social science. As in many conservative revolutions, however, the enemy was not accurately specified, but revolution required something definite to be overthrown.

If one is familiar with the history of American political science prior to 1940 (see Ricci, 1984; Seidelman, 1985), the behavioral attack on historical or "traditional" political theory is not comprehensible on its face. It might be suggested that, because the revolutionaries needed something to revolt against, the history of political theory seemed most alien to the scientific goals of behavioralism. There is also the less cynical and more historically sensitive thesis that change within the discipline had always been advanced in the name of theory. Because the history of political theory largely occupied the subfield and held the title, it became the focus of criticism. And matters like the typical postwar emphasis on science and the need to demonstrate "scientificness" in order to secure research funding, the failure of previous phases of the discipline to achieve its scientific vision, the dominance of positivism and scientism in the other social sciences and in philosophy, and the retreat from practical concerns in favor of pure science are all relevant. Yet even the composite of all these factors does not provide an adequate explanation for exactly what happened in political theory.

The fact that most of the pivotal figures in the behavioral movement had been trained as traditional political theorists might be taken as an anomaly, but it is part of the explanation and touches a matter that goes deeper than their conventional occupation with theoretical issues. Prior to 1940 there is very little to indicate any tension between science and history in American political science. Political theory had characteristically been understood as including the history of political theory, which was in turn represented largely as the progressive history of political science and democratic values. And, despite some variation in the terms employed, political science and political theory were assumed to consist of both empirical and normative propositions about politics and government.

From the paradigm-setting texts of William Dunning (1902–20) to the protobehavioral arguments of Charles Merriam (1925) to George Sabine's influential history of political theory (1937), the scientific and political ideology of the discipline had remained remarkably uniform. Despite some exceptions, the discipline was generally politically conservative although maybe at times intellectually radical in its dreams of an instrumental social science allied with a national state for the solution of social and political problems. Its propensities were distinctly pragmatic and grounded in a belief in the complementarity, if not outright identity, of scientific and liberal democratic values, along with a constant aversion to the taint of what it took to be speculative philosophy and metaphysics and their political and ideological counterparts. The history of political theory was understood as demonstrating all this and, particularly in the 1930s, offered a vehicle for democratic self-consciousness in the face of alien political challenges from both the left and right.

From 1900 to 1945 there was hardly a major figure in political theory, or political science, who was not involved in both the history of political theory and the advancement of political science as a science, and one would look in vain for any significant tension between these notions of theory. This was in part because "theory," "theorist," and "theorizing" were concepts that had been consistently understood in a rather functional manner. Political theories, in both political science and political life, were ideas about the state, whether descriptive, causal, or prescriptive and evaluative, as opposed to facts and institutions. They were, particularly as an aspect of political science, mental constructs for organizing and manipulating, both intellectually and practically, the mass of data that social scientists and statesmen confronted in the social and political world.

There are a variety of historical reasons why the profession of political science was born with a subfield called "political theory," but it was not because "theory" and its cognates had any very definite or specific meaning when the American Political Science Association was founded (1903). In some respects the history of the subfield is the history of the attempt to give "theory" meaning. It is the history of its reification. Even through the 1940s the term was largely used in a functional or categorical sense. Its reification was basically a product of the debates about theory that began in the 1950s. But the fundamental interpretative question remains – what was the root of the conflict within political theory and between political theory and political science?

The problem stemmed from the intrusion of ideas promulgated by the German émigrés of the 1930s. These individuals included Leo Strauss, Hannah Arendt, Theodor Adorno, Eric Voegelin, Franz Neuman, Arnold Brecht, Herbert Marcuse, Max Horkheimer. Although often not yet in published form, these ideas had begun, during the 1940s, to have a significant impact on the profession and discipline of political science and particularly on the discourse of political theory.

These thinkers appeared, at least from the American perspective, to be political theorists, but their ideas had been formed in the context of German philosophy and the practical experience of totalitarianism. Whether left or right in their ideological leanings, many of these individuals represented a position and orientation that threatened some of the basic premises of American political science and political theory.

American political science had been heavily influenced by German thought during its formative period in the late 1800s as well as during the first two decades of the twentieth century, and political science (and political theory) was in many respects Hegelian and Comtean in its early years. However, the general reaction against "speculative" philosophy that characterized the early 1900s had succeeded in thoroughly "Americanizing" these ideas both politically and philosophically. The world-historical visions of the third great wave of German influence were not easily assimilated in either style or substance. Although there were many specific problems stemming from the attachment of these thinkers to Marxism, certain theological doctrines, and other alien perspectives, a more basic and general difficulty was their historical pessimism and their depreciation of both liberalism and science.

The perspective introduced by Voegelin, Strauss, Arendt, and Marcuse entailed the idea that the history of politics and political theory in the West, at least in recent times, was one of decline. This notion was tied to a critique of both liberalism and science. Liberalism was construed in one way or another as decadent, as the historical threshold of fascism and nazism, and the facade of socially repressive forces. Science, scientific philosophy, and technology were conceived in similar manner, and social science was often understood as their most heinous manifestation. Science was the instrument of political oppression and the enemy of humanism.

There were numerous other antithetical elements in these new themes in political theory, but maybe most important was the resurgence of what in the earlier years would have been called "speculative" political philosophy.

Although it might not be difficult to perceive the cosmos of normative givens inherent in American pragmatism and realism, American political scientists believed not only in separating facts and values but in the relativity of values and the danger in transcendental claims. The new wave of thought, however, maintained that value relativism and the separation of fact and value were both causes and symptoms of a crisis of modernity. Almost without exception, these thinkers sought, either in history or outside it, a source of transcendental judgment for the critique of politics.

Other matters of dissonance might be detailed, but this should be sufficient to indicate that the European infusion of ideas in political theory, which began to take effect in the 1940s and was more fully visible by the 1950s, precipitated a crucial moment for the self-image of American political science. The idea of political theory as part of an empirical science of politics integrally related to the evolution of liberal thought and practice, an idea that had been at the core of American political science from its earliest beginnings, was in jeopardy. The consequence would be the end of the alliance between, if not the identity of, theory as history and theory as science and a proliferation of metatheoretical arguments in defense of each.

One would be forced to search very hard for any sophisticated and philosophically informed source of or reflection on notions about political theory as part of empirical political science before the 1950s. The basic claims about theory and science, even the language and phrasing of those claims, changed very little in the forty years from Merriam's announcement of, or call for, the creation of a systematic interdisciplinary causal "science of human behavior" (1925: 11) to Easton's statement of the "behavioral credo" and the commitment to develop "a science of politics modeled after the methodological assumptions of the natural sciences" (1965a: 8). What, increasingly, did change, however, was the relationship between philosophy and political science or between metatheoretical rhetoric and scientific practice.

It was a long time, not until well into the 1970s, before political scientists of the behavioral persuasion became fully aware of either the philosophical sources of their scientific identity or the existence of alternative images of science and social scientific explanation. But as early as 1950 Harold Lasswell, in one of the first attempts of the behavioral, or proto-behavioral, era to provide a theoretical "framework for political science," indicated that his efforts were informed by a "thorough-going empiricist philosophy of the sciences" based on "logical positivism, operationalism, and instrumentalism" (Lasswell and Kaplan, 1950: xiii, xiv). Even his collaboration on this work with the philosopher Abraham Kaplan indicated a new dimension or threshold in the relationship between political science and philosophy.

There is little evidence that would suggest that in the previous twenty years Lasswell had any very deep involvement with the philosophy of science. And his case was typical of the advocates of scientism. From the beginning, natural science had been a model, or contrast model, for the social sciences, and nowhere was this more true than in political science. What was also the case, however, was that social scientists, almost without exception and without regard to whether they wished to identify themselves with it or disassociate themselves from it, had no significant contact with or knowledge of the practices of natural science. Natural science was basically either a legitimating or a critical symbol mediated through various philosophical images.

It would require a detailed historical examination of particular cases to determine the extent to which the social sciences were influenced by philosophical accounts of science and the extent to which they employed such accounts rhetorically, either reflectively or unreflectively, for justification and criticism. The relationship was, however, an integral and complex one, and it is safe to say that eventually a change in the philosophical image of science would produce an identity crisis in the social sciences. In the history of American political science, the balance between influence and legitimation, to the extent that they can be analytically disentangled, has differed at various points.

Through 1950 there was little defection from the principle that natural science was a positive model. And, from the beginning of the discipline to the end of the behavioral era, the basic assumptions, on the part of both proponents and opponents of scientism, about the nature and demands of scientific method and explanation changed very little. Even the transition from Comtean and Spencerian images of science, dominant in the first two decades of the century, to those of logical positivism, beginning in the 1940s, did not significantly alter the basic ideas about the character of scientific inquiry. What did shift, overall, was the valence between influence and legitimation. It is necessary to exercise care in making this distinction, because even the rationalizing uses of the symbol of natural science indicate a form of influence to the degree that individuals are constrained and directed by the symbols available. But by the 1960s political scientists had become significantly more the instruments of their symbolism than in Merriam's era, despite the growth in their reflectiveness about the source.

For both internal and external reasons and audiences, Merriam had evoked and invoked the image of science for his enterprise. This was also largely true for the political scientists of the 1950s, but although Merriam, despite his lack of success in many respects, had little focused internal opposition to his program apart from critics who believed he was either too much or too little committed to practical goals, his successors believed that the survival of the traditional scientific image of political theory, as well as the basic goals of the discipline, was at risk. The symbol of science, by the 1950s, no longer commanded immediate and general respect. The historical situation seemed to signal increasing urgency about the need to realize the scientific potential of the discipline, but there was at the same time a challenge to the authority of both the general symbol of science and the specific image that had characterized political science.

It was in this context that political scientists entered into a critique of the study of the history of political theory and sought to develop a more articulate vision of their scientific commitments. Although numerous factors contributed to the resurgence of scientism that characterized the behavioral revolution, what has been neglected, and misunderstood, is the extent to which that recommitment was a reaction to the subversion of political science's scientific and political identity that was being mounted not only within the discipline but within what had traditionally been understood as its intellectual core – political theory.

It was also in this context, in part in response to the behavioral attack and in part simply because of the ideas represented in that movement, that the study of the history of political theory was transformed into a vehicle for the critique of what, by the 1960s, was becoming mainstream political science. Among the authors of this critique were both those, such as Strauss, who had begun to challenge the basic vision of liberal scientific progress and some of those more anomalously positioned individuals who had been simply "doing" the history of political theory in the usual American way. They found them-selves, somewhat inexplicably, the target of their peers, with whom they thought they shared basic premises about the compatibility of history and science. The dialogue between these protagonists, which lasted well into the 1970s, and the waves of philosophical reflection about political theory which that dialogue in part engendered were the basic cause of the contemporary alienation of political theory. And it was not merely an alienation of the spirit. Both sides began to practice what they preached.

This was not the first time in the social sciences that a *Methodenstreit* had profound disciplinary and professional effects, but this conflict largely absor-bed theoretical discussion in political science for a quarter of a century. It not only fundamentally shaped significant portions of political science, especially the subfield of political theory, but significantly contributed to the emergence of the wider field of political theory and philosophy which, despite later assumptions about its perennial character, was hardly differentiated and identifiable prior to the 1960s.

At its core, behavioralism or the behavioral movement, as something other than simply what political scientists did and came to do, was an amalgam of quasi-philosophical ideas about scientific explanation. Whether or not these ideas were reflectively instrumental, they served an ideological function within the discipline and produced a unifying force that had not been sustained in earlier years. The atmosphere of enthusiasm and the commitment to challen-ging what behavioralists characterized as the orthodoxy of historical and institutional analysis may have led some truly to believe in their extravagant claims about such matters as emulating the laws of physics. There is, however, reason to suggest that professional and disciplinary identity was the most significant goal.

Political science, more so than the other social sciences, was from its beginning, more a holding company for some loosely related fields of inquiry and research programs than a discipline with a theoretical core. The beha-vioral "revolution" and the behavioral "mood" were in part manifestations of a continuing attempt to establish a scientific and disciplinary identity. One of the factors that contributed to the success of behavioralism was the sense of urgency created by both the real and perceived external context and the sense of lagging behind other fields in scientific accomplishment, but there were also important internal factors.

One of the forces that animated political theory, particularly the history of political theory, in the 1930s was the belief in the need to construct or, more accurately, make explicit and coherent a liberal democratic ideology that would be comparable to and confront the foreign ideologies on the left and right that threatened both political mind and space. Behavioralism was doing something on this order with regard to the discipline's scientific image, but the similarity is more than analogous. The 1950s were also a period of ideological consolidation. The extent to which the creation of a value theory that would be equal to the times was part of the behavioral program is often forgotten in view of its dominant and subsequent emphasis on scientific method, but more important was the persistence of the faith in the complementarity of democracy and science that permeated the behavioral literature.

In the controversies of the 1960s over the political, and apolitical, role of the discipline, critics pointed to the extent to which behavioralism, in theory and practice, reflected and legitimated dominant liberal values. Doing science, and the particular kind of science that characterized behavioralism, was a kind of value theory. The doctrines of the priority of pure science and the separation of facts and values only appeared to be a contradiction of the professed concern with liberal democracy. The behavioral revolution was, then, a conservative one in several respects. Its basic goals and notions of science had defined the discipline from its inception, and in varying degrees of explicitness it was a defense of traditional liberalism and American institutions.

In many respects the behavioral revolution was a theoretical one – apart from the fact that, with regard to its scientific goals, it did not accomplish in practice what it claimed in theory. Not only were most of the major spokesmen by training political theorists, but the subfield of political theory was where the revolutionary and antirevolutionary debates largely took place. A transformation in theory and its uses was also to be the fulcrum for disciplinary change. But most important for the argument here is the fact that the behavioral movement, by the time this self-ascribed persuasion had become a disciplinary orthodoxy in the 1960s, produced an unprecedented metatheoretical self-consciousness that had a far-reaching impact on the practice of research as well as the evolution of images of political theory.

No matter what innovations behavioralism introduced into the research programs of political science, or what changes it effected in the orientation of the discipline toward politics, it persisted in legitimating political inquiry in terms of the authority of its scientificness. And, as in previous periods (e.g., Merriam, 1925), the history of the discipline was represented as the story of the progress of science as conceived in the present and, particularly, as the growth of theory (e.g., Almond, 1966; Truman, 1965). Theory was understood as the hallmark of science. Although it would be appropriate to write the history of many fields of knowledge as the history of the evolution of theories about their object of research, it might be more reasonable to write the history of political science from the perspective of its theory of theory. What came to characterize the behavioral era, however, was the fact that these images of theory became less and less merely legitimating myths as scientific practice became increasingly an attempt to legitimate epistemological and methodological commitments.

David Easton's claim about the "decline" of political theory and the need for its reconstitution (1951; 1953) was characteristic (although maybe the paradigm case) of a number of attacks on what came to be understood by both its critics and its defenders as "traditional theory." This meant in effect the study of what had come to be understood as the "great tradition" from Plato to the present and the normative concerns that supposedly characterized that putative tradition. The terms of this critique had, in fact, been developing steadily during the past decade as both the new European influences on the subfield of political theory were felt and the various postwar factors pointing to a need to reassert and revise the scientific image of political science took shape.

Easton's argument, and it is important to note exactly what the argument claimed, was that the tradition that had begun with the Greeks had undergone "impoverishment" in the hands of historically oriented scholars such as George Sabine who had transformed it into a history of political ideas that both lacked relevance to contemporary values and contributed little to the task of developing "a generalized theory about the relations of facts" that could serve as the "theoretical organ" of a truly scientific study of politics. What was required was a "theoretical revolution" that both released political theory from parasitic historicism and transcended the "hyperfactualism" and "crude empiricism" of previous years.

The account provided by individuals such as Easton was in many respects quite accurate with regard to its description of the character and condition of political theory and political science, but it misrepresented the intentions, motives, and work of those, such as Sabine, whom it overtly criticized. Sabine's analysis of political theory (1939), for example, was not significantly different from Easton's. Although he wrote about the history of political theory, he did not depreciate the scientific study of politics or see anything but the compatibility, even identity, of the two enterprises. The criticism was directed at a genre that harbored the incipient critics of political science but in which they were still not highly visible. Although the historians of political theory – Strauss, Arendt, and Voegelin, for example – who came into prominence in the postwar years were in fact already antagonistic toward the values of American political science, the behavioral critique crystallized and galvanized hostile attitudes and precipitated a fundamental split within the field. It would be an exaggeration to say that the arguments that emerged from the literature of the history of political theory in the succeeding years were simply a response to that critique, but they were certainly in large measure shaped by it.

Just as behavioralists had attempted to redefine and demarcate political theory, the traditionalists, who now to some extent identified themselves in terms of those who criticized them, elaborated an alternative image of theory and its past and future that at least initially was more part of a defensive maneuver than anything having to do with the normal practice of research. Individuals such as Strauss set out to diagnose what they also called the "decline of political philosophy," but they described that decline in terms of assumptions at the core of behavioralism and the liberal values with which it was associated. Furthermore, the argument, sometimes explicit and sometimes implicit, was that both the historical approach and what was to be discovered or recalled by this approach were not only far from decadent but the key to solving the problem of decline.

What is most important with respect to the argument here is that this controversy, which developed during the 1950s and came to a head in the 1960s, was not, strictly speaking, a theoretical controversy at all. Although there were various dimensions of substantive theoretical conflict about politics and political phenomena embedded in the contending claims of behavioralism and those who became its institutional critics, the dispute was about, or at least was carried on in terms of metatheoretical arguments about, the nature of theory, the history of theory, and the character and purpose of theorizing. Eventually such arguments began in many respects to overshadow and direct inquiry in these respective subfields of political science and to provide the basis for a wider interdisciplinary field of political theory which largely grew out of this realm of discourse and began to take institutional form in the 1970s.

What came to distinguish the literature on the history of political theory by the early 1960s was an increased emphasis on the tradition as a distinct and meaningful object of inquiry. From the somewhat loose construction that had characterized the work of such individuals as Sabine, there emerged the notion of the classic texts as representations of elements in an organic historical development that explained a crisis in contemporary politics and political thought. This crisis usually in some way included the condition of contemporary political and social science. In varying ways and degrees, the work of Leo Strauss, Eric Voegelin, Hannah Arendt, Sheldon Wolin, and numerous other interpreters contributed to the constitution of a paradigm that provided both a subject matter and an approach to study and research.

Either explicitly or implicitly, the message was that the study of the history of political theory was not some antiquarian enterprise devoid of relevance for contemporary politics and political values but something crucial for their understanding and a form of political inquiry far more important than that represented by modern political and social science. The account of the tradition became an etiology of the devolution of Western politics and political thought that sharply contrasted with those histories of the evolution of liberalism that had rested easily alongside the faith in an empirical science of politics. These new accounts imposed a schematic and synoptic meaning on the history of political thought, which was conceived as a unity, marked by points of beginning, reversal, and end, and presented as an entity to which one could literally apply such attributes as decline and revival. The idea of the tradition, which in various forms had been part of the study of the history of political theory since its inception, was transformed into the myth of the tradition – an elaborate myth about both the subject matter and the activity of studying it.

This myth did not turn on any single proposition. It was a syndrome of assumptions shared by academic political theorists. Among those, such as Strauss and Voegelin, who contributed to the creation of this syndrome, the precise form and content of the argument, its intention, and its purpose varied a great deal, but there were many common features. In all cases, a retrospective, analytically constituted, or stipulative tradition was reified and treated as an actual historical tradition and recast as a dramatic story with pivotal scenes and protagonists. The development of the tradition was charted by tracing a movement from one paradigmatic text and author to another – from Plato to the present – with the implication that these works were both representations and explanations of the historical period to which they were related.

Despite the variations in the historical conditions of their production, the classic texts were presented as belonging to a common literary genre that was the product of a historically identifiable activity called political theory, which was in turn distinguished by a relatively consistent set of concerns. This "great dialogue," as it was often more than metaphorically represented, was offered as the principal context for understanding a classic text. But, at the same time, counting a work as part of the tradition was what distinguished it as a classic. Although the myth was in various ways widely shared among scholars of political theory who did not themselves undertake cosmic interpretations of Western political thought and whose work was much more narrowly focused, the paradigm cases were usually associated with interpretations of the tradition that sought to provide a pathology of modernity.

The study of past political ideas and the analysis of the classic canon became a vehicle for a therapeutic exercise in discovering the intellectual source of a modern crisis and recovering certain truths, or at least important insights, buried beneath the accretions of the tradition. It was an act of deconstruction and reconstruction. In many cases, the concern was to recover the very idea of the political and reestablish its worth in an age where it had become depreciated or absorbed in other categories.

This literature contributed to the creation of a whole mythology about political theory and politics. This mythology included the notions that contemporary academic political theory was the heir to the great tradition; that it was an epic world-historical enterprise; that it was the theoretical dimension of political life and that the relationship exemplified a categorical relationship between thought and action; that ideas in general were the determinative historical forces and that, historically, modern politics could be explained in terms of classic texts; that political theory in the past and present had access to transcendental truths about politics; and that politics was an object of transcendental knowledge. But, if these claims about the tradition and its study were extravagant, they were no more inflated than the behavioralist account of theory and its role in science.

When held up to examination, both the myth of the tradition and the behavioral vision of theory seem, today, hardly credible, but their residue still lays a dead hand on many aspects of the literature of political theory. The paradigmatic statements of the behavioral notion of theory, like those associated with the myth of the tradition, varied in their particulars and especially in the degree to which they were intended literally or employed rhetorically. The tension between "traditional" and "scientific" theory led to hyperbole on both sides. But there were some common core features of the behavioral conception of theory.

Just as the idea of the tradition, so long the property of academic political theory, had been the vague but conventionally, and ultimately intuitively, accepted foundation that made the elaboration of the myth of the tradition possible and effective, the basic elements of the behavioral image of science were already embedded in the discourse of the profession. These included the ideas that there was a methodological unity of science; that empirical science was verifiable in a way that evaluative claims were not; that natural science was a model to be emulated; that true science involved generalization; that the core of scientific explanation was theoretical organization of ontologically and cognitively autonomous facts; that facts were in some way given to immediate experience and were the basis of testing generalizations even though they gained scientific significance in terms of those generalizations; and that theories were basically instrumental constructs for describing and explaining data and constructs that must be operationally defined in terms of such data.

What in part distinguished behavioralism from earlier scientism in political science was, first, the extent to which it brought these notions together and elaborated them in a relatively detailed and coherent manner. Second, it drew consistently, although often indirectly, on the philosophy of science and especially on the dominant persuasion of logical positivism and logical empiricism. Third, it did not simply employ these ideas to legitimate its research programs but attempted to realize these philosophical images of science in practice and transform them into methodological norms.

There were a number of distinct problems with the behavioralist goal of a general deductive and predictive theory of politics modeled on the natural sciences. First of all, there was a failure to consider the inherent difference between philosophical methodology and philosophical analyses of the logic and epistemology of science on the one hand and methods or intradisciplinary forms of research practice on the other hand. Second, even this philosophical image of science was largely secondhand by the time it reached political science and had been mediated through various secondary and tertiary works in philosophy and social science. There is no indication that behavioralists, at least initially, had any detailed firsthand knowledge of the philosophy of science, let alone the practice of natural science. Third, the particular philosophical tradition to which political scientists attached themselves was one that had progressively developed in isolation from any close attention to the actual history and current practice of science. Fourth, this philosophical literature seldom concerned itself specifically with matters of social scientific inquiry. Finally, even the assumption of the unity of science and the paradigm status of natural science, which were at the very core of the behavioral program, were themselves philosophical doctrines propagated by logical positivism and logical empiricism.

It was not, however, simply the failure to consider these problems that led to the alienation of theory in political science. It was also the particular philosophical model of theory and scientific explanation that was adopted and the kind of "theory" that was constructed in light of it. This involved a notion of explanation as the subsumption of particular facts under theoretical generalizations and a conception of theories as mental constructs that served as instruments for the organization and investigation of facts. Like the myth of the great tradition, this view of theory and scientific explanation had roots in the history of American political science.

Political scientists had always exhibited a fundamental ambivalence about theory that behavioralism not only failed to resolve but, in the end, exacerbated. In the early years, political scientists had defined their commitment to science and empiricism in terms of a rejection of formalism and a search for realism that would avoid the dangers of distortion inherent in metaphysics and speculative a priori claims. This translated into a demand for grasping the actual facts, the unmediated and irreducible facts, of political reality; grounding concepts and knowledge in such observable facts; and making all claims subject to their authority. Yet it was recognized that the facts did not entirely speak for themselves, that science was a business of abstraction and generalization, and that under modern conditions of inquiry the sheer amount of factual information was overwhelming without some mode of selection and organization.

From the beginning, the solution to this dilemma moved in the direction of theoretical formalism and an instrumentalist conception of scientific theory that entailed an ontological distinction between theories and facts. Theories were understood as basically conceptual tools, in themselves neither intrinsically right nor wrong, for discovering, ordering, explaining, and predicting observed phenomena, and they were to be judged according to how well they performed these functions. This position reinforced, and was reinforced by, a broader instrumentalist perspective that viewed political science as a practical science in the service of the state and directed toward political and governmental reform. This technological conception of science and theory received philosophical encouragement and validation from several sources.

Comte's and Spencer's methodological positivism and technocratic vision informed much of early political science. Philosophers and social theorists such as Karl Pearson influenced or provided support for the position of individuals like Merriam. And the pragmatic realism of John Dewey, Arthur Bentley, and C. S. Peirce further contributed to this general outlook. This practical orientation of political science made the idea of theory as a heuristic seem reasonable, but it was also supported by a more general antitheoretical intellectual propensity rooted in a tendency to believe that the conventions of the American political experience and liberalism were in some basic sense given and universal. This made the goals of generalization and factual objectivity seem feasible.

When behavioralism set out to effect its theoretical revolution, it retained this instrumental view of theory, and the dominant philosophy of science provided a basis for confirming and refining it. The latter was particularly important, because the behavioral credo emphasized the priority and autonomy of "pure" science. Instrumentalism now required an epistemological legitimacy independent of pragmatic validity. It was in part for this reason that the behavioral vision of theory became increasingly tied to the logical positivist and logical empiricist tradition that began to emerge by the early 1940s in the United States in the work of such individuals as Rudolf Carnap and Otto Neurath. In this school, theories and theoretical concepts were understood as primarily supervenient intellectual constructions or initially empirically empty logical calculi that, while organizing and explaining the relationship between facts, gained cognitive meaning by definitional ties to primitive and incorrigible observational data. This view of theory and the attending deductive model of explanation had become, by the 1950s, the "received" or "orthodox" philosophical reconstruction of science, one that gained acceptance on both sides of the argument about whether the social sciences should appropriate the methods of natural science.

Logical positivism not only supported traditional views of scientific explanation in political science but provided a new basic for other generally accepted notions, such as the separation of facts and values and the emotive and unverifiable character of value judgments. But, again, what most distinguished the behavioral attachment to this philosophical position was the extent to which it launched a program of "theory construction" and research practice that reflected this analysis of theory and science.

Theoretical endeavors in political science during the 1960s were dominated by the idea of the "conceptual framework." Although some held to the assumption that theory would arise inductively from particular empirical studies, the greatest efforts were devoted to the development of "models," "approaches," "strategies" of inquiry, and various other conceptual or analytical frameworks that were viewed as either theories or prototheories. These reflected various metaphors and analogies, but above all, variations on the idea of politics and government as a "system" were what informed this work. There was much in the history of political science that supported this strategy of inquiry in addition to the general attachment to various forms of instrumentalism, but, as Lasswell had claimed in 1950, it clearly was influenced by the orthodox philosophical theory of theory.

The basic argument was that science consisted of a marriage of theory building and data collection and that theories were abstract and somewhat arbitrary conceptual schema to be imposed on various data bases and given empirical meaning by operational definitions. It was assumed that all encounters with the facts were filtered through conceptual lenses and that science was in part a matter of making these constructs explicit and tailoring them to perform the various tasks connected with the intersubjective selection, description, and explanation of political facts. Theories were conceived as frameworks that made systematic and coordinated research programs possible.

Apart from the problems of translating a philosophical theory of theory into scientific practice, this analysis of theory distorted the character of scientific theory and obscured the extent to which theory, in science or any practice of knowledge, involves substantive claims that are constitutive of the facts. Consequently, it inhibited authentic theoretical discussion about political phenomena. But this philosophical myth also carried with it a myth about politics that operated at several levels.

First of all, it reinforced the tendency to take the facts of American politics as more than conventional. In this conception of science, the observation language for reporting and describing facts was largely that of everyday life. This incorporated the ideology of American liberalism and rendered it theoretically impervious by attributing to it the quality of factual givenness and objectivity. Second, the conceptual frameworks, despite their abstractness and apparent remoteness from political phenomena, nearly always reflected the structure and process of American politics and introduced an ideological bias that undermined the very objectivity that they were supposedly designed to achieve. They thus either idolized the political facts they reflected or fundamentally distorted configurations of political phenomena by interpreting them in terms of categories that were ultimately derived from American politics.

By the end of the 1960s, political science had officially divided political theory into three parts – historical, normative, and empirical. Although what was designated by "normative" would become more tangible as the general interdisciplinary field of political theory developed during the next decade, it was at this point more a category (largely one half of the fact/value distinction) in search of a subject and a respository for endeavors that did not fall easily into the categories of traditional and scientific theory. The tension between the history of political theory and theory as part of what by this time had become the behavioral orthodoxy had led to the differentiation of political theory and the relative autonomy of these poles with their respective images and myths of theory and theorizing. The tension had also begun to recede as behavioralism, once firmly established and identified as political science, found little need either to define itself or to defend itself in relation to the history of political theory and as the history of political theory began to focus on its own domain and internal problems.

In 1969 Sheldon Wolin undertook the most explicit justification yet of the "vocation" of political theory as one of "transmitting" theories from the past to the present in the face of the growing pervasiveness of what he characterized as the "methodism" of the behavioral movement and its "diffidence toward theory and history" as well as contemporary political problems. Wolin claimed that the "wisdom" or "tacit political knowledge" gained through studying the tradition was necessary not only for political education and practical political judgment but also for "scientific imagination" and a sense of scientific significance. He also argued for the preservation of the "vocation by which political theories are created" and which had been neglected by a discipline that was characterized by "complacency" in a time of political chaos and crisis.

Although individuals such as Strauss and Wolin might differ on a great many issues, their interpretation of the fate of political theory and its relationship to political science was indeed similar in its general character. Wolin spoke for a generation of political theorists and articulated a rationale that had been developing since the early 1950s when the enterprise of studying the history of political theory had been first called into question. But Wolin's statement was anticlimactic in the sense that it reflected a debate that was winding down. The center of the critique of behavioralism was already beginning to shift in terms of both vehicle and issues, the study of the history of political theory would be absorbed with different problems, and mainstream political science would redefine its basic mission. Wolin's eulogy, or elegy, for the vocation of political theory and Easton's call, in the same issue of the *American Political Science Review* (1969), for a "new revolution" in political science that would direct attention more explicitly to issues of public policy represented the effective termini of political theory's absorption in a debate between scientific and traditional theory. But the myths about scientific theory and the great tradition engendered by that debate did not recede, and from those myths sprang the alienation of political theory that would characterize the 1970s.

The 1970s were marked by an increasing philosophization of political theory across a number of fronts. This was in part a consequence of metatheoretical involvements spawned by the conflict between scientific and traditional political theory. It was also in some measure a result of the influence of European thought introduced by the émigrés through the vehicle of the history of political theory. But it was in large part a product of the growing professionalization and disciplinization of the field. Political theory, as a distinct and self-conscious scholarly enterprise, had almost exclusively resided in political science, but the controversy of the 1960s, as well as new aspects of the literature, had made significant elements of political theory uncomfortable and anomalous in that setting. These elements would not disappear from political science, but by the early 1970s political theory within political science tended more and more to become a microcosm of the wider and largely interdisciplinary field.

Within mainstream political science, the emphasis on theory building abated as political science refashioned its image in terms of a commitment or, more accurately, recommitment to policy science that contrasted with the behavioral emphasis on pure science. There were many reasons for this policy turn, including changes in research funding as well as considerable internal criticism within the discipline, represented for example by the Caucus for a New Political Science, regarding both the lack of politically significant research and its subtle and not so subtle political biases. Easton's proclamation of the "new revolution" in which the principal concern, at least in the short run, would be with politically relevant research produced few changes in political scientists' assumptions about scientific inquiry, but the turn away from scientism as the source of primary identity blunted the criticism that had characteristically been leveled against behavioralism.

The critique of political science in the 1970s was less in terms of its commitment to science in general than in terms of its particular assumptions about the character and demands of scientific inquiry. These assumptions had seldom been challenged directly, and the same basic image of science was shared by both behavioralists and their critics. The latter conceded the definition of science to behavioralism and identified their concerns in terms often inimical to the very idea of science. By the late 1960s, however, the challenges within the philosophy of science that had been directed against the approach and doctrines of logical positivism had begun to spill over into discussions of political theory, and by the mid-1970s arguments revolving around the work of Thomas Kuhn and others were at the center of political theory in political science (see, e.g., Gunnell, 1969; 1975).

The dependence of the behavioral image of science on the philosophy of science made it inevitable and necessary that a critique of behavioralism would involve itself with this literature. The critique exposed the unreflective dependence of the behavioral program on a particular philosophical reconstruction of the logic and epistemology of science, and it at least raised questions about the general problem of the relationship between philosophy and political theory. But it also had the effect of drawing the field of political theory deeper into a series of metatheoretical and methodological issues.

As critics probed deeper into the integrity of the behavioral image of science and became more engaged and fascinated with the dissident literature in the philosophy of science, behavioralists themselves became more self-conscious about the source of their ideas and mounted a defense through an elaboration of the counterrevolutionary arguments in the philosophy of science (see Miller, 1972). They also struggled to make the work of individuals like Kuhn compatible with their notions about science and their versions of the history of political science. More and more, both critics and defenders of behavioralism submitted to the authority of philosophy, and increasingly debates in political theory became the residue of philosophical arguments. This perpetuated the idea that political inquiry must rest on and proceed from a methodological and epistemological foundation, and such issues continued to displace substantive theoretical attention to politics and questions about the nature of political phenomena.

Often, however, political theorists did not even reach the primary literature of philosophy in joining these issues. What entered the field, beginning in the mid-1960s, was a series of mediational works that instructed political and social scientists about the nature and ways of science and either the symmetry or asymmetry between the logic of explanation in natural and social science (e.g., Kaplan, 1964). Often debates were conducted on the authority of this material. Also, the discussions were extended by the availability of a body of literature in the philosophy of social science that, like the more recent work in the philosophy of science, allowed the argument to proceed beyond the poles of science and humanism that had dominated earlier controversy.

The critique of behavioralism in terms of the philosophy of science was a somewhat negative undertaking in that it did not really provide any solutions or alternatives to the problems it surfaced. But this critique was paralleled and complemented by one drawing upon the literature in the postpositivist philosophy of social science (e.g., Gunnell, 1968). The work of Peter Winch in the Wittgensteinian tradition of linguistic and analytic philosophy and Alfred Schutz in Continental phenomenology, for example, not only challenged positivist claims about the unity of scientific method but elaborated features of a logic of social scientific explanation and concept formation which they argued was demanded by the particular nature of social phenomena. This work emphasized, like that of Weber, the intentional and purposive meaning of social action and the need for social scientific explanation to refer to that meaning and reconstruct the conventional context within which it was intelligible.

Although this literature made some general claims about the character of social phenomena, it nevertheless consisted primarily of metatheoretical arguments about the logic and epistemology of social scientific explanation. Political theorists employed these arguments in very much the same way that behavioralists, for example, had approached the claims of the philosophy of science – as if they constituted a form or method of inquiry and a way of doing social science. In some respects, however, the problem was accentuated in the case of the critics of orthodox social science. Although philosophical analyses both influenced behavioral inquiry and served to justify concrete research programs, the appropriation of new trends in the philosophy of social science produced only a philosophical *idea* of an alternative social science and the nature of theory.

By the mid-1970s it was not uncommon for these opposed philosophical images of social scientific explanation, the positivist and postpositivist, to be treated as if they were alternative modes or paradigms of inquiry or even types of theory. The various threads of the postpositivist philosophy of social science were represented as the "restructuring of social and political theory" (Bernstein, 1976). Inevitably, philosophers were quick to attempt to solve the problem by suggesting that these two broadly defined notions or classes of social scientific explanation might be viewed as incommensurable but complementary approaches that reflected different dimensions of, or perspectives on, social phenomena and different cognitive interests on the part of social science (Braybrooke, 1965; Von Wright, 1971). Many political theorists were quick to adopt some such reconciliatory position (e.g., Moon, 1975). Rather than methodology and epistemology keeping pace with the practice of social science and political theory, the latter were desperately attempting to keep up with developments in philosophy as theory, epistemology, methodology, and method were thoroughly conflated. Political theorists were, ironically, becoming increasingly imprisoned within the metatheoretical arguments to which they had repaired in search of identity and autonomy. There was good reason, by the late 1970s, to be "against epistemology" (Kress, 1979).

These excursions into the philosophy of social science were part of the growing body of literature that by the 1970s was no longer anchored in political science and its subfield of political theory. The 1968 edition of the *International Encyclopedia of the Social Sciences* not only treated political theory as part of political science but gave it a place as an additional, separate, and equal topic where it was discussed as if it were an autonomous discipline with its own history, divisions, and issues. During the next decade, the critique of behavioralism would to some extent continue to bring those elements of the subfield of political theory that were an integral aspect of mainstream political science into contact with those that reflected the wider field of political theory. But the issue nexus progressively atrophied as behavioralism became identical with political science and the various and burgeoning elements of political theory developed autonomous concerns as part of the wider and separate field that had begun to develop its own organizational structures, journals, and other accoutrements of professionalism. Those elements of the subfield of political theory in political science that represented, writ small, the more general field of political theory were increasingly a tolerated but isolated outpost disjoined from the concerns of political science.

The intellectual alienation of political theory, conceived as part of the scientific study of politics, from political theory, conceived as an independent feild of knowledge and inquiry, was objectified in the institutional distinction between political theory as a subfield of political science and as an independent field of study. It was also institutionalized in the "official" divisions of the subfield of political theory in political science. These divisions – normative, historical, and empirical – reflected the fact that there was no common structure, or even a set of issues, that constituted the identity of political theory. This situation, however, was increasingly welcomed, and a separatist mood was common among both mainstream political scientists and those in political science and other fields who labeled themselves political theorists. The displacement of the core of political theory from political science may have seemed to free it from an increasingly hostile context, but it also to a large degree deprived it of a field of action and cut it loose from any direct contact with politics and political inquiry. What most clearly distinguished the field of political theory was its philosophical self-image.

This was not merely a matter of political theory more closely identifying with what had often been understood as political philosophy, characteristically the preferred designation of those like Strauss who wished to differentiate their concerns from mainstream political science. The philosophization of political theory was a much more fundamental phenomenon. It involved a disengagement from any actual practices and problems of political inquiry, an appropriation of philosophical categories of analysis and philosophically defined political issues, and a general and often un-reflective repetition of a range of metatheoretical arguments superficially transposed into claims about political matters and problems of political knowledge.

One important line of development in this general trend and in the eventual constitution of the wider field of political theory had begun to take shape in the late 1960s as political theorists attempted to give content to the nebulous category of normative political theory and to deal with the so-called fact/value issue. What is important to note is that from the outset this was largely a philosophical or metatheoretical issue defined by the categories of logical positivism. Although it might have been intuitively related to actual problems of political judgment and political inquiry, the connection was tenuous at best. The unexamined assumptions were, first, that there were real practical problems, in general, such as justifying evaluative claims, achieving objectivity, or solving the relationship between theory and practice – that is, that these were more than *classes* of problems or analytical categories. Second, it was assumed that to the extent to which such problem definitions could reasonably be construed as identifying actual issues, philosophical solutions were tantamount to, or the basis of, practical solutions.

Part of the perceived crisis of political theory, beginning in the 1950s, had been the fear on the part of some (and the hope on the part of others) that political philosophy, as a set of metaphysical and moral claims, was in trouble. Philosophers like T. D. Weldon (1953; 1956) argued that in effect much of traditional political philosophy had rested on the mistaken belief that moral and political principles were demonstrable in some rational fashion comparable to the claims of natural science. And behavioralists were making largely the same invidious distinction. This *philosophical* dilemma about the justification of normative claims brought on by positivism and its undercutting of the idea of grounded value judgments was translated into a belief that the "tradition has been broken" and that political philosophy, as a practical possibility, "is dead" (Laslett, 1956).

At least two mistakes were involved in the definition of the crisis of political theory. The first was to assume the identity of practical and philosophical problems, and the second was to assume the historical identity of the classic canon and contemporary academic political philosophy. Consequently, it was not surprising that the appearance of postpositivist work in metaethics and related literature dealing with political values and the analysis of political concepts seemed to signal the reincarnation of political philosophy and the possibility of normative political theory. Whatever practical or political counterpart these problems might have been construed as reflecting, they were philosophical problems, formulated in a philosophical context and admitting of only philosophical solutions.

By the late 1960s it was proclaimed that "political philosophy in the English-speaking world is alive again" (Laslett and Runciman, 1967) in the form of a subspecies of autonomous moral reasoning that stood in a complementary relationship to empirical social science. Postpositivist themes in metaethics as represented by the work of Stephen Toulmin (1950) and R. M. Hare (1952; 1963), led to the conclusion that political philosophy was possible and that intercourse between facts and values was not only permissible but inevitable and fecund. Furthermore, all empirical arguments were informed by value premises, and most normative claims required factually grounded "good" reasons.

In this line of argument, political theory both functionally and, by allusion, in the form of the great tradition was factored out into two logical types of claims. Although the normative side of the equation had been temporarily called into question by positivism, its revitalization meant that the constituent parts could now be reconstituted and find a home in academic political theory and that the tradition once broken could find new life in the complementary relationship between social science and political philosophy (Runciman, 1963). Postpositivist philosophy in the form of linguistic analysis also seemed to suggest that it was once again possible to "do" political philosophy through an analysis of political concepts and that this too indicated a return to the traditional concerns of political theory. In effect, a mythological tradition, forged in part in the image of academic political theory, was declared as born again in the form of this same academic enterprise.

If there was any one work that was understood as representing the epiphany of political theory, it was John Rawls's *A Theory of Justice* (1971). This book, the commentaries it occasioned, and the type of literature that it contributed to generating were taken as confirming the guarded optimism of theory watchers who believed that the vital signs of political theory were stirring. Isaiah Berlin's faith in the perennial bloom of political theory and the impossibility of reducing such value judgments to matters of science and logic had been tempered by the admission that "no commanding work in political theory has appeared in the 20th century" (1962). Rawls was widely acclaimed as filling this void, and his work, as well as that of Robert Nozick (*Anarchy, State, and Utopia*, 1974), was hailed as having ushered in an "upswell of political and social theorizing and speculation" that confirmed that political theory "obviously flourishes, all over the English-speaking world and outside it too" (Laslett and Fishkin, 1979: 2, 5).

That outside world entered the English-speaking world in a significant sense with the translation of Jürgen Habermas's *Knowledge and Human Interest* (1971). Although Marcuse's work, more than a quarter of a century after the publication of *Reason and Revolution* (1941), had gained prominence in the literature of political theory during the late 1960s, it was probably Habermas more than anyone else who brought the so-called school of critical theory, associated with individuals like Max Horkheimer and Theodor Adorno, into the mainstream of academic political theory. His work, along with that of philosophers like Rawls, was also one of the principal factors in the institutionalization of political theory as a separate field apart from political science and other specialized disciplines such as philosophy and history. It also exemplified the alienated state of political theory.

Whatever the past of critical theory may have been, whatever practical concerns and political experience that originally motivated its founders, this literature, and the works produced by the vast academic cottage industry devoted to repeating, summarizing, and commenting on it, had little to do with existential politics. This was particularly true in the United States where it most contributed to shaping academic political theory and in which it found a congenial but domesticated home. Despite Marcuse's appeal to radical thought in the late 1960s or the relevance some found in Habermas's critique of modern capitalism, the issues provoked by this literature involved primarily metatheoretical reflection on the idea of theory and the theoretical enterprise. Rather than encouraging substantive discussions of politics, it tended to become, in itself, the interpretative object and the focus of theoretical concern. But already the problems, solutions, and arguments that characterized this literature were essentially philosophical constructions with only an allusive, and often spurious, connection with political phenomena and their historical particularities.

First of all, this literature, much like the work associated with individuals such as Rawls, was in some respects a philosophized ideology, but even those ideological roots, the connections with Marxism in one case and liberalism in the other, had become severely attenuated as the arguments were submerged and constrained by academic philosophical discourse. In the work of Habermas, for example, critical theory became largely an eclectic metatheoretical composite of arguments and concepts from philosophy, hermeneutics, social science, linguistics, psychoanalysts, and other academic fields and subfields. The problems increasingly became ones of making these often incommensurable realms of discourse compatible and of shaping them into some rationalized structure of argument. To the extent that there was an involvement with substantive theoretical issues about the nature of political and social phenomena, it was, like much of the work in the philosophy of social science, largely in support of some metatheoretical arguments about theory and social scientific explanation.

Second, although much of the focus of critical theory was on the relationship between theory and practice, or the connection between philosophy and politics, the real dilemmas associated with this range of issues, which are at the core of the problem of the alienation of political theory, were transformed into metatheoretical questions and treated accordingly. The practical problem of the relationship beween social science and society was approached as an academic issue.

Finally, what most of the arguments associated with critical theory ultimately sought, much like the literature associated with the myth of the tradition, was a rationalistic basis for the authority of philosophical and social scientific judgments about practical matters. This is an issue rooted in the very origins of modern social science, which, because of its understanding of itself as a normative and even transformational practice, has been a persistent theme in the literature of political theory. The assumption sometimes seems to have been that the demonstration of such a basis would solve the theory/ practice problem, but at a minimum the concern was to establish that authority in principle. This ultimately means at least a flirtation, but usually an affair, with transcendentalism.

It is necessary at the outset to clarify, or at least make an initial move in the direction of clarifying, this point about the relationship between the alienation of political theory and the transcendental urge. There is a significant difference between what might be called *practical* and *metatheoretical* trans-cendentalism and *internal* and *external* standards of judgment. In any practice of knowledge, whether highly disciplined as in a branch of natural science or some less easily circumscribed aspect of political and moral life, the bases of judgment and criteria of knowledge claims, whether accepted scientific theories, moral beliefs, or other fundamental principles, are in an important sense transcendental. They define experience and govern meaning, and, whether explicit or tacitly embedded in the web of conventions that constitute a practice, they occupy a privileged position. This practical or internal trans-cendentalism is significantly different from the external or metatheoretical transcendentalism characteristic of many of those second-order enterprises that make various practices of knowledge an object of inquiry.

What has characterized much of epistemology, metaethics, the philosophy of science and philosophy of social science, and other such second-order fields is the notion that they can posit metatheoretical or transpractical standards of knowledge that are, or should be, in some way practically as well as philoso-phically authoritative and applicable. And in large measure the strategy of their position involves a conflation of the distinction between these two realms. At a later point I will explore in more detail the distorted character of this understanding of the relation between what I will designate as sub-stantive, theoretical, or first-order practices on the one hand and philosophi-cal, metatheoretical, and second-order activities on the other hand. But the basic argument will be that, both historically and conceptually, the latter are parasitic. Although they are free to describe, explain, and evaluate their objects of inquiry as they see fit, they have no special intellectual authority, and obviously no necessary practical authority, over first-order practices.

A fundamental dimension of the alienation of political theory derives from its failure to deal authentically with its second-order status, but the problem is exacerbated by the fact that most of the philosophical doctrines from which contemporary political theory gains sustenance are themselves the product of alienated intellectual enterprises. It is not surprising that political theory, seeking bases of authoritative claims about politics, should be drawn to metatheoretical transcendentalism, but the idea that such bases can be meta-theoretically underwritten or destroyed, logically or in principle, simply ignores the existential relationships between political theory and political practice and renders political theory inauthentic.

In a contingent sense, metatheory may affect substantive practices of knowledge. This may be unlikely in modern settings where theoretically and metatheoretically based activities such as science and the philosophy of science are not only functionally but institutionally distinguished, but the persistent and often pernicious impact of philosophy on social science is a clear example to the contrary. The point is not that such influence is in some general sense improper but rather that metatheoretical claims have no presumptive authority, on the basis of their reflectiveness, objectivity, or rationality, over first-order practices. This includes the relationship between political theory and politics. Much of political theory, however, proceeds on precisely such an assumption, and, in doing so, not only distorts its own activity but avoids the practical problem of its relationship to politics, which it characteristically conceives and resolves, in a circular way, in metatheoretical terms. But political theory is doubly alienated in that the claims of philosophical epistemology, metaethics, the philosophy of history, natural law, positivism, and various other arguments on which it has drawn in seeking identity and authority presume, often to themselves as well as others, to have access to transtheoretical and transpractical, universal, and self-validating sources of judgment that should command practical assent.

Such philosophical transcendentalism is at the core of critical theory and the search of individuals such as Habermas for the standards of rationality based on categories of knowledge and interest supposedly revealed in history or on the logical demands of human language and communication. But the transcendental illusion touches most of political theory in one form or another. Why this is the case is in one sense quite obvious. It is what is perceived as the problem of relativism.

This is a problem that has haunted political theory, and philosophy, for a long time, and there are some historical as well as structural reasons for its persistence. One of the historical reasons was the belief, or at least the claim, of many intellectuals, including the German émigrés, that philosophical relativism was implicated in the rise of totalitarianism. This was less a substantiated argument than a typical intellectualist prejudice regarding the efficacy of philosophy in the practical world, which implied that if there was a philosophical cause there was a philosophical solution. Structurally, the idea of a metatheoretical answer to the problem of relativism is crucial to the claim of political theory's authority over practical or political judgments. Although I will be more expansive about this issue at a later point, it is necessary to indicate immediately why it is an issue that cries out for dissolution. Those who worry about this problem are those who do not, or who for various reasons do not wish to, distinguish between relativism as a philosophical problem and as a practical problem. But in both cases it is a pseudoproblem.

The only thing that relativism could mean in any practical context is the absence of defined standards of judgment. When such standards do not exist, there is no general answer to the problem and certainly no philosophical answer. To a large extent, practices of knowledge and conventional practices such as politics are defined by the existence of such standards or by ways of resolving conflicts about standards. At best, relativism could be understood as referring to a category of problems. The idea of relativism itself as a practical dilemma is a philosophical fiction. But relativism is not even a genuine philosophical problem.

Relativism as a philosophical problem is simply the logical counterpart of metatheoretical transcendentalism, and both are merely the academic memories and abstracted summaries of real problems devoid of substantive criteria and context. A sincere philosophical relativist is either an individual who naively accepts this philosophical dilemma about a nonexistent issue in a nonexistent context but spurns the fictive transcendental solution or a person who has received this pejorative label for failing to accept the pseudoproblem that philosophy has generated and, consequently, for failing to solve it according to the rules of the game. Behind the game is either philosophy's claim to parity in the problem-solving market or, more characteristically, its baseless claim to logical and epistemological authority over the conventional activities that constitute its chosen object of analysis. Philosophy, however, has been somewhat successful, at least in such quarters as social science and political theory, in perpetuating and propagating the scam that practical claims must either be grounded in transcendental philosophical criteria or fall into the abyss of relativism.

Transcendentalism appeals to academic political theory for a number of reasons. Political theory wishes to cast itself in the mold of its own constructions of epic actors in the great tradition; it seeks political authority without engaging in political action and leaving the academy; it may, in some more sophisticated instances, believe in the necessity of practical or political transcendentalism and seek to keep the noble lie alive; it wants to find a basis for allaying its fears about its scientific and political virility; and it of course has conjured up alienated images of those real problems that in practical life demand solutions. But it seeks a chimera and, paradoxically, probably condemns itself to practical irrelevance. It is, nevertheless, the transcendental urge that animates many of the elements of political theory throughout the ideological and philosophical spectrum.

Because the problem of relativism and transcendentalism has in some respects been an import from the Continent, it is not entirely fair to evaluate much of European academic social thought, including projects such as that of critical theory, simply in terms of what is discussed here as academic political theory. Its indigenous circumstances are somewhat different from the principal universe of discourse under consideration both in terms of its relationship to politics and in terms of the intellectual context that governs its meaning and significance. To the extent that such a contrast is relevant, it points up the degree to which that universe is a peculiarly American, or maybe Anglo-American, invention and the manner in which European ideas have been transformed as they have been integrated into that complex.

By the middle of the 1970s, the cluster of issues that had given a certain measure of identity to political theory had been largely dissipated. Although the residue of those issues was visible in the various constituents of the field, the origins were often forgotten and the themes attenuated. One might speak of this period as one of differentiation or, somewhat more critically, as the "dispersion" of the field and its subject matter (Gunnell, 1983b) or, still more harshly as I have here, as part of the alienation of various elements of political theory from each other. But what is clear is that there was a disappearance of any issue center that brought these elements together in terms of either dialogue or debate.

Although political theory had gained autonomy as an independent field of study, its parts were largely colonies of various philosophical sovereignties, and, to the extent that they existed, controversies that might have given rise to creative and substantive theorizing were transformed into outposts of philosophical argument in such areas as the philosophy of social science. The enclaves were all represented and tolerated in an increasingly pluralistic atmosphere (e.g., Deutsch, 1971) in the subfield of political theory in political science, but they had little relevance to the main discipline which was increasingly concerned with consolidating the "new revolution" and ratifying the image of political science as a policy science (Eulau, 1973; Leiserson, 1975; Ranney, 1976). Not only was it less exercised about its scientific image, but some of the strongest proponents of behavioralism were even willing to reject much of the scientific platform that had distinguished the movement (Almond and Genco, 1977; Eulau, 1977). By the mid-1970s the discipline's emphasis on theory, which had characterized the 1960s, had largely disappeared, and any clear notion of the identity of theory and its place in the field was difficult to ascertain.

Assumptions about science and theory embedded in political science did not, however, change a great deal. One area in which they once again became highly visible was the increasingly distinct area of formal, positive, or social choice theory, which its advocates began to advance as the mainstream of scientific development and identified in terms of the same logical positivist models of science derived from the philosophy of science that had characterized the behavioral program (e.g., Riker, 1982; 1983; Riker and Ordeshook, 1973). Despite concerns among some leading political scientists about the "paucity of theoretical concerns" (Wahlke, 1979) and the failure to recognize alternative theoretical perspectives (Lindblom, 1982), there was a return to the same arguments about scientific explanation that had been so severely criticized and had contributed to the poverty of substantive theory in the discipline. But there was now little reaction either in the literature of political science or in the wider field of political theory – a fact that attests to the absence of an issue center. Much like the myth of the tradition that was still very much alive in the Straussian project and other theoretical relics, this image of theory not only survived but found vitality in isolation and the atmosphere of pure tolerance that came to characterize the late 1970s and early 1980s.

One of the basic elements in the wider field of political theory during the 1970s was the appearance of the "new" history of political theory, This development was in part the consequence of professional historians entering the field and the recognition that much of the practice of the history of political theory was not, by most conventional standards, really historical in terms of either purpose or approach. It was political and philosophical commentary. The new history claimed to offer a "truly" historical method for understanding the meaning of the classic texts and other material in the history of political ideas and for locating and tracing the "actual" historical traditions to which they belonged (Pocock, 1971; Skinner, 1969).

Although a considerable body of literature appeared that was associated with this approach, its status as a candidate for replacing the "old" history was far from clear. It promised to extract the study of the history of political theory from such alienating intellectual structures as those surrounding the idea of the great tradition and at least make the history of political ideas a real object of study. To some extent it accomplished this goal, but in other ways it contributed to the alienation of political theory by identifying its program in terms of metatheoretical images of historical explanation grounded in the postpositivist philosophy of science and, often, divorcing itself from any general concern with the field of political inquiry.

The real concerns of the new history, despite its emphasis on exegetical accuracy and the recovery of the authorial intention, had little to do with the interpretation of texts, and much of its concern about the non- or ahistorical character of previous work was actually a reflection of its unhappiness with a particular kind of historical analysis that was based on materialist or Marxist premises. The "new" history was in fact part or an extension of a well-established contextualist idealist historiographical tradition, and, apart from its substantive research contributions, what was new about it was basically its extended metatheoretical justification of its endeavor and the critique of what it took to be its rivals. Its actual theoretical assumptions were submerged and undeveloped, and what it proposed as a "method" was in fact a philosophical argument about historical explanation that generated another dimension of the *Methodenstreit* in the philosophy of social science and political theory.

To some extent, the methodological emphasis that became the hallmark of the new history was a function of its search for legitimation as a mode of doing the history of political theory, but metatheoretical reflection was also a consequence of the growing autonomy of the history of political theory and its disengagement both from the more political concerns that originally had motivated traditional scholarship and from the role of critic that it had played in political science. In any event, there was some irony in these trends, not the least of which was the fact that concerns about method came to the fore as the defining characteristic of the historical approach to political theory after two decades of historians of political theory attacking political science for its "methodism." There was also irony in the fact that, although behavioralists had attacked traditional scholarship for being too historical, the new historians now attacked it for being inadequately historical. But my concern is principally with the manner in which the debates on these issues exacerbated the alienation of political theory.

The discussion generated by the new history was not, for the most part, about competing historical claims or even about theoretical claims regarding the character of historical phenomena. Because one of the purposes of the new history had been to establish, or reestablish, the legitimacy of the study of the history of political theory on the basis of a metatheoretical warrant and to establish the historicity of a particular kind of historical practice, it was a methodological argument that most clearly defined this literature. It constituted neither a theory of the text or of social phenomena in general nor a method of historical inquiry, and the only ground on which the claims could be joined was metatheoretical. The result was to move discussions in the history of political theory into the realm of the philosophy of history, hermeneutics, and the philosophy of social science. Once again political theory became an extension of philosophical arguments that it seldom either critically examined or extended. As in other cases, political theory's search for identity and purpose ended in a loss of autonomy.

By the mid-1980s political theory, then, both in the discipline of political science and as a more general field, had settled into a number of relatively discrete enclaves governed by alien universes of discourse and had become estranged, through philosophical myths about theory, tradition, science, and politics, not only from the particularities of politics but from substantive theoretical analyses of the nature of political phenomena. It had largely become a series of metatheoretical claims about metatheoretical objects and issues; yet even the metatheoretical enterprises to which it attached itself were often unreflectively embraced and inauthentic in their own right. Even to say that political theory had devolved in a series of intellectual fads might not be to put too fine an edge on it.

What is often taken as the recent philosophical renaissance in political theory even evokes in some of its partisans "a nightmarish feeling that 'the literature' has taken off on an independent life of its own and now carries on like the broomstick bewitched by the sorcerer's apprentice" (Barry, 1980). The image that comes to my mind is an old "Monty Python" skit, parodying television game shows, where the contestants, racing against a time clock, were set the task of summarizing Proust. As it turned out that no one could possibly win the game, the prize was awarded on the basis of purely subjective criteria. However this simile might best be applied to political theory, the enterprise often does seem like an arbitrary exercise in recapitulating the work of Rawls, Habermas, and the variety of cult figures from whom political theorists seek a basis for pursuing some less than well-defined, reflectively and autonomously chosen end in a series of games that go by the name of critical theory, formal theory, and the like.

Because there is hardly any decline and, in fact, maybe a "glut" (Barry, 1980) in the literary production of political theory and philosophy and the professional and scholarly activities that compose its various domains, there are encouraging signs for those who would measure the health of the field in terms of prolificacy and prolixity. For many this is an adequate measure of the "possibility" of the enterprise, and the pluralism and fertility of contemporary political theory and its institutional independence, both in and outside political science, are an indication that it has recaptured what many have believed to have been its "grand manner" of the past (e.g., Freeman and Robertson, 1980: 1, 11). I would suggest a different assessment of the current situation.

Whatever criticism one might offer with regard to political theory during the fifties and sixties and well into the seventies, there were general issues in and about the field that were joined. There was also a deeper sense of the problem of the relationship between political theory and politics. Many, in both mainstream political science and political theory, may applaud the separation of the two and the growth of pluralism, but there is now little in the way of common concern and controversy and little sense of what the identity of political theory is or might be. Political theory has largely withdrawn from a critique of modern political science except in the most abstract terms, and political science has little that could be identified as theoretical controversy in its literature. Similarly, one would be hard pressed to indicate problems that bring into contention the various elements of the wider field of political theory. The final word would seem to be that any significant dialogue has disappeared – both within political theory and between political theory and politics.

References

Adorno, Theodor W., et al. 1976. *The positivist dispute in German sociology.* New York: Harper and Row.

Almond, Gabriel A. 1966. Political theory and political science. *American Political Science Review* 60: 869–879.

Almond, Gabriel A., and Genco, Stephen J. 1977. Clouds, clocks, and the study of politics. *World Politics* 29: 489–522.

Arendt, Hannah. 1958. *The human condition.* New York: Doubleday.

Arendt, Hannah. 1961. *Between past and future.* New York: Viking.

Barber, Benjamin. 1981. Political theory in the 1980s: prospects and topics. *Political Theory* 9: 291.

Barry, Brian. 1980. The strange death of political theory. *Government and Opposition* 15: 276–288.

Baumgold, Deborah. 1981. Political commentary on the history of political theory. *American Political Science Review* 75: 928–940.

Berlin, Isaiah. 1962. Does political theory still exist? In Peter Laslett and W. G. Runciman, eds, *Philosophy, politics, and society*, 2d ser. New York: Barnes and Noble.

Bernstein, Richard. 1976. *The restructuring of social and political theory.* New York: Harcourt Brace Jovanovich.

Bernstein, Richard. 1983. *Beyond objectivism and relativism.* Philadelphia: University of Pennsylvania Press.

Braybrooke, David, ed. 1965. *Philosophical problems of the social sciences.* New York: Macmillan.

Brecht, Arnold. 1959. *Political theory.* Princeton, NJ: Princeton University Press.

Brodbeck, May, ed. 1968. *Readings in the philosophy of the social sciences.* New York: Macmillan.

Cobban, Alfred. 1953. The decline of political theory. *Political Science Quarterly* 68. Reprinted in James A. Gould and Vincent V. Thursby, eds, *Contemporary political thought.* New York: Holt, Rinehart and Winston, 1969.

Deutsch, Karl W. 1971. On political theory and political action. *American Political Science Review* 65: 11–27.

Deutsch, Karl W., and Rieselbach, Leroy N. 1965. Recent trends in political theory and political philosophy. *Annals of the American Academy of Political and Social Science* 360: 139–162.

Dunning, William A. 1902, 1905, 1920. *A history of political theories.* 3 vols. New York: Macmillan.

Easton, David. 1951. The decline of modern political theory. *Journal of Politics* 13. 1: 36–58.

Easton, David. 1953. *The political system.* Chicago, IL: University of Chicago Press.

Easton, David. 1965a. *A framework for political analysis.* Englewood Cliffs, NJ: Prentice-Hall.

Easton, David. 1965b. *A systems analysis of political life.* New York: Wiley.

Easton, David. 1966. Alternative strategies in theoretical research. In David Easton, ed., *Varieties of political theory.* Englewood Cliffs, NJ: Prentice-Hall.

Easton, David. 1969. The new revolution in political science. *American Political Science Review* 63: 1051–1061.

Eulau, Heinz. 1967. Segments of political science most susceptible to behavioristic treatment. In James Charlesworth, ed., *Contemporary political analysis.* New York: Free Press.

Eulau, Heinz. 1977. The drift of a discipline. *American Behavioral Scientist* 21: 3–10.

Eulau, Heinz. 1973. The skill revolution and consultative commonwealth. *American Political Science Review* 67: 169–191.

Freeman, Robert and Robertson, David, eds. 1980. *The frontiers of political theory.* New York: St. Martin's Press.

Gunnell, John G. 1968. Social science and political reality: The problem of explanation. *Social Research* 34: 159–201.

Gunnell, John G. 1969. Deduction, explanation, and social scientific inquiry. *American Political Science Review* 63: 1233–1246.

Gunnell, John G. 1975. *Philosophy, science, and political inquiry.* Morristown, NJ: General Learning Press.

Gunnell, John G. 1978. The myth of the tradition. *American Political Science Review* 72: 122–134.

Gunnell, John G. 1979. *Political theory: tradition and interpretation.* Cambridge, MA: Little, Brown (Winthrop).

Gunnell, John G. 1980. Method, methodology, and the search for traditions in the history of political theory. *Annals of Scholarship* 1: 26–56.

Gunnell, John G. 1982. Interpretation and the history of political theory: Apology and epistemology. *American Political Science Review* 76: 317–327.

Gunnell, John G. 1983a. In search of the political object: beyond methodology and transcendentalism. In JohnS.Nelson, ed., *What should political theory be now?* Albany: State University of New York Press.

Gunnell, John G. 1983b. Political theory: the evolution of a sub-field. In Ada Finifter, ed. *Political science: the state of the discipline*. Washington, DC: American Political Science Association.

Habermas, Jürgen. 1971. *Knowledge and human interest*. Boston, MA: Beacon Press.

Habermas, Jürgen. 1973. *Theory and practice*. Boston, MA: Beacon Press.

Hare, R. M. 1952. *The language of morals*. Oxford: Oxford University Press.

Hare, R. M. 1963. *Freedom and reason*. Oxford: Oxford University Press.

Kaplan, Abraham. 1964. *The conduct of inquiry*. San Francisco: Chandler.

Kress, Paul. 1979. Against epistemology. *Journal of Politics* 41: 526–542.

Kuhn, Thomas S. 1970. *The structure of scientific revolutions*. Chicago, IL: University of Chicago Press.

Laslett, Peter, ed. 1956. *Philosophy, politics, and society*. 1st ser. New York: Barnes and Noble.

Laslett, Peter, and Fishkin, James, eds. 1979. *Philosophy, politics, and society*. 5th ser. New Haven, CT: Yale University Press.

Laslett, Peter, and Runciman, W. G., eds. 1962. *Philosophy, politics, and society*. 2d ser. New York: Barnes and Noble.

Laslett, Peter, and Runciman, W. G. 1967. *Philosophy, politics, and society*. 3d ser. New York: Barnes and Noble.

Lasswell, Harold, and Kaplan, Abraham. 1950. *Power and society*. New Haven, CT: Yale University Press.

Leiserson, Avery. 1975. Charles Merriam, Max Weber, and the search for synthesis in political science. *American Political Science Review* 69: 175–185.

Lindblom, Charles E. 1982. Another state of mind. *American Political Science Review* 76: 9–21.

Marcuse, Herbert. 1941. *Reason and revolution*. New York: Oxford University Press.

McDonald, Neil A., and Rosenau, James N. 1968. Political theory as an academic field and intellectual activity. *Journal of Politics* 30: 311–344.

Merriam, Charles. 1925. *New aspects of politics*. Chicago, IL: University of Chicago Press.

Miller, Eugene F. 1972. Positivism, historicism, and political inquiry. *American Political Science Review* 66: 796–873.

Moon, J.Donald. 1975. The logic of political inquiry. In Fred I. Greenstein and Nelson W. Polsby, eds, *Handbook of political science*, vol. I. Reading, MA: Addison-Wesley.

Nelson, John S., ed. 1983. *What should political theory be now?* Albany: State University of New York Press.

Nozick, Robert. 1974. *Anarchy, state, and utopia*. New York: Basic Books.

Pocock, J. G. A. 1971. *Politics, language, and time*. New York: Atheneum.

Ranney, Austin. 1976. The divine science of politics: political engineering in American culture. *American Political Science Review* 70: 140–148.

Rawls, John. 1971. *A theory of justice*. Cambridge, MA: Harvard University Press.

Ricci, David M. 1984. *The tragedy of political science*. New Haven, CT: Yale University Press.

Riker, William H. 1982. The two-party system and Duverger's law: an essay on the history of political science. *American Political Science Review* 81: 753–766.

Riker, William H. 1983. Political theory and the art of heresthetics. In Ada Finifter, ed., *Political science: the state of the discipline*. Washington, DC: American Political Science Association.

Riker, William H., and Ordeshook, Peter C. 1973. *An introduction to positive political theory.* Englewood Cliffs, NJ: Prentice-Hall.

Runciman, W. G. 1963. *Social science and political theory.* Cambridge: Cambridge University Press.

Sabine, George. 1937. *A history of political theory.* New York: Holt, Rinehart and Winston.

Sabine, George. 1939. Political theory. *Journal of Politics* 1: 1–16.

Schaar, John H., and Wolin, Sheldon S. 1963. Essays on the scientific study of politics: a critique. *American Political Science Review* 57: 125–150.

Schutz, Alfred. 1967. *The phenomenology of the social world.* Evanston, IL: Northwestern University Press.

Scriven, Michael. 1958. Definitions, explanations, and theories. In Herbert Feigl, Michael Scriven, and Grover Maxwell, eds, *Minnesota studies in the philosophy of science,* vol. 2. Minneapolis: University of Minnesota Press.

Scriven, Michael. 1959. Truisms as the grounds for historical explanation. In Patrick Gardner, ed., *Theories of history.* Glencoe, IL: Free Press.

Seidelman, Raymond. 1985. *Disenchanted realists.* Albany: State University of New York Press.

Skinner, Quentin. 1969. Meaning and understanding in the history of ideas. *History and Theory* 8: 3–53.

Skinner, Quentin. 1970. Conventions and the understanding of speech acts. *Philosophical Quarterly* 20: 118–138.

Skinner, Quentin 1971. On performing and explaining linguistic actions. *Philosophical Quarterly* 3. 1: 1–21.

Toulmin, Stephen. 1950. *An examination of the place of reason in ethics.* Cambridge: Cambridge University Press.

Toulmin, Stephen. 1961. *Foresight and understanding.* Bloomington: Indiana University Press.

Truman, David B. 1965. Disillusion and regeneration: the search for a discipline. *American Political Science Review* 59: 865–873.

Von Wright, Georg Henrik. 1971. *Explanation and understanding.* Ithaca, NY: Cornell University Press.

Wahlke, John C. 1979. Pre-behavioralism in political science. *American Political Science Review* 73: 68–77.

Weldon, T. D. 1953. *The vocabulary of politics.* Harmondsworth: Penguin Books.

Weldon, T. D. 1956. Political principles. In Peter Laslett, ed., *Philosophy, politics, and society,* 1st ser. New York: Barnes and Noble.

Wolin, Sheldon S. 1969. Political theory as a vocation. *American Political Science Review* 63: 1062–1062.

3 American political science, liberalism, and the invention of political theory (1988)

This chapter, most narrowly specified, is part of an account of the discursive history of academic political theory in the United States. It can, however, for at least two reasons, be construed as a study in the history of political science. First, the period under consideration, 1940–50, was a crucial one in the development of this discipline, and the issues that arose in the subfield of political theory were determinative with respect to its subsequent evolution. Second, the discourse of political theory was also the basic vehicle for reflection on the state of the discipline, its past, and its future prospects. But the relationship between political science and political theory has, since the beginning of the period in question, been an uneasy one. The principal purpose of this chapter is to explain that relationship and to explore the origins of a controversy that fundamentally shaped the structure and content of contemporary academic political theory.

Political theory today has little to say to or about its parent field, and much of political theory is of marginal interest and intelligibility to many political scientists. This estrangement cannot be explained merely in terms of normal trends in professional differentiation. It is in part the legacy of an old quarrel that was one of the principal factors in the emergence of the independent interdisciplinary field of political theory. Since the early 1970s, the subfield of political theory in political science, once understood to be the core of the discipline, has tended to reflect concerns generated within the wider, more autonomous field that has evolved its own institutional structure, issue nexus, and self-image.

This situation has sometimes been perceived as a problem, but it has seldom occasioned great concern among either political theorists or political scientists as a whole. In some quarters, both in political theory and mainstream political science, there is a sense of relief that the tension between field and subfield that had characterized the behavioral era has been ameliorated by intellectual distance. There are narrow but weighty professional pressures that tend to lead to the validation of separatism but that are rationalized in terms of notions of intellectual pluralism. Often the problem is depreciated by noting that it is more apparent than real if one takes into account the manner in which the policy turn of the postbehavioral era has produced a convergence between normative and empirical research. But the propensity to confront the issue on a superficial level conceals both the historical source of the problem and some very basic difficulties that cannot easily be dismissed.

A readily accessible and familiar explanation of the alienation of political theory from political science locates the cause in the conflict that arose in the course of the behavioral revolution and its attack on the study of the history of political theory as antiquarian and inmimical to the development of empirical theory and a scientific study of politics. This explanation is not incorrect, but it is incomplete. It is necessary to reach a deeper historical sense of the genealogy of political theory and to recover some of the more fundamental issues that occasioned the controversy we associate with behavioralism and its aftermath. By the early 1950s some of these issues had already been submerged in the rhetoric and legitimating philosophies that characterized the debate between "traditional" and "scientific" theory. A pivotal transformation in the discourse of political theory, which occurred during the 1940s, was obscured. An understanding of that transformation is also important for exploring the general problem of the relationship between academic political inquiry and politics – a problem that was at the heart of the controversy about political theory as it originally developed.

The real history of political theory

The basic images of political theory of and by which we are now possessed, images of theory as both a product and activity and as both a subject matter and mode of inquiry, have been generated within, and have little meaning outside, the language of political theory as an academic field. Attempts to endow political theory with world-historical significance by seeking its past in a great tradition from Plato to the present, by categorically defining it as the reflective and critical dimension of political life, by understanding it as a tributary of theory in the natural sciences, or by creating other putative identities that would enhance the authority of this professional field and provide foundations for its claim to knowledge, cannot withstand much analytical scrutiny (Gunnell, 1986). Although we have become accustomed to thinking of the history of political theory as the chronologically ordered canon of classic texts, such history is in fact largely a reified analytical construct. What we might call the "real history of political theory" is the history of the academic field that created this image as its subject matter and projected it as its past. Furthermore, despite the current distance between political theory and political science, these images, and the field of political theory itself, were largely an invention of U.S. political science.

Although it is important to investigate the early development of the concept of political theory as well as the academic practice that gave rise to it (Gunnell, 1983), the current species of both essentially came into existence after 1940 in the wake of the emigration of refugee scholars from Germany. Although the émigrés did not, for the most part, come to the United States understanding themselves as political theorists, this eventually became their identity. The adoption, appropriation, or discovery of this identity and the propagation of their image of, and concerns about, liberalism, as well as a related conceptual cluster including positivism and relativism, precipitated a scholarly and ideological conflict within political science that was manifest in a debate about political theory. Although the behavioral revolution was hardly one-dimensional, it was in an important respect initially a conservative rebellion catalyzed by, and directed against, the encroachment of a vision that was hostile to the traditional values of U.S. political science.

Notions of theory as the history of political ideas and as part of empirical social-scientific inquiry had, through the 1930s, been consistently understood as either complementary or even merely diachronic and synchronic modes of the same endeavor, which involved explaining politics by linking behavior and ideas. Charles Merriam, despite his emphasis on jettisoning or surpassing history as a form of inquiry, neither disparaged the paradigmatic studies of the history of political theories associated with his mentor, William Dunning, nor perceived any serious discontinuity between such studies – in which he himself participated significantly – and the advancement of social scientific theory. But a more significant factor in explaining the lack of tension was an underlying intellectual consensus that transcended various scholarly and ideological divisions between empiricism and idealism, history and science, and statism and laissez-faire. The history of political theory was understood by all as the history of the development of scientific knowledge about politics and as a story of the progress of the symbiotic relationship between such knowledge and the evolution of liberal democratic thought and institutions.

The notions of political theory and the disciplinary practices that developed between the late 1800s and the 1930s were, to be sure, the receptacle for the discourse that emerged in the 1940s. The arguments, for example, of someone such as Leo Strauss about the rise and decline of the great tradition would not have taken hold if the basic idea of the tradition had not already gained conventional acceptance in the work of George Sabine and his predecessors, and there was nothing in the behavioral credo that had not been already articulated as an ideal to which political science should aspire. But the transformation was dramatic. The dominant consensus was frontally challenged for the first time, and political theory, as the focus of controversy, became an essentially contested concept.

The great change began almost unnoticed, or at least uncomprehended, as the claims of Strauss, Hannah Arendt, Hans Morgenthau, Theodor Adorno, Eric Voegelin, Franz Neumann, Arnold Brecht, Max Horkheimer, Herbert Marcuse, and others, in varying ways and degrees but inexorably, reshaped the discourse of political theory. Despite some very great differences in ideological and philosophical perspective, they looked much alike to the successors of Merriam as they uniformly and on very similar bases challenged the liberal, scientific, relativistic, historicist perspective that dominated political theory and political science. What might be taken as the politically conservative arguments of individuals such as Voegelin were initially more professionally visible than those on the Left associated with the Institute for Social Research, but they all propagated the thesis that liberalism, either inherently or because of its degenerate condition, was at the core of a modern crisis and implicated in the rise of totalitarianism.

It would be far too simplistic to suggest that the behavioral revolution should be understood exclusively as a reaction to this challenge, but we have lost sight of the degree to which its arguments were originally formed in response to it. The attack on liberalism and science and the rejection of the progressive-pragmatic vision of history were too basic to allow any syncretic resolution. The sense of liberal givenness, which characteristically allowed U.S. theorists to embrace relativism and the idea of the separation of facts and values while remaining totally committed to definite political ideals, was incompatible with the transcendental speculation and philosophies of history, whether of the Marxist or natural-law variety, that marked the new literature. Since at least the turn of the century, such ideas had traditionally been specifically what most U.S. political theorists had understood themselves as rejecting.

I seek to specify as precisely as possible how the controversy commenced and how it shaped the discourse of political theory. The situation as it first emerged was not clear to many of the participants. The new ideas had often not taken distinct and published form when the conflict began, and some of those involved in the controversy were at first truly perplexed. Individuals such as Sabine, whose influential analysis of political theory was not significantly different from that of those devoted to empirical political science, found himself the target of those whose ideas he largely shared simply because he represented the history of political theory. Similarly, proto-behavioralists and the founders of the behavioral movement, such as David Easton, saw not only a growing tendency toward historical and evaluative analysis that was pointedly at the expense of the idea of a scientific study of politics and liberal values but one that was being mounted within the genre of political theory, which had heretofore reflected the constitutive conventions of the discipline of political science.

The transformation of political theory

Apart from textbooks, there was at the beginning of the 1940s, a dearth of literature distinctly understood as political theory, and institutionally, as a subfield of political science, it had all but disappeared. The revitalization of discourse could be construed as beginning with the publication of Sabine's 1939 article, "What is Political Theory?" in the first issue of the *Journal of Politics* and with the appearance, in the same year, of the *Review of Politics* (which became a principle vehicle for the work of the émigrés). The resumption of discussion about political theory and its place in political science was in part prompted by an increasing concern about the status of the scientific study of politics which, despite the work of Harold Lasswell and others connected with the Chicago school during the 1930s, had received limited attention after Merriam's enthusiastic claims in the 1920s. More than a decade before the behavioral revolution, Benjamin Lippincott (1940) argued that in practice the discipline of political science was much as it had been at the turn of the century and that the greatest deficiency was theoretical. What passed as political theory had been devoted to the recounting of past ideas, and even among those committed to science, there was an "aversion" and "hostility" to theory (p. 130). But most important was the renewed reflection on liberal political values and the beginning of the impact of newly arrived European scholars who severely questioned the scientific faith and liberalism as well as the historical vision that united them.

A pointed "challenge" to political scientists was advanced by William Foote Whyte in an article published in 1943. This piece (quite accidentally) served as the principal catalyst for the incipient controversy. Whyte was a social anthropologist who had been studying political organization in a slum district, and there is no indication that he had any notion of the nerve endings that would be agitated by his comments. He suggested that the war had occasioned a concern about democratic values that had led political scientists to "write political philosophy and ethics" and neglect the study of "plain politics." He argued that "a scientific study of politics" required "the discovery of certain uniformities or laws" and that political scientists should direct their attention to "the description and analysis of political behavior" (pp. 692–93).

The most immediate response to Whyte was by John Hallowell (1944a) whose work would become one of the principal conduits through which the ideas of the émigrés entered political theory and whose voice would come to represent the new mood in the field. The response, however, moved the discussion to a very different context. Whyte, much like Lippincott, was writing from the perspective of traditional American social science, but Hallowell identified this critique, as well as the general commitment to science in the discipline, with an intellectual position that was not only alien but unfamiliar to most U.S. political scientists. Hallowell suggested that Whyte's views reflected "increasingly positivistic" trends that threatened to undermine "all belief in transcendental truth and value" that could serve as a barrier to intellectual and political "nihilism" (pp. 642–43).

The political-theory research committee of the American Political Science Association had been largely inactive in the early years of the war, but in 1943 it met, under the chairmanship of Francis G. Wilson, and attempted to sort out the issues that were beginning to surface. Wilson noted that there was now a "deep cleavage among political theorists in the area of primary ideas" on an "ultimate issue" (Wilson et al., 1944: 726–27). The exact nature of this issue and cleavage was something that he had some difficulty in specifying. One facet of the issue, or one way of stating it, involved a conflict between those who, like the "great political thinkers," took metaphysics seriously and those who believed that philosophy was relevant only as "logical thought." Was scientific "detachment" from traditional philosophy a sign of "progress" or "ineptitude"? Another definition of the problem was in terms of a clash between the "theological approach" and the "empirical" or "positivistic/scientific, or liberal technique of social study." A theological perspective was considered by some as necessary for understanding both the past and contemporary society, but there was a question of what constituted such a perspective and the manner in which it might conflict with the "approaches of idealistic and rationalist liberalism" that were more characteristic of political science (p. 727).

There was also a recognition of a conflict between those who stressed "value-free discussions in political science" and those who believed that there was "more in politics than simply clinical observation." All agreed that it was important to "formulate and criticize values" and that there should be "a frontal attack" on the problem of "value in American political society," and many believed that in some sense it was necessary and possible to arrive at "valid social and political principles." There was much the same kind of discussion about knowledge of regularities regarding "political behavior." Most were willing to compromise at some point and acknowledge that both "utopia" and the "facts" should be given consideration (pp. 727–28, 730), but it was clear that the consensus in political theory was breaking down.

Some believed, Wilson reported, that the fundamental cleavage was manifest in the differences between the thought of the Middle Ages and that of the modern age, between natural law and natural rights. There was also a division between those who argued that the United States needed a consciousness of history and that an examination of our philosophy of history was in order and those who wanted to concentrate on practical questions of political choice and the "ends-means relationship." There was also a general, but maybe less than enthusiastic, agreement that there was a need for a greater availability of the "texts of the great thinkers" and that "the political tradition of the West must be subjected to close scrutiny." The "ancients" should be studied as really "modern" and "timeless" because we belong to the same tradition but maybe also because there is an "essential nature of moral man or the moral universe (or even Satanic man and the Satanic phase of the universe)" to be discovered (pp. 730–31).

Wilson, who was a specialist in American political thought and a consistent spokesman for a U.S. brand of conservatism, did his best to report and make sense of the various and sometimes novel notions of theory that surfaced in these discussions and to reconcile them. Neither task was easy. The issues being formulated were radically different from those that had been characteristic of American political science and political theory.

In the symposium, Benjamin Wright (who had written on the American tradition of natural law) claimed that the greatest need of the period was for a statement of objectives in terms of ideals, since there was no "clear conception of what we are fighting for, what goals we should seek to attain, even in this country, after the war." We had "been too inclined to hide timidly behind the excuse of objectivity" (Wilson et al. 1944: 739–40). In this respect, he maintained, interpretations of the history of political thought and analyses of current doctrine could make great contributions to the future of democracy in the United States. Ernest S. Griffith, on the other hand, argued that "research in political theory hitherto has been largely synonymous with searches for the origin, growth, and decline in ideas, principles, and doctrines," while what was required, if there was to be "precision" in the field, was more attention to "the basic concepts that underlie all theory" and to the definition of these concepts. Such research, he cautioned, should not be understood as a search for "*correct*" concepts, since theorists have too long looked for absolute principles and failed to recognize that principles are subjective and historically relative to various institutional arrangements (pp. 740–42).

The claims of Wright and Griffith could easily be situated within the characteristic discourse of the field and did not necessarily represent sharply conflicting attitudes; Wright's notion of natural law, for example, was largely functional or instrumental. The increasing tension between such positions, however, indicated a different kind of influence. Voegelin, who had fled to the United States in 1938, was beginning to make his mark on professional discussions of political theory during this period, and in this symposium he presented at some length the basic research scheme and thesis regarding the derailment of modern political thought that would inform his *New Science of Politics* (1952) – a book that would epitomize one of the poles of political theory during the 1950s and 1960s.

Voegelin suggested that the study of the history of political ideas had been represented with distinction by individuals like Dunning and Sabine and was of particular importance to U.S. scholars who had done the most to develop this field, over which they had held a "monopoly." He claimed, however, that it was now necessary to rethink the field in light of the vast new historical knowledge available and in terms of the general philosophy of history. Dunning, he argued, had made the first real step beyond earlier work by focusing on "political theory" as a special category, but his work was somewhat distorted by his emphasis on the notion of "progress." Sabine had taken the further step of making political theory distinctly subordinate to the structure of political history, and it now remained, Voegelin suggested, to pursue this task in a much more "philosophical" manner (pp. 746–51).

The increasingly pivotal issue of relativism was, at this time, grounded in a concrete concern about the defense of liberal democratic principles. The war and the domestic political crises of the 1930s that preceded it had prompted an uneasiness about the lack of an articulate and philosophically grounded democratic ideology. And the work of individuals like Charles Beard and John Dewey had already incited a controversy about historicism and relativism as a threat to both political values and scientific objectivity. The concern about relativism, then, was not without precedent. But as the issue entered the literature of political theory, it took on a reconstituted identity based on new claims about the origins of totalitarianism. The assessment advanced by émigré scholars, and by Hallowell, was that the problem of totalitarianism was at root a problem of science, liberalism, and relativism and that it was susceptible in large part to a philosophical or religious solution.

If we want to understand fully the behavioral animus toward "traditional" political theory, it is necessary to take account of the extent to which what had actually been traditional in American political theory was being fundamentally challenged. The unhappiness with liberalism and science that would mark much of the major work in the history of political theory by the 1960s (Strauss, Voegelin, Arendt, and others) was already taking shape. And it propagated the image of a crisis and decline in Western political history and thought. Hallowell, in reviewing Brecht's account of the decline of the German republic, argued (1944b) that Brecht did not sufficiently stress the degree to which that decline was "a direct consequence of the liberal's lack of conviction in his own philosophy." The solution, for Hallowell, was a renewal of what he believed were the religious and spiritual foundations of liberal democracy.

Hallowell had developed this thesis in an earlier article (1942) and book (1943) in which he argued that the decline of liberalism as an ideology and the rise of totalitarianism were directly related to positivism and historicism and that a reconstruction of liberalism could be effected by a grounding in modern theology as characterized by the work of Niebuhr, Tillich, and Berdyaev. Voegelin reviewed the book sympathetically – suggesting only that Hallowell might seek the roots of the decline of liberalism further back than the nineteenth century. Voegelin was at this time working on a general (but later temporarily abandoned) history of political ideas that attributed the decline of the West, which culminated in Marxism, to the secularization of Christian history during the Enlightenment (1975). Where the tradition of political philosophy went wrong and led to the decadence of modern politics and political thought would become the principal concern of a new wave of historians of political theory.

Hallowell's attack on liberalism became strident (1947), and the substance of his argument was hardly congenial to American political science. Merriam, for example, had stressed the danger of theology to liberalism while Hallowell was suggesting that secular liberalism, with the disintegration of religious conscience, led to anarchy and tyranny. Much of the tradition of U.S. social science had grown out of an attempt to replace religion as a cohesive social force with a science of social control and public policy that would realize liberal values, but now "political theorists" were claiming that liberalism and "the liberal science of politics" were a failure and the breeding ground of totalitarianism.

It would be a mistake to assume that political scientists committed to the scientific study of politics were unconcerned with values – either as an object of study or as premises and goals of empirical inquiry. As Herman Finer put it (1945), "the need was for an ideology that would accomplish for democracy what Marxism had done for Soviet Communism" (p. 239). These claims would be overshadowed by the renewed commitment to scientific inquiry by the end of the decade, but the "value-free" stance of behavioralism did not entail a rejection or neglect of what it understood as liberal democratic values. Gabriel Almond, for instance, who had studied with Merriam and Lasswell, spoke out strongly at this time for the ethical involvement of political scientists and against Whyte's suggestion that values should be the province of the philosopher. Almond even argued that the "chief challenge" of the day was to seek "a valid theory of natural law" (Almond et al., 1946). The problem was not that the new influences in political theory stressed values but that behavioralism could not countenance the idea that science and liberalism exemplified social and intellectual decline.

The symposium, "Politics and Ethics," in which Almond participated was conceived as an attempt to explore further the issues that had been raised by Whyte. But, for the most part, the participants talked past one another, and the arguments were by now far removed from Whyte's actual concern and understanding. Whyte claimed that he did not recognize the target of Hallowell's criticism – that he had never even met anyone who represented the position attributed to him. He stated that he was not interested in the "philosophy of science" and "positivism" and that Hallowell had gone off on a "tangent" and created a "straw man" (p. 301). Hallowell was caught up in a realm of ideas and issues that were distinctly European and closely related to the arguments of individuals such as Brecht. Brecht's work constitutes a particularly interesting and illuminating case. Although he posed the problem in a paradigmatic form, his solution was not quite consonant with the claims of Voegelin and Hallowell.

Brecht had been a political actor and administrator who did not enter academia, or what he understood as the pursuit of "science," until he came to the United States and the New School of Social Research in 1933 after a period of Nazi harassment. Around the turn of the decade, he published several articles dealing with the question of relativism, absolutism, and science that eventually became the basis of his book. *Political Theory: The Foundations of Twentieth-Century Political Thought* (1959). Brecht did not directly attribute the rise of national socialism to a philosophical context, but, like many others, he was concerned about the influence of legal positivism and relativism on judges and lawyers who applied laws that were morally reprehensible. He believed, however, that it was impossible to seek a form of "scientific" proof or some rationalistic equivalent for moral principles and natural law. Moral judgment was a matter of human volition even though no less lacking in validity. Brecht argued that scientific value relativism, as expounded by Max Weber, Hans Kelsen, Gustav Radbruch, and Lasswell, had once seemed a liberating philosophy, but in the face of Nazism it became a paralyzing one. In a search for intellectual authority to combat totalitarianism, intellectuals, however mistakenly, "turned from being political scientists to becoming ethical philosophers or theologians (if not simply bad logicians) and *they called this science*" (1970: 434, 490). For Brecht, the great dilemma of modern political theory was that there was no scientific knowledge of values. His solution was to teach "the *limits* of science" and urge other ways to bridge the *is* and *ought* (p. 494), He was an intensely religious Lutheran, particularly in his later years, and in his own way he attempted to ground political theory in faith and religious values.

In 1947, Brecht reported on a round-table ("Beyond Relativism in Political Theory") that included Francis Coker, Roland Pennock, Lippincott, Wright, Voegelin, Hallowell, and Almond. Kelsen was unable to attend, but he sent a message indicating that despite the growing unpopularity of value relativism in the United States, he was still an adherent and remained a critic of moral "absolutism." Kelsen's legal positivism was a prime target of those such as Hallowell who wished to ground political theory in religion and natural law, but for Kelsen, as well as for most U.S. political scientists and theorists, value skepticism and relativism were understood as the foundations of liberal democratic theory. Only on this basis, they believed, could liberal democracy be justified. Moral absolutism signaled political absolutism for émigrés like Kelsen, while for Kelsen's erstwhile student, Voegelin, relativism abetted and reflected the decline of the West.

Brecht suggested that the paradox of modernity was that "modern science and modern scientific methods, with all their splendor of achievement, have led to an ethical vacuum, a religious vacuum, and a philosophical vacuum." He argued that the situation had come to a point where social science found it impossible to distinguish between right and wrong, good and evil, and justice and injustice. Political science was particularly affected by this dilemma, because it dealt most directly with the phenomena of nazism, fascism, and communism, which had "settled down" in this vacuum. Brecht claimed that "no political theorist can honestly avoid the issue" posed by "scientific relativism" (pp. 470–71). Most participants in the symposium offered little in the way of a concrete recommendation for getting "beyond relativism." Hallowell made his characteristic case for Christianity as the basis of political theory, but Wright and Lippincott, speaking for the more traditional conception in American political science, warned against any such retreat to commitment.

There has not been sufficient recognition of the degree to which the transcendental urge and historical pessimism manifest in the émigré literature affected political theory. It contributed to the split between political theory and political science during the behavioral era and to the eventual constitution of political theory as an independent field. Although the behavioral revolution, or counterrevolution, in many ways transformed the mainstream practice of the discipline, it was, at least theoretically, a reaffirmation of past ideals – ideals that did not rest easily alongside the arguments that characterized the new literature of political theory. Although the behavioralists singled out the study of the history of political theory as requiring displacement, transformation, or supercession, this was more because it was the genre to which most of the offending arguments happened to belong than because the literature characteristic of the field before 1940 actually embodied the problems with which behavioralists were concerned.

By 1950, there was an antiscientific, antiliberal sentiment in political theory even though neither the medium nor the message were always entirely clear. Although, for example, Arendt had published widely during the 1940s in a variety of journals, her first major work in English, *The Origins of Totalitarianism*, did not appear until 1951. Much of Strauss's *Natural Right and History* was originally presented as Walgreen lectures at the University of Chicago in 1949, a year after his appointment, but the book was not published until 1953. Strauss had already announced in his work on Hobbes (1936) some of his distinctive themes, including the depreciation of both liberalism and the new science of politics, but the book received little attention and surely not much comprehension. The same could be said of Herbert Marcuse's *Reason and Revolution* (1941) and Horkheimer's *Eclipse of Reason* (1947). In an article-length review of Strauss's book, Carl Friedrich, himself an earlier émigré, praised the effort but clearly did not understand the project. He wished that Strauss had been more forthcoming about his own views, but he believed that it was safe to conclude that Strauss was a "historical relativist" (1938).

Although these attacks on science, liberalism, and the legitimacy of the modern age had not yet coalesced into a definite oppositional force in political science, they were at least engendering an alien mood that had a considerable professional impact. There were all sorts of reasons to reassert the scientific image of political science in the postwar years, and the new voices in political theory were not only failing to do so but were inimical to such an image. The need for scientific theory was the theme of William Anderson's survey of political science in 1949. What was required, he argued, was an "established body of tested propositions concerning the political nature and activities of man that are applicable throughout the world and presumably at all times" (p. 309). It was, he claimed, necessary to distinguish between politics and science and pursue the latter, and the way to do this was to study individual "human political behavior" or the "political atom" and produce knowledge in the "field of scientific method" (pp. 312–14).

Behavioralists, beginning in the 1950s, would increasingly emphasize their dedication to a vision of pure science, but the underlying concern at the end of the decade was still the articulation and realization of a science of *liberal* politics. In two articles, on Bagehot (1949) and Lasswell (1950), that closely preceded his analysis of the "decline of political theory" (1951), Easton made clear that the pursuit of science was a means and not an end and that the belief in the complementarity of scientific realism and liberal democracy was still alive. The ultimate purpose remained political rationality, but the immediate goal was to create a theoretically grounded science of politics equal to this task. The priority for the moment was an emphasis on what Lasswell and Abraham Kaplan termed the "contemplative" as opposed to the "manipulative" dimension of science (1950).

The individuals most responsible for affecting and sustaining the behavioral revolution had almost without exception been primarily trained in the field of historical and normative political theory, as traditionally conceived. While the debate within the discipline would eventually often be understood as a conflict between political *scientists* and political *theorists,* it really signified a split between different conceptions of theory. Few of the early behavioralists understood themselves as antitheoretical, and probably very few initially understood their concern with scientific political theory as a rejection of their earlier education. To some extent, what was involved was a lag between the graduate educational establishment and the new literature and mood of political theory. The theorists trained in the 1930s and 1940s had, for the most part, not been exposed to the arguments of the new wave of European thought that was appearing in political theory, and they felt a good deal more at home with the traditional goals of the field than with the perspective that characterized this literature. Ultimately they felt compelled to choose between political theory and political science, and the choice was as much ideological as professional. But by the mid-1950s, the behavioral critique of political theory was forcing the same polarizing choice on theorists concerned with historical and normative issues.

In 1950, Lippincott attempted, as he had a decade earlier, to make sense of what constituted political theory in the United States and to provide a critical analysis of the field. His discussion did not gain the attention received by some of the testaments of the behavioral movement that would be advanced during the next few years. But it indicates the degree to which the basic tenets of behavioralism had already been formulated and enunciated by individuals like Lippincott, who were hardly enemies of "traditional" political theory but who were clearly worried about the direction that the enterprise was taking and about its relationship to political science.

Lippincott suggested that political theory was at least potentially – and as correctly understood – the "most scientific branch" of political science. It was, however, an area in which political scientists had "produced little," if theory were defined, as he believed it should be, "as the systematic analysis of political relations." It should, he argued, be concerned with "general" claims about the "actions" and "behavior" of men and with particular events and institutions only as objects for testing its principles (pp. 208–9). Up to this point, Lippincott argued, "the greatest effort has been devoted to writing the history of political ideas" and "defining and classifying terms and principles of politics." The methods in political theory had been basically historical, and the "emphasis placed on the history of political ideas has meant very largely the abandonment of the aim of science" (pp. 209, 211, 214).

The call for science was increasingly accompanied by an attack on the existing practice of political theory. Theory was often described as historical, teleological, utopian, moralistic, ethical, and generally obscurantist. There was more going on in these critiques than was readily visible, and the exact target of the criticism was often not clearly or easily specified. By 1950, however, Hallowell had brought together his arguments in a comprehensive work (*The Main Currents of Modern Political Thought*), and to understand fully the image of political theory that behavioralism would invoke, this work must be examined. It reflected and summarized claims that had emerged in the discourse of political theory during the 1940s, and it initiated a genre that would find its classic expression in the work of Strauss, Voegelin, and others during the next decade. Even a work such as Sheldon Wolin's *Politics and Vision* (1960), which ideologically and philosophically was far removed from the positions of Hallowell, Voegelin, and Strauss, was still a story of liberalism and the decline of modern politics. The imprint of the 1940s was fundamental for the future of political theory.

Although Hallowell's book was about "modern political thought," a large portion was devoted to a synoptic reconstruction of the development of political ideas from ancient times up through the emergence of what he designated as "integral liberalism," which he claimed was an outgrowth of the ideas of individuals like Grotius and Locke. The image projected was one of a seamless web of history that moved from the classical world through the evolution of modern science, the Renaissance, and Hobbes to the rise of liberalism. However, the story of modem political thought was now a story of decline – a decline as organic as the upward slope of the past and one that was offered as an explanation of modern political problems and "the crisis of our times" exemplified in socialism, Marxism, the Soviet Union, fascism, and the theory and practice of totalitarianism in general. But the most basic problem was the decadence of contemporary liberalism and its inability to defend and maintain itself.

In Hallowell's saga, the main villain was positivism, which in turn he viewed as a direct outgrowth of the Enlightenment, utilitarianism, and German idealism. His notion of positivism was the very general one of an "attempt to transfer to the study of social and human phenomena the methods and concepts of the natural sciences," and he believed that it was represented by the work of Comte, J, S. Mill, Herbert Spencer, Frank Lester Ward, and Ludwig Gumplowicz. Positivism, with its attendant separation of fact and value, and relativism undermined liberalism and allowed the rise of antiliberal political movements. For Hallowell, the answer to the modern crisis was once again Christianity and the reconstitution of decadent liberalism on the basis of religious values. This particular work, although reasonably influential in political theory, was seldom the specific focus of behavioral criticism, but it represented the kind of claims that in large part evoked that criticism.

Some émigrés like Kelsen (1948) and Felix Oppenheim (1950) would continue to argue, like U.S. liberals, that relativism and empiricism were more conducive to democracy than moral absolutism. They claimed that there was a root connection between democracy and the spirit embodied in the scientific method. The imminent debate between "scientific" and "traditional" political theory would be far from simply a debate about method and political inquiry or even about an emphasis on values as opposed to facts. It was, in the end, a debate about liberalism, its foundation, and its fate – and about the relationship between political theory and politics.

By the 1950s, the dispute in political theory was projected on the wider screen of academic philosophy and issues about the nature of science. This was already quite evident in the 1950 volume of the *American Political Science Review*. J. J. Spengler, speaking from the perspective of an economist, claimed that it was time that political science was "transformed into a full-bodied social science" (p. 375). What was required, T. I. Cook argued in a discussion of this thesis, was the development of a general unified science of theories and postulates similar to that "developed in natural science before, and first completed by, Newton" (p. 388). Wilson, commenting on these claims, observed that U.S. social science had now come to share a common conception of theory, knowledge, and social reality that was based on scientism, empiricism, pragmatism, instrumentalism, positivism, relativism, and operationalism.

In a symposium on "The Semantics of the Social Sciences," which was basically a statement of the philosophical and social-scientific position of the Chicago school, Charner Perry, a Chicago philosopher and long-time editor of *Ethics*, argued that natural science had made its great advances by going beyond the lore and common sense embedded in "anthropomorphic and teleological" language. In political science, however, there still was "no important contribution in the field resulting from the application of scientific method." This could be attributed to the "theological, normative, or even moralistic terms" of "political theory" which "belong to subjective or fictitious universes of discourse quite inappropriate to a general science of society" (1950: 397–99).

There was an increasingly extravagant dimension to the rhetoric on both sides of the debate. Actual research and publication in the field hardly matched the picture of "positivism" that was painted by the critics of scientism, and the image of moralistic political theory on which the protobehavioralists focused was equally unreflective of the literature. To claim, as Perry did, that political science was "mostly history and ethics" was simply counterfactual, and to argue that "the propositions of political theory have a character of 'unreality' and futility that bars out any serious interest in their discussion" (pp. 399, 401) was clearly to speak generically on the basis of a narrow and unspecified body of literature. But there was, ironically, a sense in which each faction was now beginning to fulfill the image conjured up by its opponents.

Herbert Simon, George A. Lundberg, and Lasswell participated in the discussion and pressed, as they would in many forums, for making the language of social science scientific. Although they did not specify their sources, they were clearly no longer strangers to the positivist philosophy of science. Simon enunciated a model of science as a system of predictive-cum-explanatory general propositions from which could be deduced other propositions about concrete observables that were therefore testable. Science was conceived methodologically as a unity, and human action as an object of inquiry was viewed as requiring no departure from the methods of natural science.

For Simon, it was essential that political science adopt what he considered to be the more advanced methods of the other social sciences, and he insisted that central to this task was a *transformation and redefinition of political theory* that would entail "consistent distinctions between political theory (i.e., scientific statements about the phenomena of politics) and the history of political thought (i.e., statements about what people have said about political theory and political ethics)" (p. 411). Lundberg, a sociologist, who was a major advocate of positivism in the social sciences during this period, confirmed Simon's image of science and stressed the need to "adopt the orientation of modern natural science," which would involve as a first step finding out "what the methods of natural science are" and thus provide a means for getting away from the a priori philosophy characteristic of the humanities (p. 421).

Lasswell warned against getting too involved in the question of what "science" means and neglecting the practical end toward which scientific inquiry was ultimately directed, that is, "to decrease the indeterminacy of important political judgments," but he advocated "more attention to the construction of theoretical models" that would guide research (pp. 423, 425). Exactly what was entailed *by* the commitment, or recommitment, to science was not very clearly defined, but there definitely was a new philosophic dimension to the argument. Lasswell's collaboration with Kaplan, who had been a student of Carnap's, was one obvious point of intersection. And they had stated in the introduction to their book (1950) that it reflected a new scientific outlook informed by "a thorough-going empiricist philosophy of the sciences" based on "logical positivism, operationalism, instrumentalism" (pp. xiii–xiv). Maybe their position was actually more justified than informed by this philosophy, but in the face of new philosophical challenges, political scientists attempted more self-consciously to ground and articulate their scientific faith.

By 1950, some mainstream political scientists were becoming uneasy about the implications of the new scientism. Paul Appleby (1950), speculating on the direction of political science during the next 25 years, argued that a much broader value-oriented vision was required than the one that was then developing in the discipline, and for many the concern was still to link science to problems of practical politics (White, 1950). Easton's call for the reconstruction of political theory has quite reasonably often been construed as the first shot fired in the behavioral revolution. But although *The Political System* (1953) was, to be sure, a critique of the study of the history of political theory and a plea for the creation of scientific theory, it is sometimes forgotten that it was an explicit challenge to the new "mood" in political theory and an attempt to find a basis for the reconciliation of political science and political theory that would at the same time sustain and advance liberal democratic values. By mid-decade such mediative integrating efforts had largely given way to the alienating forces that pushed political theory and political science along different paths. And in an important sense the language and agenda of political theory, for at least a generation, had already been set.

Conclusion

The literature of political theory is, and since the late 1930s has been, saturated with discussions about liberalism and its tradition, rise and decline, faith, dangers, limits, collapse, challenges, agony, paradox, irony, spirit, development, end, poverty, and crisis and its relation to innumerable things, individuals, and other political concepts. Even when the concept is not specifically a focus of discussion, the concern about liberalism significantly structures the discursive universe of political theory. An understanding of this situation requires a grasp of those initiating issues that informed the invention of political theory and that fundamentally shaped its real history. The enthusiastic reception of European thought in recent years, such as that associated with Habermas, is directly related to its perpetuation of the critique of liberalism, and surely some of the literature that has had the greatest impact on the field has been devoted to attempts, such as that of John Rawls, to provide new foundations for liberal theory.

Although the tension between political science and political theory was, and in large part has remained, the product of a disagreement about liberalism, the controversy quite early on became detached from concrete political issues. From the beginning, there was a tendency for the debates about liberalism to escape the political concerns that had given rise to them. For the émigrés, the experience of Weimar and totalitarianism was determinative and came close to confirming the idea that in Germany, as in Athens and Rome, liberalism was the manifestation of political decline and the threshold of tyranny. No matter how much individuals like Strauss and Marcuse might disagree on various grounds, they were at one in extending the analogy to contemporary politics in the United States. And even their specific critiques of liberalism were not all that different. For U.S. political scientists also, the rise of totalitarianism and its attendant ideologies during the 1930s, as well as the domestic problem of rationalizing the conflict between government and the economic enterprise, indicated a need to rearticulate and ground the principles of liberal democracy. If a sense of crisis regarding liberalism, in theory and practice, had not been part of the world of political science, the arguments of the émigrés would likely not have carried the weight that they did.

On both sides of the controversy, however, there continued to be an alienating displacement of the issues. In the case of the émigrés, there was a philosophization of their experience and a projection of the analysis onto recalcitrant political circumstances in the United States as well as the ambiguous screen of world history. This produced an estrangement between academic political theory and politics that has plagued the subsequent evolution of the field. The defense of liberalism among political scientists also became oblique. Either it became the validation of an image that was not easily related to political realities, or it took the form of a philosophy of science, conceptual frameworks, and empirical findings that often seemed to confirm the existence and efficacy of liberal society.

The debate about relativism was also originally grounded in a practical issue that was eventually obscured by the philosophical formulation of the problem. This was the problem of the relationship between academic and public discourse or between philosophy, political theory, and political science on the one hand and politics on the other. This concern about the authority of political inquiry and the intellectuals who engaged in it was equally prominent in the work of both the émigrés and the practitioners of traditional American political science, but the responses were different.

Although relativism, as a philosophical problem, may arise in reaction to crises in substantive practices such as science and politics, it more basically and frequently reflects a crisis in the understanding of the relationship between first- and second-order discourses, that is, between, for example, academic political theory and politics. It is a problem in part because second-order inquiry conceives its mission as the proprietory one of discovering, validating, or explicating the grounds of judgment in the activity it has appropriated as its subject matter. But the problem is often only tangentially one of the possibility and integrity of practical judgment. The pursuit of a solution to the problem of relativism is a quest for a comprehensive answer to the infinitely complex and contextually diverse questions attending the nexus between theory and practice. It most essentially reflects a crisis in the self-image of political theory and the foundations of its claims to knowledge.

The world of the émigrés was one of not only political but intellectual and professional insecurity, and the problem of relativism was a philosophical expression of their anxiety. The question of the authority of academic inquiry was an important concern for political science, but there were several reasons why the discipline tended not to perceive relativism as a threat. Easton's remedy for the decline of political theory, for example, called for the reconstitution of value theory without jettisoning the liberal belief in the relativity of values and their emotive nontranscendental basis. One reason that political science was able to absorb the issue of relativism was because it was an essential part of the pragmatic liberal creed of fallibility and progress in both scientific inquiry and politics. But the liberal science of politics had its own grounds of certainty.

There was, first of all, the belief that history validated liberalism and that liberal values were embedded in the basic institutions of U.S. politics. Relativism never was taken as implying that one value was as good as another but only that values reflected contexts and perspectives. Furthermore, certainty was to be achieved through science. Although science could not yield values as such, it seemed to select, confirm, and discredit them in various ways, and, again, there was the belief that the logic and procedures of science and liberal democracy were inherently mutually supportive and that both rested on a pragmatic notion of truth and the eschewal of absolutist speculation. Finally, political science was, much more than the emerging autonomous enterprise of political theory, an established disciplinary practice with its substantive criteria of judgment and, despite continuing concern about its public role and possibilities, a sense of practical efficacy and professional identity. It was, consequently, less daunted by the philosophical phantom of relativism that haunted émigré political theorists.

The discipline of political science constituted a context that profoundly and singularly shaped the institutional form and ideational content of political theory. Political theory, in turn, was deeply implicated in some of the most fundamental changes that took place in political science, including both the behavioral and postbehavioral revolutions. Today, political theory has largely retreated from an involvement with, let alone critique of, political science, and political science has, for the most part, afforded political theory the ultimate disdain of pure tolerance. This situation has allowed many important issues, both explicit and implicit, to slide into obscurity or to become, as in the case of liberalism and relativism, detached from the practical concerns that originally generated them. Professional pressures, under the guise of intellectual principle, continue to push in the direction of separatism, but the results are debilitating. Both political science and political theory have been diminished. The former has lost its most important critical and reflective dimension, and the latter has lost its congenital and maybe most authentic field of action.

References

Almond, Gabriel, Lewis Dexter, William Whyle, and John Hallowell. 1946. Politics and Ethics – A Symposium. *American Political Science Review* 40: 283–312.

Anderson, William. 1949. Political Science North and South. *Journal of Politics* 11: 295–317.

Appleby, Paul. 1950. Political Science, the Next Twenty-five Years. *American Political Science Review* 44: 924–932.

Arendt, Hannah. 1951. *The Origins of Totalitarianism.* New York: Harcourt, Brace.

Brecht, Arnold. 1947. Beyond Relativism in Political Theory. *American Political Science Review* 41: 470–488.

Brecht, Arnold. 1959. *Political Theory: The Foundations of Twentieth-Century Political Thought.* Princeton, NJ: Princeton University Press.

Brecht, Arnold. 1970. *The Political Education of Arnold Brecht.* Princeton, NJ: Princeton University Press.

Easton, David. 1949. Walter Bagehot and Liberal Realism. *American Political Science Review* 43: 17–37.

Easton, David. 1950. Harold Lasswell, Political Scientist for a Democratic Society. *Journal of Politics* 12: 450–477.

Easton, David. 1951. The Decline of Political Theory. *Journal of Politics* 13: 36–58.

Easton, David. 1953. *The Political System.* Chicago, IL: University of Chicago Press.

Finer, Herman. 1945. Towards a Democratic Theory. *American Political Science Review* 49: 249–268.

Friedrich, Carl I. 1938. Thomas Hobbes: Myth Builder of the Modern World. *Journal of Social Philosophy* 3: 251–257.

Gunnell, John G. 1983. Political Theory: The Evolution of a Subfield. In *Political Science: The State of the Discipline*, ed. Ada W. Finifter. Washington, DC: American Political Science Association.

Gunnell, John G. 1986. *Between Philosophy and Politics: The Alienation of Political Theory.* Amherst: University of Massachusetts Press.

Hallowell, John H. 1942. The Decline of Liberalism. *Ethics* 52: 323–349.

Hallowell, John. 1943. *The Decline of Liberalism as an Ideology.* Berkeley: University of California Press.

Hallowell, John. 1944a. Politics and Ethics. *American Political Science Review* 38: 639–655.

Hallowell, John. 1944b. Review of Arnold Brecht. Prelude to Silence: The End of the German Republic. *Journal of Politics* 6: 466–469.

Hallowell, John. 1947. Modern Liberalism: An Invitation to Suicide. *South Atlantic Quarterly* 46: 453–466.

Hallowell, John. 1950. *The Main Currents of Modern Political Thought*. New York: Holt, Rinehart & Winston.

Horkheimer, Max. 1947. *Eclipse of Reason*. New York: Oxford.

Kelsen, Hans. 1948. Absolutism and Relativism in Philosophy and Politics. *American Political Science Review* 42: 906–914.

Lasswell, Harold, and Abraham Kaplan. 1950. *Power and Society*. New Haven, CT: Yale University Press.

Lippincott, Benjamin. 1940. The Bias of American Political Science. *Journal of Politics* 2: 125–139.

Lippincott, Benjamin. 1950. Political Theory in the United States. In *Contemporary Political Science*, ed. W. Ebenstein. Paris: UNESCO.

Marcuse, Herbert. 1941. *Reason and Revolution*. New York: Oxford University Press.

Oppenheim, Felix. 1950. Relativism, Absolutism, and Democracy. *American Political Science Review* 44: 951–960.

Perry, Chamer. 1950. The Semantics of Social Science. Discussion by Max Radin. George Lundberg, Harold Lasswell, and Herbert Simon. *American Political Science Review* 44: 394–425.

Sabine, George H. 1939. What is Political Theory? *Journal of Politics* 1: 1–16.

Spengler, J. J. 1950. Generalists versus Specialists in Social Science: An Economist's View. Discussion by Thomas I. Cook, Stuart Rice, and Francis G. Wilson. *American Political Science Review* 44: 353–393.

Strauss, Leo. 1936. *The Political Philosophy of Thomas Hobbes: Its Basis and Genesis*. Chicago, IL: University of Chicago Press.

Voegelin, Eric 1952. *The New Science of Politics*. Chicago, IL: University of Chicago Press.

Voegelin, Eric. 1975. *From Enlightenment to Revolution*. ed. John H. Hallowell. Durham, NC: Duke University Press.

White, Leonard D. 1950. Political Science, Mid-Century. *Journal of Politics* 12: 13–19.

Whyte, William F. 1943. A Challenge to Political Scientists. *American Political Science Review* 37: 692–697.

Wilson, Francis G., Benjamin F. Wright, Ernest S. Griffith, and Eric Voegelin. 1944. Research in Political Theory: A Symposium. *American Political Science Review* 33: 726–754.

Wolin, Sheldon. 1960. *Politics and Vision*. Boston, MA: Little, Brown.

Part II
Interpretation and action

4   Political theory and the theory of action (1981)

The purpose of this chapter is to present the basic elements of a theory of human action and to suggest their relevance for claims about political phenomena. Although it would be desirable to offer the analysis of action without an introduction and justification, there are at least two reasons why such a move might be problematical. First, this type of analysis, and even the idea of what is referred to here as "theory," does not have an accepted place within the disciplinary matrix of contemporary political science. Although my principal concern in this chapter is neither to demonstrate the need for such a theory in political science nor to explore its possible implications for prevailing forms of research,[1] a summary statement of the arguments and assumptions relating to such matters is required. Second, although the theory is in certain respects related to accounts of social scientific explanation that advocate what has been variously described as an interpretative, hermeneutical, or phenomenological mode of inquiry, there is a fundamental logical difference. It is a claim about *action* as a kind of phenomenon rather than about the *explanation of action.* This is a crucial distinction which, along with several other issues raised by this analysis, will be discussed briefly in Sections I and III. Section II presents the substance of the theory, but the argument is necessarily very compressed in this context.[2]

Social scientific theory and the theory of social science

Theorizing in political science and social science in general (in the sense of making substantive claims about the character of political phenomena) has been severely inhibited by the influence of certain aspects of academic philosophy. This problem became acute during the behavioral era when the discipline turned to the philosophy of science (that is, theories about science), and particularly the logical positivist and logical empiricist reconstruction of the logic and epistemology of scientific explanation, as a rationale for, and guide to, the practice of empirical inquiry, but it did not end there. Neither the advocates of behavioralism nor their critics avoided the dilemmas arising from the relationship between social science and philosophy.

During the past decade, the assumptions about science which characterized behavioralism as a philosophy of inquiry and which continue to inform the conception of science held by many, and maybe most, political scientists were subjected to an intensive critique from the perspective of alternative views in the philosophy of science.[3] It is not surprising that political science, in attempting to establish itself, practically and reputationally, as a form of science came into contact with a body of literature that made what seemed to be authoritative claims about scientific theory and explanation. And it is not surprising that the revolt within the philosophy of science, associated with the work of individuals such as Kuhn, against the arguments of logical positivism and logical empiricism provided a basis for the critique of behavioralism in political science. This mode of criticism was necessary, and maybe inevitable, since the behavioral image of science had been predicated on assumptions derived from the philosophy of science. But this development had certain unfortunate results.

Although it may be difficult to assess precisely what effect behavioral doctrines about science had on the actual conduct of inquiry, one thing is quite clear: the philosophical origin of these doctrines propelled discussion in a metatheoretical direction. The critique and defense of behavioralism became largely a philosophical debate about the nature of scientific explanation rather than a confrontation between substantive claims about politics or the character of political phenomena. Methodological issues in political science became largely the residue of controversies in the philosophy of science, and political theory gave way to epistemology.[4] Political scientists began to pose for themselves such questions as "What is the logic of scientific explanation?"; "What is the relationship between theory and fact?"; "How is objectivity possible?" But these are philosophical or metatheoretical questions to which there are only philosophical and metatheoretical answers. They are questions about the character of social science stated in the language of philosophy and not, strictly speaking, questions that arise in the practice of social science. When social scientists treat these questions as theoretical questions and assume that the answers provide some sort of methodological guide, the difficulties begin. But this fascination with the philosophy of science was only one aspect of the "philosophization" of political theory.

The critique of behavioralism from the standpoint of issues in the philosophy of science was paralleled, and complemented, by the introduction of a number of anti-positivist arguments about social scientific explanation which were derived from the philosophy of social science and which addressed themselves to the question of the logic of inquiry demanded by the character of social phenomena. Often these philosophical accounts largely accepted the positivist representation of the character of explanation in natural science and, building upon the methodological work of individuals such as Weber and upon more recent but related philosophical arguments associated with phenomenology and linguistic analysis, they set out to demonstrate that social scientific inquiry was logically distinct. These accounts, advanced by individuals such as Alfred Schutz, Charles Taylor, and Peter Winch, generally objected to what was understood as the "naturalistic" or behavioristic implications of the positivist view of science and its demand for logical symmetry between explanation in the natural and social sciences, and they attempted to describe and prescribe the basic features of the explanation of social action. Opponents of behavioralism in political science soon discovered this literature and found that it provided a more sophisticated basis for a critique than some of the earlier attacks on scientism.[5] This literature also seemed to suggest a somewhat more positive alternative to behavioral research than the dissident literature in the philosophy of science, since it did say something about character of social phenomena.

These arguments were caught up, however, in the problem of differentiating between social science and natural science and the general question of the possibility of "man as a subject of science."[6] They offered general characterizations of social phenomena (purposive, intentional, rule-governed, meaningful, etc.) and social inquiry, and the work of political scientists influenced by this literature often simply constituted abbreviated repetitions and recapitulations of these philosophical accounts of the character of social scientific explanation. This pushed discussions in the discipline further in the direction of metatheory. Just as behavioralism had made the mistake of thinking that such philosophical claims about scientific explanation provided a basis for scientific practice, many of those who embraced these arguments in the philosophy of social science believed that they had found an alternative approach to social and political inquiry when all they had in fact found was a philosophical claim about what takes place, or should take place, in social scientific inquiry.

The difficulty is that philosophy has become the source of the self-understanding and aspirations of the social sciences as well as, in some instances, the norms of its practice. However, it is not intercourse with philosophy as such that is the problem but rather the belief that metatheoretical accounts, either descriptive or prescriptive, of social scientific explanation are equivalent to theories of social phenomena and/or constitute approaches to inquiry. But arguments *about* science, even if correct, are not the basis for doing science anymore than aesthetics is the basis of artistic virtuosity. Theories *of* science are no substitute for scientific theories. Yet the problem persisted. Arguments about how to do science were enunciated in philosophical terms, challenged in these terms, and lately it is clear that there has been a movement toward a resolution in these terms which once more reflects the course of recent discussions in philosophy.

Certain philosophers have now begun to suggest that the debate over "naturalistic" versus "nonnaturalistic" explanation in social science can be solved by realizing that these are in fact complementary modes of inquiry or perspectives that reflect a concern with different aspects or dimensions of social phenomena. This argument has been quickly seized upon by political scientists as a way out of what seems to be a methodological impasse.[7] It is now suggested that political science, confronted with two paradigms of inquiry, must develop a synthetic approach which accommodates the dualistic character of social phenomena. What is actually involved here is neither a theoretical issue about social phenomena nor a conflict between actual approaches to explanation but rather an abstract confrontation between two kinds of philosophical claims. The proposed conceptual reconciliation is not very satisfying, since the reconstruction of scientific explanation by logical positivism and empiricism and the account of the nature of social science by its opponents are not really comparable alternatives. Furthermore, such a third party proposal for a compromise is not likely to satisfy proponents of either philosophical persuasion. But the real difficulty is that "theoretical" controversies continue to be dramas written by philosophers. The "restructuring of social and political theory" is equated with philosophical arguments about the character of social scientific explanation.[8] The metatheoretical search for a solution to metatheoretically generated issues simply moves discussion further away from substantive theoretical issues.

Philosophical claims about social scientific explanation do not, and cannot be expected to, provide a basis of empirical inquiry. The problem of what does provide the basis of a mode of scientific practice or how such a practice evolves is not easily answered, but one thing is quite certain. It is more a theory of what is to be explained than it is a theory of explanation. But it is not simply methodological discussions cast in the mold of philosophical arguments that have prevented substantive theoretical work in political science. It is also the pervasive impact of a particular philosophical conception of theory. No doctrine from the philosophy of science has had a greater influence on the political scientist's view of science than the instrumentalist analysis of scientific theory which, in its various forms, has persistently characterized the schools of logical positivism and logical empiricism.[9]

Although most contemporary logical empiricists, and the defenders of this position in political science, would deny adherence to a strict operationalist/instrumentalist interpretation of scientific theory and theoretical terms, the language of the instrumentalist account has provided the basic framework for the analysis of theory in this philosophical tradition. This theory of theory, or at least its imprint, is still apparent in the most recent statements about the cognitive status of theory and its relationship to the specification of facts which have been made by such representatives of this school as Carl Hempel. But it was the earlier and more radical formulations of this thesis in the philosophy of science which formed the basis of the characteristic view of theory in political science, and social science in general, as set forth by individuals such as David Easton, Karl Deutsch, and Talcott Parsons.[10]

The principal feature of this "orthodox" analysis of theory was the postulation of a universe of "given" facts that was epistemologically prior to, and cognitively independent of, theory. Such facts were understood as both the object and foundation of scientific knowledge, and theories were understood as principally logical calculi of deductively related propositions which could be clamped on to empirical data and serve as instruments of description and explanation. Theories were believed to gain empirical content by correspondence rules or operational definitions which tied them, or at least certain key theoretical terms, to the primitive language of the observational framework. It is difficult to ascertain the extent to which political scientists correctly understood this philosophical argument. They certainly were mistaken in assuming that it was intended, or suited, to serve as a guide for theorizing. But the basic idea of theories as instruments for explaining facts was seized upon. Despite a great emphasis on the priority of theory in science and the "theory-laden" character of scientific statements and factual assertions, the instrumentalist notion that theories are essentially somewhat arbitrary intellectual constructs applied to, and evaluated in terms of their utility for dealing with, cognitively independent observable data became an accepted feature of political science. Theories, like values, were understood as part of the inevitable structure of preconceptions in terms of which facts are selected and ordered. It was maintained that, for scientific purposes, these preconceptions must be made as systematic and explicit as possible in order to perform as intersubjective heuristic devices for economically describing, explaining, and predicting relations between facts.

Theories were not understood as basic claims about the world to be judged in terms of their ultimate truth or falsity but as devices which are evaluated in terms of their usefulness for accomplishing a range of scientific tasks. Theoretical terms, like theories as a whole, were assumed to be initially empty of empirical meaning. They were to be tied down to the language of an observational framework in which the facts of immediate experience are specified in order to be meaningful and applicable. Theory in political science has often been equated with a range of approaches, strategies, conceptual frameworks, and systems of propositions which, while they did not meet the standards of what was conceived as the law-like explanatory devices of natural science, were nevertheless viewed as prototheories or theoretical constructs. Theories have been likened to models or "as if" constructions that in various ways enable investigators to gain a knowledge of, or insight into, the complexity of the world of observed facts.

The adoption of assumptions derived from the instrumentalist theory of theories has tended to blind political scientists to the most important function that theory performs in any viable science. Theories are not prior to facts in that they provide a perspective on facts and categories for analyzing them but in that they constitute primary or "realistic" conceptions of the world and the facts that inhabit it. The belief of logical positivism that some class of things called "facts" was a philosophically specifiable given datum (in terms of sense data, molar physical objects, etc.), and not merely a concept for referring to what science at some particular time and place takes to be "true" or "existing," distorted the extent to which theories in the practice of science are only pragmatically distinguishable from facts. Theories are not sets of high order functional tools for investigating a separate factual world and finding one's way about but rather amount to a vision of some aspects of the world. To say that something is a fact is to specify what kind of a thing it is, and this amounts to making a theoretical claim. It is such a claim that provides the criteria of explanation, description, and evaluation in any context of inquiry. Theories are not a way of conceptualizing facts but rather are the conceptual constitution of facts. To view theories as tools to be applied in solving research problems and to be judged by their applicability or usefulness is to fundamentally misunderstand their character. Theories are not supervenient frameworks imposed on facts. It is theory which gives meaning to the language of factual observation, but it does so not by providing a language for naming separate facts but by specifying what kinds of things the facts indeed are and that they "are" in fact. A theory is an ontology. Although one might speak metaphorically of theories as explaining facts, this tends to be an echo of the language of instrumentalism. Theories and facts are only analytically distinguishable within a particular paradigm of reality. Theories in science do not so much explain facts as provide the conceptual context in terms of which explanations (and descriptions) – which are particular context bound claims – take place and are evaluated.

The reason that instrumentalist assumptions about theory must be dispelled is not simply that they are philosophically inadequate but that the application of such assumptions in political science has prevented the problem of political reality from being confronted directly, and, consequently, theory inheres somewhat randomly and unreflectively in the usually unexplicated ontology implicit in everyday language of common-sense observation, in the concepts imported from various disciplines, and in reified analytical constructs. Theoretical claims might be available in such arguments as those of behaviorism, sociobiology, psychoanalytic theory, theism, and Marxism, but, for the most part, political scientists have treated these as complementary perspectives on given phenomena rather than incommensurable theories of social life. Political scientists talk about actions, their causes, and their effects and employ a whole category of terms often associated with the language for talking about action such as intention, purpose, and motive. And they enter into all sorts of discussions that imply certain assumptions about the relationship between language, thought, and behavior, but at present there are few systematic and reasoned claims about human behavior or action that give coherency to these assumptions.

What follows is in many respects derivative of contemporary work in the philosophy of action and the philosophy of language. To the extent that philosophy is concerned with the phenomenon of action itself rather than issues relating to the explanation of action, it is not a metatheoretical literature as far as social science is concerned but logically equivalent to theory in social science. The argument presented is not intended as a definitive or exhaustive analysis of action, but as a set of preliminary claims about very basic features of action which are relevant to the specification and explanation of political phenomena. It is an attempt to provide criteria for distinguishing the units and boundaries of political analysis to the extent that political objects are actions (and action artifacts such as institutions, texts, etc.). More specifically, it is an attempt to explicate and clarify the relationship between a family of action concepts, to sort out some of the problems involved in specifying a political action, to present an elementary analysis of the structure of action phenomena, to distinguish between designations and descriptions of actions, and to indicate the difference between actions, their antecedents, and effects.

The analysis of action

It is often noted that actions are a species of human behavior distinguished by what people "do" as opposed to what happens to them. But not all that might be considered "doings" are actions – for example, what one "does" accidentally. Also it would seem that many things that people might be said to "do" in the course of performing actions are not actions in themselves. Often actions are demarcated in terms of what a person does intentionally or purposively, but although this may be helpful as a general characterization and as a basis for differentiating action as a species of behavior, the concept of intention is as difficult to deal with as that of action itself. It should be apparent that issues such as these are interminable without reference to some general theoretical principles.[11]

The individuation and structure of actions

To perform an action normally involves several analytically distinguishable, but simultaneous and logically linked, acts or doings which may be considered components, aspects, or dimensions of a fully intelligible and autonomous action. First, in most cases, there is a *physical act* which could be construed as giving a certain "objectivity" or extension to actions. This usually involves bodily movements, vocables, or inscriptions. Such a physical act is a condition for, and often the means for, performing a *conventional act*, and in doing the latter, one necessarily does the former. But not every physical act qualifies or succeeds as a conventional act which requires conforming to, or acting in relation to (even contravening) certain conventions (grammatical, semantic, social) or performing the physical act in certain circumstances that give it meaning and significance. Yet such conceptually discrete and conventionally specifiable and recognizable acts are, in themselves seldom fully intelligible. In general, to perform a conventional act is also to perform an *intentional act* which involves using or doing the conventional act in a certain way or meaning something by performing it. "Intentional" and "meaning" here do not necessarily indicate "conscious" in the sense of "reflective," and neither refer to any psychological or mental state nor gain their identity from criteria privately accessible to the actor. This need not imply, however, that the criteria are behavioral. It is perfectly possible to develop a theory of action that avoids both behaviorism and mentalism which are, in fact, doctrines that tend to surface more in claims about the explanation of action than in the analysis of action itself.

The conventional act is thus a collateral act necessary for the performance of the intentional act, and, in many contexts, quite different conventional acts could conceivably be employed to perform a particular intentional act just as various physical acts could be used to perform a particular conventional act. Although every conventional act has *significance*, it is the intentional force or *meaning* which renders it intelligible. These intentions, however, are also related to conventions in the sense that the intention, which individuates or gives identity to an action, is necessarily always conventional (as opposed to nonconventional rather than unconventional). There are no private, in the sense of publicly inexpressible, intentions anymore than there are private languages, although a person can always keep one's intentions to oneself or have intentions prior to acting much in the same way that it is possible to "talk" to oneself. The point is that every intention is an instance of a convention just as every speech act must be formed from, and conveyed in, a language in order to be communicated. An action is both meaningful (understandable) and expressible, because its performance belongs to a public social context. Finally, in performing an action, one often does something which, like the physical and conventional acts, but yet in another way, is not an action in itself. While the physical and conventional acts are components or dimensions of an action, the performance of an action may constitute a *causal act* which generates events which are distinct from the action itself.

The causal act is defined in terms of the effects, results, and consequences (either purposive or nonpurposive) of an action. Such "eventuations" of an action are, in principle, only contingently related to the action, although in certain instances there may exist certain conventional connections between a particular action and the production of certain events (including other actions). But there are no logical (necessary) connections between an action and its eventuation in a causal act in the sense that the relationship between an action and its component (physical, conventional, intentional) acts involves logical or necessary connections. The causal act is not a dimension or element of an action. An action may be performed in order to accomplish something, or it may cause something to happen, but these outcomes are not themselves actions that the agent performs even though they may be purposive, that is, brought about in order to accomplish some end. However, what is "caused" may be another action performed by someone else.

There is a very crucial difference between the specification and analysis of an action on the one hand and such things as the description, evaluation, and categorization of an action on the other hand. Actions can be described in many ways, and there are all sorts of statements which can be made about them (which may or may not reflect their identifying intention and conventional context). But all this must be clearly distinguished from individuating an action and analyzing its components. In order to illustrate this point, as well as the preceding arguments, it may be helpful to offer some simple hypothetical examples that present a schematic analysis of action and indicate the distinctions discussed in this chapter.

Table 4.1 A schematic analysis of action

Nonlinguistic action	Theoretical designation of type of action
Conformative political behavior	Stipulative category (from language of political science, for example)
Political activity	Socially constituted and identified symbolic form
Following the party line	Description, evaluation, etc.
Electing Jones	Causal act
Voting for Jones	Intentional act individuating the action
Marking "X"	Conventional act
Moving arm	Physical act
Linguistic action	Type of action
Citizen participation	Stipulate category
Political activity	Symbolic form
Campaigning	Description
Convincing Brown	Causal act
Recommending Jones	Intentional act
Uttering "Jones is the best man"	Conventional act
Making vocal sounds	Physical act

What must be rejected immediately is the persistent idea, which in various forms continues to influence much of contemporary work in the philosophy of action, that bodily movements are somehow primitive in analyzing actions either in the sense, which is argued by the behaviorist or reductionist, that actions can be conceptually reduced to such movements or, in the sense which is argued by many anti-reductionists, that actions are redescriptions of such movements which in certain circumstances can be *seen* as actions or can *count* as actions. This same assumption about the primacy of physical acts is also often behind the arguments of those who hold that there are theoretically specifiable basic actions which are irreducible uncaused causes of other actions as well as those who defend some version of the identity thesis or the idea, for example, that electing Jones, voting for Jones, and marking "X" are three descriptions of the same event (moving the arm).

The notion that bodily movements are either primitive actions or the basic subject of action predicates can no more be sustained than the idea that the intentional force of an action derives from some nonconventional meaning in the mind of the actor. Actions and bodily movements cannot be viewed as logically equivalent, since any number of various movements might conceivably be used in the performance of a particular action, and the same movements might, in different circumstances, be components of entirely different actions. Furthermore, not all bodily movements (reflective behavior, for example) are even dimensions of action, and probably not every action can be construed as involving such movements. Bodily movements are often aspects, or even pre-conditions, of the execution of an action, but they are neither logically nor perceptually primitive. The idea that one basically "sees" such movements or "hears" noises and then makes an interpretation or inferential move that places it within an action framework is no more compelling than the idea that what we see and hear are sense-data or some other class of transcontextual facts. What we see and hear are actions, and only by retrospective analysis can we abstract out a physical act or bodily movement and show its place in the performance of an action.

The whole idea of nonconventionally or transcontextually specifiable basic actions, in the forms that it has been traditionally advanced, should be abandoned.[12] Whether or not an action is basic depends on situational not epistemological criteria. The assumption that certain actions by their very nature are basic usually involves confusing an action component with an action, failing to distinguish between an action and its effect, or conflating an action and its description or category. Either all actions are basic or else some may be singled out as basic in a particular context (such as the case of voting in American politics). To argue that certain actions are basic in the sense that they are the cause or condition of other actions, involve the exercise of a repertoire of certain supposedly innate human capacities, or are "simple" rather than "complex" is usually to mistake an aspect or dimension of an action for an action.

Moving one's arm in order, for example, to mark an "X" on a ballot would, according to some versions of the basic action thesis, be considered a standard case of causal generation. The action of moving one's arm is, it is suggested, basic because it is the exercise of a fundamental faculty and is not caused by any other action, while marking "X," voting for Jones, and so on, are complex derivative actions caused, or in some other way generated by, the simple or basic action of moving the arm. But once it is recognized that not all the things that one does when performing actions are themselves actions, the problem of isolating so-called basic actions disappears. The problem is to isolate *what* action is performed. Moving one's arm is a dimension or component of the action of voting, but it is not another more primitive action. In another context, marking "X," or even moving one's arm, could constitute an action, but what kind of action it would count as is essentially a matter of the intentional force. Whether or not the action is basic is either a matter of where it stands in a conventional context and/or a matter to be decided by some kind of criterion imposed by an observer. Just as it is important to discriminate between actions and their components, it is necessary to discriminate between actions and their outcomes. In the above example, convincing Brown is not an action resulting from a series of simpler more basic actions but rather the effect of the action of recommending Jones.

All actions are simple in the sense that they are not made up of other actions, and all actions are complex in the sense that they have act components. The language of "simple" and "complex" actually has little utility in talking about actions although it may be useful in discussing forms or patterns of social action. In analyzing politics or various political activities, it is apparent that they are often made up of different kinds of actions. Complexity is an attribute best ascribed to activities. But, in another sense, it is not really either actions or activities that are simple or complex but rather their descriptions, but this brings us directly to the problem of the relationship between the individuation and analysis of actions on the one hand and the description of actions on the other hand – a problem which is crucial for social scientific inquiry as far as maintaining cogency and clarity in this endeavor.

Description, evaluation, and categorization

In an influential article published nearly two decades ago, Donald Davidson suggested a solution to this problem, but I believe that his now widely accepted, and discussed, position must be rejected.[13] Davidson maintained, in his classic example, that by flipping a switch, turning on a light, illuminating a room, and alerting a prowler, a person is not doing four things but one which is described in four different ways. Although I would argue that, assuming a few facts, it is plausible to maintain that only one *action* has been performed (turning on the light), it is apparent that more than one thing has been done. The problem is to distinguish these items and make sense of the relationship between them. But setting aside for the moment the distinction between actions and the more general category of "doings," a question arises, with regard to Davidson's analysis, about the identity of the one thing that supposedly has been done and variously described. To speak of describing something implies that the subject of the description can be specified. Although Davidson did not address this question directly, he appeared to assume that some undesignated bodily movement is the bearer of these descriptions. In a later piece, Davidson made this explicit. He argued that bodily movements are primitive basic actions and that all descriptions can be ultimately reduced to a description of such a movement.[14]

It is difficult to sort out all the difficulties that attend Davidson's argument. Clearly, the idea of bodily movements as basic actions is involved, but he also fails to distinguish between an action and its description or between *specifying* an action and *describing* an action. There are two aspects to this failure. First, even if it is assumed that the reference in each of the four instances is to the same thing, what Davidson has offered are multiple designations or names for that same thing rather than what would normally be considered descriptions. But, second, what leads him to this conflation of actions and their descriptions and to his version of the reducibility thesis is in part at least what appears to be an assumption that actions can be construed as particulars or particular events, that is, discrete happenings that are temporally and spatially bounded. If actions were particular events, then descriptions (and various designations) could be taken as referring to properties of the event (or to properties which are exemplified by the event or of which the event is an instance). But actions, and "doings" in general, cannot easily be analyzed as particulars. Rather, they can be more reasonably construed, like linguistic meanings, as universal predicates ascribed to persons or agents who instantiate the action by performing it.[15] The *performance* of an action is a particular event and can be described as such – how, when, where, and so on. The performance of an action could be given four descriptions, but Davidson's four "descriptions" are actually ascriptions of acts or doings.

One might suggest, then, that Davidson's example does not involve four descriptions of a single action but rather four actions performed at the same time.[16] But although it could be said that four things have been *done*, interpreting this particular example as a performance of four distinct but simultaneous *actions* does not seem convincing. Assuming a few contextual facts, it is possible to view this situation in terms of our model. What is specified is one action, turning on the light, which is ascribed to a person. What individuates or identifies this action is the intentional act of turning on the light. In performing this action, the actor performs the collateral conventional act of flipping the switch as well as some physical act such as moving his hand. Illuminating the room and alerting the prowler are causal acts or the production of events which are, respectively, the purposive and nonpurposive consequences of the action. The action, as well as its components and effects, could be described and categorized in many ways, but descriptions and categorizations of actions are different from the specification and analysis of actions.

A number of philosophers, including Davidson, have been quite taken with what is sometimes termed the "accordion effect" in the description of action, that is, the fact that descriptions of actions can be compressed or expanded according to one's point of view or particular interest.[17] As it stands, this idea might seem quite unexceptionable, but often those who introduce it are either those who wish to demonstrate that beneath the various layers of description, there is a basic action or those who assume that there are as many actions as there are descriptions. In both cases, there is usually a failure to distinguish between the designation and the description of an action. Both the notion that every statement about an action reduces to a description of some basic physical act and the notion that what action has been performed, or how many, is simply relative to an observer's concern and description must be rejected. The "accordion effect" is a quality of the description, evaluation, and categorization of actions and not a quality of the actions themselves.

Voting for Jones and recommending Jones are not, at least in this instance, descriptions of actions but specifications of actions which in turn could be described and evaluated in various ways and in varying degrees of complexity. In addition, they can be subsumed under various categories, related to various activities, and judged and commented on in an infinite number of ways. But this does not change the action. Not all statements about actions – whether descriptions, evaluations, or the like – are equally correct (a matter which depends on contextual criteria), but certainly an action can have, for example, more than one description although not more than one correct designation. But, again, what is necessary is to stress the distinction between actions, their components, their effects, and the many things that can be said about them. Such distinctions must be carefully clarified before approaching the question of the explanation of action.

Explanation and understanding

It would be a mistake to assume that there is any one kind of operation that constitutes the explanation of action, but before confronting the general issue of the scope of action explanations, I want to discuss briefly the problem of the meaning of action. Although it would be too limiting simply to equate the explanation of an action with illuminating its meaning, the very character of the phenomena demands that a certain precedence be given to this aspect of the analysis of action. If to explain a phenomenon is to make it intelligible and produce understanding, then just as an essential aspect of explaining a speech act is, in most cases, to clarify its meaning, explaining actions in general usually involves demonstrating their conventional import. Since a good deal of the literature that is relevant to the problem of the meaning of action has focused on speech acts, it is reasonable to concentrate initially on linguistic actions if one assumes, as I do, that there is a fundamental structural symmetry between linguistic and nonlinguistic action and that they are simply two types of the same basic phenomenon.

Despite the continuing debate in philosophy about whether the performative or illocutionary force (intentional act) of speech is to be taken as part of its meaning or whether meaning is to be restricted to something such as sense and reference (conventional act), it seems reasonable to speak of the meaning of a linguistic action as a whole as long as both aspects of meaning are recognized and the relevant distinctions observed. However, there are further distinctions. First, with regard to the conventional act, it is important to differentiate between an *utterance* as an object (such as a sentence, for example) and *what is said* (conventional meaning or sense and reference). The latter can be ambiguous. For example, "Jones is the best man" could refer to a wedding. Second, it is necessary to take account of what the speaker *intends or means to say,* since it is not always true that one "says" what one means. Third, what a person means to say, in performing the conventional act of saying something must be distinguished from the *intentional force* of the action, and, since intentions can misfire, from what the person actually *means to do* and *wants to be understood as doing* by uttering the utterance. Finally, what one is doing by performing an intentional act must be distinguished from the causal act or the *effect that the utterance has* and *the purpose for which it is performed* (in addition to the purpose of being understood). All these distinctions are relevant to discussions of meaning, and they apply equally to linguistic and nonlinguistic action. Thus it is necessary to distinguish between the

conventional act as an object in the world and as something which has conventional meaning, between what the actor does and what the actor means to
do in performing a conventional act, between what the actor intends to do by
doing what is done and how this intention is understood, and between the
intentional act (or the action as a whole) and what one may mean to do or
cause to happen by performing the action.

There is more than one dimension to the relationship between intentions
and conventions. The meaning of the conventional act depends on the
meaning of the intentional act in the sense that conventional acts do not have
a use in themselves but rather are used in the course of performing an action
which is individuated by an intentional act. But although they may be said to
be the means of performing an intentional act, conventional acts also place
limits on the intentional act both in the sense that they provide a stock of
vehicles for actions and in the sense that some are better suited than others in
certain circumstances for satisfactorily performing an action. Furthermore,
what is merely a conventional act in one context, for example, "flipping the
switch," might well be an intentional act in other circumstances. The intentional act expresses or signifies what one is doing, but its meaning is a matter
of convention. An intention could not be formulated or communicated apart
from conventions, and although it is the intention that gives identity to an
action, intentions are always conventionally expressed. There is no way of
specifying intentions or talking about them or ascribing them to actors except
in terms of an analogical extension of the language for talking about conventions. As far as a theory of action is concerned, it is reasonable to treat
intentions as an attribute of the language or the "grammar" of action, since it
adds nothing to refer to a psychic state of the agent. Also it is worth men-
tioning once again that when speaking of convention in this context, "conventional" must not be interpreted as opposed to "unconventional" but rather
as opposed to nonconventional. There are certainly unconventional intentions, but there are no nonconventional intentions (or actions), that is, intentions that can be specified without reference to conventions. This is true even
with regard to actions that contravene conventions.

The conventions relating to linguistic actions, those pertaining to grammar
and syntax as well as the performatives governing intentional force, may seem
more easily identifiable than those relating to nonlinguistic action. But nonlinguistic action has its "grammar and syntax" also and, even in the case of
linguistic actions, the conventions which determine their meaning and constitute the vehicle for their expression and understanding involve more than
strictly linguistic conventions – particularly in cases where intentional force is
not conveyed by an explicit verbal performance such as "I recommend
Jones," but rather by some statement such as "Jones is a good man."
Although philosophers have devoted considerably more attention to the systematic analysis of the linguistic conventions governing the use of ordinary
language than to those relating to other forms of action, understanding the
meaning of any action involves locating it in a conventional context which

renders the various levels of meaning as well as the intention intelligible. However, the analysis of the conventions peculiar to particular forms of action such as politics is not so much a task of theory as it is a task of taxonomy and empirical investigation.

To move from a discussion of the meaning of action, which is part of an analysis of action, to the general problem of the explanation of action, is, as pointed out in Section I, to move away from theory to metatheory. Whether conducted by philosophers or social scientists, analyses of the phenomenon of action are part of a theoretical discussion about an object of social scientific inquiry, while the problem of the explanation of action concerns what social scientists do or should do. Here the activity of the social scientist is the object of inquiry. Scientists are engaged in theorizing and explaining, while philosophers of science are engaged in analyzing the character of theories and explanations in science. Scientists seek general explanations while philosophers of science, or social science, seek to generalize about explanations. I do not want to belabor this distinction, or argue that theory and metatheory should be insulated from one another, but, as I emphasized in Section I, this distinction does point up a difficulty that plagues the literature of both political science and the philosophy of social science.

A theory of action yields a phenomenon about which a number of questions can be asked, and, consequently, explanation will take different forms according to the various questions that can be posed within the theoretical context. The kinds of explanatory claims offered and the types of evidence adduced are variable within those limits. Sometimes to explain an action may involve simply a specification of its meaning, but it may also involve such things as putting it in a chronological sequence, locating it in a particular activity or cultural setting, determining its antecedents (including other actions as well as nonaction events), and indicating the structure of conventions in society which allow or even determine its manifestation. The possibilities are legion. When questions about explanation are viewed from the standpoint of the social scientist and against the background of a substantive theory, that is, a theory of action rather than a theory about the explanation of action, it becomes clear that what constitutes explanation is a scientific or empirical problem and not a philosophical problem. There is, in fact, no such general problem for the social scientist at all. *The* problem of explanation is the residue of a philosophical discussion *about* explanation. A good example is the case of the controversy about whether explanations of action are, or can be, causal explanations.

While some philosophers wish to equate explanations of action with causal explanation, others insist on extracting them from this category, but often the debate seems to revolve around issues which are quite far removed from substantive theories and problems of inquiry. A typical instance is the debate about whether explanations of actions fall under the Hempelian covering-law model. The metatheoretical question of whether there is a logical difference between the explanation of natural phenomena and human action is philosophically significant, but often those on both sides of the issue begin by accepting the validity of the Hempelian reconstruction of scientific explanation as a model of causal explanation in natural science, and the argument amounts to little more than a discussion about the universality of the model and its extension to social phenomena. Although opponents of the model may attempt to establish the differentia of social phenomena and their explanation, it is usually in terms of some equally broad characterization. The point is that this has no more relevance for empirical claims in social science than academic philosophy of science has for claims in natural science.

In many respects, the debate about whether social scientific explanations are causal is not even a very interesting philosophical issue. The point of many of the anti-causalist arguments is clear enough, that is, to demonstrate that the explanation of action involves such things as a reference to an agent's reasons and thus entails a language and logic which is different from that characteristic of the natural sciences and the explanation of physical events. But at the same time their view of natural science is often very limited and involves little more than an identification of natural science with some particular philosophical image. The search for the criterion that would distinguish natural science from social science requires moving to such a high level of abstraction that it has little relevance to the conduct of inquiry in any field. "Natural science" and "social science" are categories and not the names of branches of science. But what separates explanations in natural science from those in social science is ultimately much like what separates explanations in one particular branch of science from those in another, that is, the fact that they take place in the context of different theories and involve different phenomena. Explanations *within* natural science and *within* social science are variable to the degree that they are related to different theories. Those who have attempted to solve the longstanding debate in the philosophy of social science between "explanation" (cause) and "understanding" (meaning) by suggesting that they are logically autonomous but complementary modes of achieving social scientific knowledge have a point in the sense that they recognize that social science is not exclusively limited to the study of one kind of phenomenon. Yet what they undertake is really an attempt to synthesize two philosophical reconstructions of social scientific explanation by attributing a kind of dualism to social phenomena. Confronted with the philosophical problem of a conflict between two philosophical accounts of social scientific inquiry and social phenomena, they do little more than give each argument its due. If divorced from a comparison of concrete theories in natural and social science, and the explanations that proceed from them, such arguments about differences in explanation tend to be philosophical arguments about philosophical fictions.

A number of post-Wittgensteinian philosophers have set out to destroy the Cartesian notion of human behavior as a causal interaction between mental and physical events as well as to free the idea of action explanation from various kinds of mechanistic or deterministic models and reconstruct the concept of human agency and put it on a firmer basis than that provided by earlier arguments. But all this has involved some very narrow construals of causality. Critics have been quick to point out, for example, that many non-mechanistic types of action explanation can be viewed as causal. It is tempting to suggest that there is little at stake in many of these discussions and that they amount to little more than quibbling over the use of "cause." There is an important philosophical problem here and that is to illuminate the logic of action explanations and differentiate them from other kinds of explanations. But in the absence of a fully articulated theory of action, it is useless, or at least frustrating, to argue about the criteria of such explanations just as it is a sterile endeavor to inquire into explanations in natural science without looking closely at actual explanations and theories. This difficulty is quite apparent in the controversy about whether the reason for an action can be interpreted as a cause or whether such an explanation must be considered, for example, teleological in nature. What is characteristic of these debates is the same attempt to solve the problem of the explanation of action prior to an extended analysis of action and the place of the concept of reason in that analysis. Only when the concept of reason is located in a theory of action is it possible to discuss its role in the explanation of action. It is not possible to divorce questions about the logic and epistemology of social science from questions about the ontology (theory) of social phenomena. The former can only be cogently discussed in view of the latter.

Many of the concepts commonly employed in talking about action have a legitimate ambiguity that results from the various ways in which they are employed in everyday contexts as well as in diverse theories of human behavior, and to use them in relation to a particular theory of action requires some legislation of meaning. It is necessary to give some account, however tentative, of some of these concepts in terms of the theory that I have suggested. Specifically, I wish briefly to discuss *reasons* and *purposes* in relation to the pivotal concept of *intention*.

I have explicated the concept of intention in terms of a theory of conventional performatives, and I assume that this is roughly what Wittgenstein had in mind when he stated that "an intention is embedded in its situation, in human customs and institutions. If the technique of the game of chess did not exist, I could not intend to play a game of chess."[18] "Intention" here does not refer to some phenomenon hidden behind an action. It is a dimension of an action, and to explain an action in terms of its intention is to illuminate a dimension of it and not some empathetic divination of a prior mentalistic event. Intentions may be construed as an actor's meaning but that meaning is part of the action event or action artifacts such as texts and institutions. There is no need to refer to any "psychological" data. What is assumed in this theory is a basic logical symmetry between language, thought, and action. There is no way to speak of one except in terms of an analogy with the other.

It is possible to speak of forming an intention before acting, but this is best conceived as something on the order of a "rehearsal," since there is no way logically to separate an intention and the specification of an action. Intentions, then, are not factors in explaining why an action comes about, but reasons *are* such factors and can be viewed as antecedents, or even causes, of action as well as elements in a justification. All actions are intentional but not necessarily rational (in the sense that reasons can be specified). In addition to the reasons for an action, there are, or may be, purposes why an action is performed which relate to the causal act and the consequences or results of actions. Not all actions are purposive, but explaining an action may involve referring to the purpose for which it was performed or what one wished to accomplish by performing it. The difficulty with most attempts to discuss the nature of rational action and the function of reasons, purposes, and intention is that the model which emerges is often a culturally limited one that reflects modes of action in modern Western society – and maybe even a narrow aspect of that particular form of life.

It may seem that what has been presented here deals largely with actions, while social scientists are primarily concerned with modes or forms of action or activities. But I would suggest that this distinction, that is, whether we start with games or players, does not raise any questions of major theoretical significance. Although some work on the theory of action has emphasized individuals as agents of action and explicated the concept of action in those terms, my concern has been with action, and not with its instances. All action is social, and the level at which a question about action is posed is a matter to be decided in the course of empirical investigation. In terms of the theory presented here, particularly in view of the discussion of convention and intention, the great debate about whether individuals or society are the basic datum is nullified, and the question of whether groups can be actors is relegated to an empirical issue. Action exists wherever the criteria for applying action predicates is present, individuals, associations, and organizations could probably in many instances qualify as actors but usually not social classes, generations, technology (e.g., Jacques Ellul), and so on. Yet, although it is not a theoretical question, I do not want to slide entirely by the relationship of a theory of action to the practice of political and social science. Theories are not schemes to be applied, but they certainly have implications for the practice of science.

Theory and empirical inquiry

First, it should be noted that a theory of action does not in itself provide a program for social science or rules about its uses (explanation, critical, etc.). Not everything that social scientists do is explaining, and not all explanations in social science can be presumed to be explanations of action. The practice of political science is not anymore than the practice of any natural scientific discipline, coincidental with one theory or the investigation of one class of phenomena. Second, it may be necessary to point out once more that a theory is not a method and that from a theory one cannot analytically derive a set of imperatives and procedures for empirical inquiry. A theory does, however, indicate what questions can or should be asked, the kinds of empirical problems that can be formulated, and the criteria for answering questions and solving problems. The theory which has been proposed here carries with it the idea that social science, to the extent that it deals with the description, evaluation, and explanation of human action, is a mode of what, for want of a better term, might be designated *symbolic* or *interpretative analysis*, and a few brief selective comments about this kind of analysis may be appropriate.

Symbolic or interpretative analysis can be defined as the form of inquiry required when the object of study is conventional phenomena. As an approach within social science, it presents certain epistemological parallels, despite differences in method and purpose, with other disciplines (or certain approaches within other disciplines) such as philosophy, history, literary criticism, and hermeneutics, where the subject matter consists of symbolic artifacts. However, despite obvious epistemological differences, some care must be exercised in pressing the distinction between this form of analysis and enterprises such as natural science. For example, theory functions in the same manner in both cases in that the conceptual constitution of the facts is a function of theory. The difference is that, in the case of symbolic analysis, the phenomena or facts are in a sense other "theories" or the objective residue of other theories, that is how people conventionally conceive of the world and act in it.

To suggest, as I do, that certain modes of explanation in social science should involve illuminating conventional forms of action is sometimes characterized, or criticized, as entailing the assumption that the language of social science must in effect be the language of the actors and involve some kind of immersion in their form of life in order to effect understanding. But this is not the case. Symbolic analysis or interpretation logically requires a distinct and autonomous language. One cannot, for example, translate or learn a language outside the framework of another language, and, to a large extent, symbolic analysis is a species of translation with all the limitations and difficulties that translation implies. The language of social science and the language of a theory which together constitute a large portion of a disciplinary matrix are entirely necessary for the systematic investigation of politics. In addition, translation is not reproduction, and the idea that the aim of such an endeavor in social science is some sort of a reproduction or reliving of action should be finally laid to rest. It does, however, require making *reference* to a preconstituted conventional universe. Finally, there is no need to assume that the validity of an explanation depends on its being intelligible to the actor, since the language of social science is not the language of the actor. There is no need to assume that actors are necessarily conscious of the character of their actions and the conventions that constitute the context of these actions anymore, for example, than most individuals are aware of, or even capable of formulating, the conventions of grammar to which they conform in speaking their native language.

Although one might accept the idea that a theory of action would require something in the way of symbolic analysis, it is not uncommon for critics of such a project to ask how such analysis is, in the end, really possible. But what is the significance of this question? It could be, and should be, simply a request for the criteria of explanation which amounts to asking for a theory, but usually it involves a subtle move from theory to metatheory and to a series of open questions predicated on some metatheory.

Such a question is often informed by the assumption that there is some peculiar problem involved such as getting access to other minds and that the mind is some sort of private place where the events that produce physical behavior take place. It amounts to the same thing as posing a question about how to get somewhere when the conception of a destination presupposes that the journey is impossible. It belongs to a class of questions that include "How is objectivity possible?" (when it is assumed that objectivity involves referring to some extra-propositional datum) or "How is rational argument in morals possible?" (when it is assumed that rational argument involves empirically verifiable claims). Another kind of assumption that sometimes prompts these questions is that which is behind such queries as "How is science possible?" It is not inconceivable that these could be reasonable questions from some perspective, but often, since the grammar is similar, they are assumed to be like "How do you isolate a virus in solution?" where what is called for is a method or procedure. But it is no more reasonable to ask how social science is possible than to ask how physics is possible and expect an answer that would supply a recipe.

To the question of how social science is possible in terms of the theory proposed here, the only reply is to attempt to elaborate the theory at those points where specific problems are raised. How we explain an action can present numerous pragmatic difficulties, and in some instances it may not be possible at all, but in principle it is the same as translating a language, explaining a foreign culture, interpreting a text, or even understanding what someone says to us. When the obdurate skeptic asks if we can ever *really know* such things, we need only ask for the criteria *of really knowing*. The philosophy of systematic skepticism, or any other epistemological position, for that matter, is not a theoretical stance.

The final, and maybe most important, point to be made with regard to the implications of this theory is to anticipate the obvious objection that this is not a specifically *political* theory. The answer to this objection is that in one very important sense there can be no such thing as a theory of *political* action. Politics is one species, or conventional form, of human action which is not historically, culturally, or biologically given, and the specification of the "political" is a particular research problem rather than a theoretical undertaking. It is, of course, always possible to define the units and boundaries of politics in some stipulative manner and term phenomena encompassed by such a framework a "political system." From the instrumentalist's perspective in contemporary political science, this has traditionally been taken to constitute a "theoretical" endeavor, but it is much more like natural history than the natural science it professes to emulate. But although in one sense the theory of social action is not, and cannot be, a theory of politics, there is an even more important sense in which it does constitute such a theory. It makes a claim about what political phenomena are as such, whatever their particular character and configuration, it gives meaning and coherence to the language of action which is characteristically used as a basic observation language for talking about politics and engaging in political inquiry, and it provides a critical instrument for evaluating or challenging conflicting ontological assumptions or tacit theories of action and political reality which are often embedded in the use of that observation language by either political actors or observers of political action.

Notes

1 For a more detailed discussion of these matters, see John G. Gunnell, "Political Science and the Theory of Action: Prolegomena." *Political Theory* 7 (February 1979): 75–100; "Philosophy and Political Theory," *Government and Opposition* 14 (Spring 1979): 198–216: "Encounters of a Third Kind: The Alienation of Theory in American Political Science," *American Journal of Political Science* 25 (1981): 440–61.
2 Earlier versions of portions of this argument may be found in John G. Gunnell, "Political Inquiry and the Concept of Action: A Phenomenological Analysis," in Maurice Natanson, ed., *Phenomenology and the Social Sciences* (Evanston, IL: Northwestern University Press, 1973); "Political Science and the Poverty of Theory," in Maria Falco, ed., *Through the Looking Class: Epistemology and the Conduct of Inquiry* (Washington, DC: University Press of America, 1979).
3 See, for example, John G. Gunnell, *Philosophy, Science, and Political Inquiry* (Morristown, NJ: General Learning Press, 1975).
4 See Paul Kress, "Against Epistemology: Apostate Musings," *Journal of Politics* 41 (May 1979): 526–42.
5 For an early argument from this standpoint, see John G. Gunnell. "Social Science and Political Reality: The Problem of Explanation," *Social Research* 55 (Spring 1968): 159–201.
6 See, for example the arguments of A. R. Louch, *Explanation and Human Action* (Berkeley: University of California Press, 1966), and A. J. Ayer, *Man as a Subject of Science* (London: Athlone Press, 1964). For a more recent discussion, see Martin Hollis, *Models of Man* (Cambridge: Cambridge University Press, 1977).
7 In philosophy, for example, see Georg Henrik Von Wright, *Explanation and Understanding* (Ithaca, NY: Cornell University Press, 1971); and in political science, J. Donald Moon, "The Logic of Political Inquiry: A Synthesis of Opposed Perspectives," in Fred I. Greenstein and Nelson W. Polsby, eds, *Handbook of Political Science*, Vol. 1 (Reading, MA: Addison-Wesley, 1975).
8 See, for example. Richard Bernstein, *The Restructuring of Political and Social Theory* (New York: Harcourt, Brace, Jovanovich, 1976).
9 For a historical and analytical discussion of this position, see Frederick Suppe, "Introduction," in Suppe, ed., *The Structure of Scientific Theories* (2nd edn, Urbana: University of Illinois Press, 1977).
10 See Gunnell, *Philosophy, Science, and Political Inquiry*, Chs. 5, 6.
11 This analysis draws directly upon the argument of J. L. Austin in *How To Do Things With Words* (Cambridge, MA: Harvard University Press, 1962), as well as other analyses of speech acts in contemporary philosophy such as that of John R. Searle, *Speech Acts* (Cambridge: Cambridge University Press, 1972).

12 For a classic statement of the basic action thesis, see Arthur Danto, "Basic Actions," *American Philosophical Quarterly* 2 (April 1965): 141–48. Cf. Jane R. Martin, "Basic Actions and Simple Actions," *American Philosophical Quarterly* 9 (January 1972): 59–68. For a theory of action based on a version of the basic action argument, see Alvin Goldman, *A Theory of Human Action* (Englewood Cliffs, NJ: Prentice-Hall, 1970).

13 Donald Davidson. "Actions, Reasons, and Causes," *Journal of Philosophy* 60 (November 1963): 685–700.

14 Donald Davidson, "Agency," in Robert Binkley et al., eds.,*Agent, Action, and Reason* (Toronto: Toronto University Press, 1971).

15 See Charles Landesman, "Actions as Universals: An Inquiry into the Metaphysics of Action," *American Philosophical Quarterly* 6 (July 1969): 247–52, and *Discourse and its Presuppositions* (New Haven, CT: Yale University Press, 1973).

16 Cf. Arthur B. Cody. "Can a Single Action Have Many Different Descriptions," *Inquiry* 10 (1967): 164–80; Monroe Beardsley, "Action and Events: The Problem of Individuation," *American Philosophical Quarterly* 12 (October 1975): 263–76.

17 For a standard statement, see Joel Feinberg, "Action and Responsibility," in Max Black, ed., *Philosophy in America* (Ithaca, NY: Cornell University Press, 1965).

18 Ludwig Wittgenstein, *Philosophical Investigations* (New York: Macmillan. 1968), par. 337.

5 Interpretation and the history of political theory
Apology and epistemology (1982)

A panel at the 1977 annual meeting of the American Political Science Association was devoted to a discussion of the "New History of Political Theory." At that time, few may have been able to connect this label with any well-defined body of scholarship, but it did at least refer to an increasingly recognizable set of critical theses about contemporary research as well as prescriptions for its future conduct which had been advanced by individuals such as J. G. A. Pocock (1971), Quentin Skinner (1969), and John Dunn (1968). Their work has been the object of considerable comment, and there is now a more extensive and well-defined literature that might be understood as a product of the "New History." But neither the advocates of this persuasion nor their critics have adequately clarified the arguments associated with this position nor satisfactorily assessed its implications for the history of political theory as a field of study, particularly as it relates to the discipline of political science. Now, five years after the suggestion that there is a "New History," it may be possible to present a more definitive account of this endeavor.

It is possible to adopt a critical attitude toward past research in the history of political theory without endorsing the tenets of the "New History," and it is also possible to analyze critically the claims of the new historians without rejecting their enterprise (Gunnell, 1980). I do not wish to maintain that the goals enunciated by those who view themselves as setting out a new route are misguided. My basic concern is to clarify some of the complex issues which are raised by their arguments about historical knowledge and textual interpretation and to consider the problem of the relationship between these epistemological and hermeneutical arguments on the one hand (such as those represented in the headnotes) and substantive historical and interpretative claims on the other. One point on which I will insist is that hermeneutics, or arguments about the nature of textual interpretation, is neither the theoretical dimension of interpretative practice nor a method for pursuing that practice. However, it is often used as a justification of the norms involved in such practice. A second point that I will stress is that although many of the assumptions that have informed some of the most influential secondary literature in the history of political theory have been implicitly and explicitly challenged by the arguments of the new historians, neither their hermeneutical philosophy nor their substantive historical practice provide the basis for the reconstruction of the field.

The new history

It is necessary to be cautious about claims that past scholarship was "unhistorical" and that the subject matter must be now approached with the "methods of the historian" (Pocock, 1971: 9). It would be to miss the point of much of the earlier literature to see it as a series of historiographical mistakes, and exactly what constitutes historicity is far from uncontentious. Although David Easton and other political scientists of the behavioral persuasion deprecated what they considered to be the historical approach to the study of political theory, there are reasonable grounds for suggesting that the work of those scholars, from William Dunning to George Sabine, who engendered and worked within the paradigm of the great tradition of political theory, was informed more by a practical than a historical attitude. And, despite the form of the arguments, neither the goals nor the concerns of their successors such as Leo Strauss, Hannah Arendt, Eric Voegelin, and Sheldon Wolin, who focused on what they conceived as a decline of this tradition, were historical if judged by the criteria of what many intellectual historians do or think they are doing (Gunnell, 1979). The claims of these commentaries were ostensibly predicated on knowledge of the past and an access to the meaning of the classic texts; thus the status of this knowledge and the question of how to achieve it was always treated as a matter of some importance. Strauss, for example, repeatedly stressed the need to understand the thinkers of the past in the manner in which they understood themselves, but seldom were the issues confronted directly. The influence of the idea of the tradition is by no means extinguished, and it can be expected that the intellectual and emotional investment in this notion is too extensive to allow any wholesale retrenchment of research informed by it. Many continue to assume that the concept of the tradition is a given in any discussion of the history of political theory and to insist that "*it is simply not the case* that there is no '*tradition* of political thought!'" (Schocket, 1974: 270). But although there are numerous senses in which it might be reasonable to talk of tradition with regard to the study of political theory, arguments such as those associated with the new history have challenged both the subject matter and mode of inquiry which have dominated the field.

Notwithstanding the implications of arguments by individuals such as Skinner and Pocock, the history of ideas is not a very distinct genre and certainly not a discipline under which the history of political theory can be subsumed. If there is a problem with the past scholarship, it is not simply a failure to meet the criteria of some easily specifiable practice. The new history involves a plea for restructuring the study of political theory along the lines of a particular norm of historical inquiry and in terms of a particular philosophical (hermeneutical) model of historical explanation and textual interpretation. What is most easily and generally attributable is a claim about the need for, and possibility of, a truly historical approach, or even method, that will make it possible to achieve an accurate reconstruction of the actual meaning of historical texts as distinguished from their significance for the reader, their subsequent influence, and their philosophical cogency. This is not to say that the latter issues are viewed as unimportant, but rather than any intelligent discussion of these matters presumes a prior understanding of what a text does in fact mean to say. The explication of the meaning involves recovering the intentions and motives of the authors which in turn requires determining the activity in which they were engaged, specifying their audiences, and in general reconstructing the context in which they wrote. Heretofore, it is alleged, much of the secondary literature in the history of political theory was informed by considerations that led to reading the present into the past and to the imposition of alien concerns and categories. The result has been anachronistic and ideological interpretations and conceptual confusions which have yielded distorted nonhistorical characterizations more concerned with evaluating than describing. The goal of past interpretation has been more philosophical than historical. The point is not that the philosophical analysis is untoward, or even that it is possible to eliminate completely bias and evaluation from an account of the past and put aside all preconceptions, but only that the ideal of historical interpretation demands that a construal of a text be as objective as possible; this requires discovering what the authors said, what they intended to say, and what they were doing when they said what they did.

The assumption is that the recovery of this meaning is possible because the object of analysis is a linguistic artifact and the product of linguistic activity in which the meaning is embodied and objectified. By locating the text in a wider structure of literary genres, conventions of public speech, and social activity, it is, at least in principle, possible to develop hypotheses about what an author intended to say and therefore what a text means. This process is only pragmatically different from understanding social action in the present. Interpretation is a matter of finding contexts in which a text is intelligible and then closing the context as tightly as possible in an attempt to eliminate alternative readings. One of the basic assumptions is that most of the texts of political theory were developed in the context of practical political issues and belong to distinct traditions of political discourse, and thus they may be viewed as ideological arguments. Thus a central task of the history of political theory is to focus on elaborating those ideological contexts in which the texts are located. Finally, although the basic goal of analysis must be to understand the political thought of the past, it is assumed that such analyses have relevance for explaining politics in the past as well as for illuminating the general relationship between politics and political ideas.

Such a sketch may convey the general character of the argument under consideration, but it does not provide a satisfactory understanding of exactly what kind of argument it is, and it does not constitute an adequate basis for a critical examination of the issues involved. Few of the individuals who might be taken as representative of this position have developed their views explicitly and extensively enough to allow such an understanding and examination. Quentin Skinner, however, has attempted in a series of pieces to state, elaborate, defend, and deploy his position. His work has been extensively discussed and criticized (more extensively than some may feel is warranted but often less scrupulously and fastidiously than would seem fair), but for the most part the criticisms that have been offered relate to a different set of issues from those that I wish to pursue here. Although I wish to present an accurate reconstruction and critical analysis of Skinner's position, my primary concern is neither to discuss the viability of his notion of interpretation nor to evaluate the goal toward which it is directed but rather to demonstrate the manner in which his arguments exemplify a certain problem in the relationship between the philosophy and practice of political inquiry.

Epistemology, theory, norm, and method

This problem has become endemic, or maybe has always been endemic, in history and the social sciences. It is a tendency to confuse, conflate, and otherwise entangle epistemological and methodological (in this case hermeneutical) claims; theories; research norms and goals; and methods or techniques. In speaking of epistemology and methodology, I am referring to arguments that usually are generated within the academic discipline or philosophy and are directed toward or are about a practice of inquiry. Theories are a range of claims of varying degrees of generality within a form of inquiry which specify what is being investigated and which form an ontology of the subject matter. Given a range of possible choices allowed by the conception of what is being studied, a research norm is a statement of the goal to be achieved and the problems to be solved in the conduct of inquiry. Finally, a method or technique is a claim about how, or through what procedures, a norm should be practiced. What individuals such as Skinner and Pocock refer to as a historical method is in fact an amalgam of these four types of propositions. The character of, and relationship between, these elements of inquiry will become clearer in the course of discussing Skinner's work, but some preliminary elaboration is necessary.

To explain, describe, evaluate, or in any other way talk about something is to say at least implicitly what kind of thing it is. Theories provide the criteria for making and evaluating substantive claims. They may take the form of a relatively focused and detailed discussion of a class of phenomena, but in most disciplines theory is often simply embedded in particular claims about instances of those phenomena. The case of epistemology and methodology is quite different. Although one might argue that there are epistemological and methodological assumptions in any practice of inquiry, that is, notions about knowledge and how it is, or should be, gained and validated, they constitute a distinct realm of discourse which has largely become part of academic philosophy (of science, of history, of social science, etc.). This is not to suggest that epistemology cannot or does not influence or reflect substantive inquiry, but at least in the modern age it is a separate field of argument. No one would suggest, however, that theory could be separated from science and become a branch of formal philosophy. Norms of inquiry and methods are, like theory, part of the matrix of inquiry and emerge in varying degrees of explicitness. Since epistemology, norms, and methods are prescriptive or at least often couched in prescriptive language and deal with how knowledge is acquired, they are easily confused, but as with theory, one criterion of demarcation is that norms and methods are necessary elements of the actual conduct of inquiry. The point of this brief digression is to prepare a foundation for my argument that even if Skinner's particular theoretical statements, philosophical or hermeneutical claims, practical norms, and methods of inquiry are defensible, he confuses them and does not accurately represent their respective functions.

The theoretical component of Skinner's work appears principally in his discussions of conventions, speech acts, and linguistic meaning (1971; 1970; 1969). Whatever the ultimate adequacy of Skinner's analysis of speech acts, it falls under the category of a theory of the text and of social action in general. My first quarrel with Skinner, however, centers around his belief that an analysis of speech acts, such as that which he has adopted and adapted from the work of philosophers such as J. L. Austin and John Searle, constitutes, or even yields, a method of historical interpretation. My point is not that a theory has no implications for methods or norms, since it would seem to suggest certain directions of inquiry and to proscribe some procedures and prescribe others. But Skinner has consistently maintained that it is possible to deduce, or at least extrapolate, interpretative methods and norms from the theory of speech acts. This is no more convincing than the idea that theories in physics constitute norms and methods for investigating physical phenomena. The relationship between theories on the one hand and norms and methods on the other is contingent. Whatever some philosophers and social scientists might claim, theories are less like road maps that provide instructions for how to proceed than they are like geodetic surveys that indicate the way things are and the limitations and possibilities of proceeding. What Skinner sometimes refers to as a method is basically a temporalized sketch of speech act theory that provides no actual procedure or rules for textual interpretation. It is a claim about the nature of speech and language. Furthermore, it appears that his theory of speech acts was adopted as a consequence of a prior commitment to a particular philosophy of interpretation, that is, an epistemological or hermeneutical claim about what understanding and interpretation involve.

This is the real core of Skinner's notion of method – the assumption that epistemology is the foundation of inquiry. But this is as mistaken as the idea that the philosophy of science is the basis of scientific practice. Although such philosophies characteristically contain normative and descriptive statements about scientific explanation, they are only defeasible philosophical claims about scientific practice and do not constitute scientific methods. In the case of the neo-idealist epistemology embraced by Skinner, some of the more characteristic soft points of this position, particularly with regard to how to make objective statements about subjective meaning and mentalistic phenomena such as intentions, seemed to be solved by the "linguistic turn" in philosophy and arguments such as those of Austin and Wittgenstein. The theoretical component of Skinner's argument is in large measure used to support a particular philosophical claim which, I will argue, actually functions as a legitimation of a particular practical norm and form of historical practice rather than as a method for that practice.

Although Skinner, as well as many commentators on his work, sees his substantive historical research as the application of his philosophical principles, these principles are in fact a justification for a particular norm of historical practice, that is, the reconstruction of historical contexts and the interpretation of texts by locating them in those contexts. There is an important sense in which Skinner is quite correct when he claims that his approach is "truly historical" if "historical" is equated with what many intellectual historians actually do. He fails, for the most part, to confront other hermeneutical arguments such as those associated with the work of H.-G. Gadamer (1976; 1975) and Paul Ricoeur (1976), as well as that of a wide range of individuals in literary criticism who stress the autonomy of the text and the authority of the reader in establishing meaning. These claims give a quite different meaning to the notion of historicity. This failure, however, is consistent with Skinner's instrumental use of epistemological claims. It is necessary to look more closely at Skinner's arguments before pursuing these critical comments any further, but these comments provide the framework for the following discussion.

History and hermeneutics: the case of Skinner

The limited and selective manner in which Skinner has addressed himself to the theory of meaning and speech acts indicates the extent to which this material is directed toward the support of his philosophy of interpretation. There is a vast theoretical literature dealing with action and speech (and such particular issues as the structure and individuation of actions and the question of basic actions) which Skinner does not pursue, but which would be essential to confront if one wished to elaborate fully a theory of the text and written discourse (Gunnell, 1981b). For example, in a symposium on the explanation of action, the important question of whether or not different descriptions designate and entail different actions is implicitly raised, but Skinner evades this issue by simply stating that even though there are different descriptions, "there is surely only one action at stake" (1978a: 9). Such a conclusion is defensible, but an unexplicated "surely" is not sufficient to settle this complex problem in the theory of action and to clarify issues which attach to it. Another significant problem in the theory of action which Skinner treats somewhat summarily involves the problem of intentionality (and other mental concepts) and language.

Skinner by no means neglects the problem of intentionality, but his concern is to defend the epistemological claim that intentions can be known and that the recovery of intentions constitutes interpretation and historical explanation. He argues that an author must necessarily express intentions in public conventions which in principle make those intentions accessible to the reader. But at the same time it would appear that he assumes that intentions are psychic states or mental phenomena expressed in speech acts and actions which are in turn the objective traces of ideas and prior thoughts. Again, this is a popular position in the philosophy of social science and a theory in the literature of the philosophy of action and philosophy of language, but it is by no means uncontested. In fact, the weight of argument may now even be in the other direction, toward the notion that intentionality is a function of language. Such a notion could well find support in the work of Austin and Wittgenstein. The reference of mental terms in Skinner's arguments is never entirely clear, but his distribution of emphasis is continually indicative of separating thought and action and suggesting that the former explains the latter. He speaks of speech acts as the expression of "attitudes" (1979: 210) and of texts as the products of "mentalities" (1978b: xi), but the theoretical status of such concepts (as well as ideology, beliefs, ideas, motives, intentions, and thought) and their relationship to language and social practice are never sufficiently clarified or explored. Speech act theory is used by Skinner to bolster or resurrect hermeneutical claims that are rooted in the work of individuals such as R. G. Collingwood and closely related to the theories of such contemporary advocates of the authority of original or auctorial meaning as E. D. Hirsch (1976; 1967). It is not part of an extended analysis of the phenomenon of a text, the character of meaning in language, and the relationship between thought and action.

Skinner explicitly supports (and, given the character of his argument, must support) the idea that philosophy (epistemology) provides a basis for explanatory practice in the human sciences. He states that "with the ebbing of confidence in empiricist epistemologies and their accompanying claims to provide us with a methodology for the human sciences, *those of us who try to practice these disciplines ... come to feel an increasing need to look for renewed philosophical help*" (1978a: 69). This statement must be taken very seriously; it indicates much about the assumptions and purpose of his work. What Skinner elaborates is a philosophical claim about the nature of historical explanation which he views as a species of the explanation of human action. Although claims about the explanation and the nature of action are seldom entirely separable (since the former presuppose certain general assumptions about the latter, and since both are usually found in the literature of philosophy), there is a significant difference. It is the difference between epistemology and theory. It is quite clear that most of Skinner's methodological arguments belong to the epistemology of the social sciences or hermeneutical philosophy (1972b). Skinner repeatedly notes his concern with recovering the *"historical* meaning of the text,"* writing the history of political theory "as real history," using a "strictly historical approach," "excluding unhistorical meanings," fulfilling "the promise of historicity," being "historically minded" and "historically orientated," writing "genuine histories," and producing arguments of a "genuinely historical character" (1974: 297, 281, emphasis added; 1977: 8, 14; 1978b: xi). But the only criteria of historicity offered are a version of a standard philosophical model of the explanation of action.

Skinner believes that this model is not merely of philosophical (or what he terms theoretical) interest but has a distinct "methodological value" that has been sometimes "overlooked or even repudiated by practicing historians" (1978a: 65). He claims that the model yields an *"appropriate methodology for the history of ideas"* (by which he means method) and for "investigating the motives of political theorists and the character of their political thought" (1969: 49; 1977: 24). He contends that it is the source of what he refers to as his "method" which constitutes "a particular way of approaching the study or interpretation of historical texts" (1978b: 10). But although Skinner points to an individual such as John Plamenatz as an example of someone who believes interpretation is only a matter of "simply reading the text over and over again" or to C. B. Macpherson as an example of someone whose arguments are "unhistorical" (p. 1978b: xxxi), he neither examines in any detail the work of any particular historian of political theory nor identifies and analyzes any systematically developed alternative position, such as Marxist or structuralist, in the philosophy of interpretation. Gadamer, for example, maintains that understanding never involves the recovery of an author's intention; interpretation is always a matter of encountering a text from the present perspective. The closest that Skinner comes to confronting directly a concrete counterargument is his discussion of certain literary criticism that defends claims about the autonomy of the text (1975–1976; 1972a). But in this discussion it is possible to grasp the logical level and realm of discourse to which much of Skinner's argument about method belongs. Theories of literary criticism are principally defenses and codifications of practical interpretative norms.

Certain elements of Skinner's epistemological argument (such as his earlier claim that the ultimate authority for judging the adequacy of a description of an actor's or author's intentions must always lie with the individual agent) have been elaborated and amended (1972a; 1969), but the general position has remained consistent. The principal and necessary element in textual interpretation, he maintains, is understanding, and although there may be a sense in which it is possible to understand authors better than they understood themselves, the basic task is to discover what an author "intended to mean, and how this meaning was intended to be taken" (1969: 49). In order to accomplish this task, it is necessary "to delineate the whole range of communication which could have been conventionally performed on the given occasion of the utterance of the given utterance, and, next, to trace the relation between the given utterance and this wider linguistic context as a means of decoding the actual intention of the given writer" (1969, p. 49). This may sound like a piece of procedural advice, but it is logically equivalent to, and about as practical as, some general philosophical precept regarding scientific explanation, such as "seek generalizations with the greatest empirical content and test them by comparison with the widest range of observations." But Skinner is defending a practical norm of historical inquiry and interpretation, that of reconstructing the historical context of a text. In pursuit of this defense he relies on hermeneutics and the philosophy of social science.

Although he concedes that there are various senses in which a text might be said to have meaning, he maintains that the meaning of what is written is "actually *equivalent*" to the author's intentions in writing it, and thus recovery of this meaning and a grasp of what the author was doing must always be "*amongst*" the interpreter's tasks. It is the "necessary condition" of all other tasks the interpreter might take on and "indispensable" for attributing any other types of meaning (1972a: 404, 406; 1975–1976: 214, 219). The "decoding" of these intentions embodied in the "nonnatural meaning" and "illocutionary force" of speech acts and logically linked to the meaning of what is said (semantically) in a text must be supplemented by a recovery of the motives which "prompted those particular speech acts" and indicated what an agent meant by performing them (1975–1976: 214; 1972a: 400). Finally, it is necessary to determine if, given the circumstances, the action "would be appropriate" for a rational actor in that situation (1978a: 60). If it seems appropriate, then the action must be deemed explained, since "to exhibit a social action as rational is to explain it." He claims that rational action is its own explanation. Otherwise, it is necessary to explain why the agent "*believed* it was rational" to act in that manner and that the actor did so because of this belief (1974: 295). This, again, represents a highly contested position in the philosophy of social science which is associated with the work of individuals such as Martin Hollis (1977) and which Skinner less elaborates or defends than uses to justify the norms that he advocates.

Skinner maintains that "most historians appear in practice to accept the view that the explanation of action is a matter of recovering meanings and motives," and he wants to determine "whether it is possible to lay down any general rules about how to interpret a literary text." Such rules would specify how to proceed with "'getting at the message' of a text, and of 'decoding and making' explicit its meaning, such that the 'best reading,' rendering … the 'best meaning' can be obtained" while still recognizing that it is never possible to "arrive at '*the* correct reading' of a text, such that any rival readings can then be ruled out" (1978a: 64; 1972a: 393). In response to the skeptical claim "that it is actually impossible to recover a writer's motives and intentions," Skinner states that since such a view "seems straightforwardly false, I assert this as obvious, and shall not attempt to prove it" (1972a: 400). The general rules that Skinner puts forward for recovering meaning are, first, to "focus not just on the text to be interpreted, but on the prevailing conventions governing the treatment of the issues or themes with which the text is concerned," and, second, to "focus on the writer's mental world or his empirical beliefs" (1972a: 406–7). Surely, for someone actually seeking a rule or method, these instructions must seem a bit disappointing. They are not practical rules at all, but only elements of a philosophical methodology.

Skinner explicitly rejects the crude argument that a text is simply a product of its context and that its message can be deduced from the context, but he actually often moves very close to this position. It does seem clear at least that what he describes as a historical approach tends to depreciate the text in favor of the context. Although he claims that the goal is the interpretation of texts, he sometimes seems to equate an interpretation with detailed descriptions of a historical context "from which the elements which seem most significant can then be abstracted" (1966: 214–15). His claim is that a text is "a meaningful item within a wider context of conventions and assumptions, a context which serves to endow its constituent parts with meaning while attaining its meaning from the combination of its constituent parts" (1975–1976: 216). This is simply a description of one aspect of the famous hermeneutical circle, but Skinner's conception of the recovery of an author's meaning, the process which he terms "illocutionary redescription," makes it necessary to stress viewing authors in terms of the "general social and intellectual matrix out of which their works arose" and "to surround a given text with an appropriate context of conventions as an indispensable key to decoding the meaning of the text itself." Skinner claims that "when we attempt in this way to locate a text within its appropriate context, we are not merely providing historical 'background' for our interpretation; we are already engaged in the act of interpretation itself" (1978b: x, xiv; 1975–1976: 221, 224). A recognition of this point is essential in grasping the kind of historical practice that Skinner is attempting to defend. Although he is willing to allow that some texts are more "autonomous" than others, that is, less ideologically engaged with their contemporary world, he believes that even the least "heteronomous" require the aid of history to establish the meaning (1975–1976: 217).

When Skinner addresses the particular problem of interpreting texts in the history of political theory, he appears to assume that he is dealing with largely heteronomous pieces of literature, since not only does he wish to approach them as "the record of an actual activity" but as "the history of ideologies." The principal justification he gives for engaging in such historical research is that it would not only provide "a realistic picture of how political thinking in all its various forms was carried on in the past" but "would thus enable us to begin to establish the connections between the world of ideology and the world of political action" (1974: 279–80). Skinner does not indicate exactly where this division lies or how ideology can be separated from action and used to explain it, but he wants to suggest that political theory is a type of political ideology and its study should be seen as a study of the "process of ideology formation and change" (1974: 281). This is clearly an empirical proposition about the literature of political theory, but Skinner wishes to raise it to the level of a regulative research principle. It does, however, serve to support his claim that understanding a text in political theory requires locating it in "the prevailing conventions of political argument at the time" and looking at it in terms of relevant "*genres* and traditions of discourse" (1974: 287). It is necessary to "surround these classic texts with their appropriate ideological context" in order to recover their meaning (1978b: xi). Precisely because of this assumption that much of the history of political theory must be construed in ideological terms, Skinner believes that it is necessary to introduce into the standard model of action explanation yet another piece of "regional" hermeneutical advice that in the case of the history of political theory should almost justify a special kind of historical investigation. This is the study of the use of political principles as rationalizations.

This notion, to which Skinner gives considerable attention, is of great importance to him since it is obvious that some of the alternative epistemologies that he is at least implicitly challenging, as well as conflicting theories and norms, would hold that political ideas are epiphenomenal and basically rationalizations, either conscious or unconscious, of particular political circumstances. Although Skinner believes that it is too simple merely to take the principles cited by an actor or author as either an account of motives or as sufficient causes of action, it is incorrect to adopt the Namierite view that they are not relevant explanatory factors. Since principles are often used to legitimate an actor's behavior or arguments, there is a sense in which there is always a "causal-connection between the principles for the sake of which he professes to act and his actual social and political actions." Even when the actor does not believe in the principles, "he will be obliged to behave in such a way that his actions remain compatible with the claim that these principles genuinely motivated them." Thus principles are always relevant, since "the course of action open to a rational agent in this type of situation must in part be determined by the range of principles which he can profess with plausibility." To study principles even when they are rationalizations is to study one of the "key determinants of his decision to follow out any particular line of action" (1974: 292, 299–300).

My concern in discussing this aspect of Skinner's argument is not to inquire into the validity of this proposition which, if pursued, would soon seem to run afoul of a large body of literature on rational action ranging from very technical formal philosophy to game theory in social science. My purpose is to suggest the extent to which this argument is a somewhat *ad hoc* thesis to meet a characteristic criticism of the philosophical model of the explanation of action that Skinner adopts to defend his notion of historical inquiry. The rationalization argument allows Skinner to maintain that to explain a political action or interpret a text *always* requires an investigation of "appraisive" terms or "the general concepts which serve at once to describe and evaluate political life," that is, "commend and legitimate, or question and condemn."

It requires a study of the "divergent normative vocabularies" which are available to the actor or writer and a determination of "how these various languages function in, and contribute to, political life" (1977: 5–6; 1979: 209). It is then necessary to determine why the writer picked the language he did – that is, to discover the "ideological aim" (1977: 21). Skinner also believes that this type of approach holds promise for bringing "the connections between political theory and explanation of political behavior into a closer relationship" (1978b: xi; 1977: 8). The "capacity to explain political action is actually dependent on a willingness to study the available languages of political thought," and the "'relevance' of the history of political ideas must be sought in studying changes in political vocabularies over time, revealing their role in the formation of ideologies and in this way the dependence of political action on political thought," and "the exact ways in which the explanation of political behavior depends upon the study of political thought" (1977: 15; 1976: 386).

In this statement it is possible to grasp the basic character and purpose of Skinner's argument. It is a statement of a standard position in the philosophy of social science tailored to legitimize a certain kind of historical explanation and an emphasis on contextual reconstruction and to shore up the prevalent idealist belief in intellectual history that mental phenomena (for example, ideas, attitudes, beliefs, and ideology), objectified in language, are the explanation of overt action. To confront these claims at the level of method makes little more sense than, for example, the controversy about whether Peter Winch's idea of a social science constitutes a practical alternative to positivist modes of inquiry in social science. What actual methods or techniques are involved in, or could be attributed to, the practice of the "new history" is difficult to specify in any very general manner. There is a great reliance on other secondary literature in reconstructing contexts, and this raises certain obvious problems about the interpretation of those works and the extent to which they can be offered as explanatory data. But a discussion of such methods would require a detailed analysis of a range of substantive work in the field. Whatever these methods may involve, they have not been carefully articulated by those who practice them.

As a set of philosophical claims about historical understanding (such as the need for recovering the author's meaning), Skinner's method might well be taken as representing a wide range of individuals from Sabine to Strauss, and the question of who, in practice, was being genuinely historical would still not be resolved. There really is no way to arbitrate empirical claims by epistemological standards, because there are no given conceptual linkages. The question of "historicity" is either a question to be settled or debated at the level of epistemology, or it is a matter of confrontation between different modes of substantive historical practice. It is never an issue that can be fruitfully joined between hermeneutical philosophy and interpretive inquiry. Since Skinner does not engage philosophical rivals in any direct and systematic manner, and since, despite the fact that he does raise certain theoretical issues as well as offer certain field-specific programmatic recommendations such as viewing political theories as ideologies, his basic emphasis is neither theoretical nor procedural, it must be assumed that his argument serves essentially to describe and justify what he and many intellectual historians do and the interpretative norms they embrace. In this sense Skinner is quite correct when he speaks of this as a "genuinely" historical approach to the study of political theory. However, no matter how great his concern with the "philosophical status of this activity" (1966: 230), it does not solve the many practical difficulties that are inherent in much of the work that might be associated with the new history of political theory. In fact, it contributes to those difficulties.

Text and context in intellectual history

One of the difficulties with some of the work that might be identified (or identify itself) with the new history is what would appear to be the often striking gap between hermeneutical wind-up and interpretative delivery. By pointing to this problem, I do not wish to imply judgments about the quality of the research, but rather further demonstrate the nature of the enterprise. According to individuals such as Skinner, the historical approach will make it possible to elicit the meaning or message of a text, but from a reading of Skinner's work, for example, it would be difficult to gain the impression that the aim of situating a text in its appropriate context is primarily instrumental, and that the ultimate purpose is to move toward a closer textual analysis. There are probably few historians of political theory who would disagree with John Dunn's claims that it is necessary to "return to the contexts of the utterances which men produce" and that "the problem of interpretation is always the problem of closing the context," or even the idea that the achievement of "historicity" in the account of a text is "its sufficient and its sole legitimate immunity from our philosophical prejudices" (Dunn, 1968: 98–99). But such abstract pronouncements neither guarantee the goal nor provide a method for pursuing it. They do, however, often serve to make legitimate an approach that does not so much concentrate on a deep systematic textual analysis as on general characterizations of a work and its place in a reconstructed historical context.

When we turn to Skinner's most ambitious substantive work, *The Foundations of Modern Political Thought* (1978), it seems much more reasonable to read his account of method as a defense of this type of project rather than a statement of the procedures that made it possible. Skinner claims in this work to first "offer an outline account of the principal texts of the late medieval and early modern political thought," and, second to "indicate something of the process by which the modern concept of the State came to be formed" (Skinner, 1978b: ix). Although it might be possible to quibble over the meaning of his statement of the first goal and to argue about the extent to which he has achieved it, he has done an excellent and valuable job of synthesizing primary and secondary sources and constructing a historical and literary frame for locating and exhibiting what have conventionally been taken as the major texts of political theory for the period under consideration. The second aim and consequently the degree to which he has accomplished it is more ambiguous since there appears to be very little of the work directly addressed to this issue, and it is not at all clear what Skinner has in mind by "a process" through which a concept comes into formation or the locus of that formation (texts, politics, modern political vocabulary, institutions, etc.). It is, however, Skinner's third aim which would seem to be the most problematical.

He claims that this study serves "to exemplify" his arguments about the character of historical interpretation and that in this work he has "practiced" his "method." The goal of his "method," he asserts, is "the interpretation of historical texts" (1978b: ix). But although Skinner's book might be construed as an aid to interpreting some of the texts of early modern political thought by demonstrating the historical background and indicating the literary setting and the continuities and contrasts with earlier, later, and contemporary work, it would be more difficult to defend the claim that there is much in the work that constitutes interpretations of those texts or that confronts in any detail the range of issues that have been raised about their meaning. There are general characterizations of the works and their purposes and intentions, but little that could qualify as a reconstruction of a text and its argument. Setting the text in a context and arriving at descriptive generalizations about its intention and purpose may be precisely what Skinner means by the notion of interpretation, but it is exactly such concrete practical questions which are not answered by his philosophy of historicity. Skinner's discussion of Machiavelli illustrates some of these difficulties and ambiguities.

Skinner makes a strong and lucid case for the extent to which *The Prince* shared in the preexisting genre of "advice-books for princes," but his argument that the work "at the same time revolutionized the genre itself" is more questionable (1978b: 118). He does not really demonstrate the influence of Machiavelli on later pieces of advice to princes; if the point is simply that Machiavelli developed a critique of humanist political thought and gave a different meaning to concepts such as *virtù*, it is scarcely a novel insight.

Skinner offers a number of generalizations on such matters as what constitutes "the heart of Machiavelli's message" (nothing matters as much as keeping up appearances) and "the essence of Machiavelli's advice" (model one's values and conduct on both the lion and the fox), how "the whole of Machiavelli's advice is governed by a highly original sense of what should be taken to constitute true *virtù* in a prince," and how "the basic value around which Machiavelli organizes his advice is that of security" (1978b: 132, 136, 138, 156). But even if all these characterizations are compatible, it is difficult to see this type of descriptive generalization as an interpretation of *The Prince* or even as the basis for any significant interpretation of the work. There is, for example, no detailed analysis of the structure of the text (or even a discussion of whether it has one); no theme, argument, motif, or symbol is systematically pursued through the work; there is no extended discussion of the relationship of Machiavelli's many other works to *The Prince*; no consideration is given to his intentions in writing the book beyond the generally accepted, but not uncontested, view that he wished to win employment with the Medici; and there would seem to be a neglect of numerous other problems surrounding the text. For example, when we have considered all that Skinner offers, there is nothing that would rule out hypotheses that the work was a satire, that it was, as Rousseau suggested, written for Republicans, that it was an attempt to manipulate princes into actions that would prepare the foundations for a republican regime, or that numerous other defensible notions of Machiavelli's meaning and motive are possible. Not only is a careful examination of the text not evident, but even the literary and historical context seems far from closed.

When we turn to Skinner's discussion of the *Discourses*, the same problems are apparent. There is no structural analysis and no extended examination of what Machiavelli was doing as a whole or why he was doing it. The problem of dating and the relationship to *The Prince* is briefly considered and a conclusion is drawn which would not easily satisfy many scholars – "Machiavelli almost certainly began to compose his *Discourses* only after he came to realize that his hopes of gaining employment under the Medici were misplaced." We are told that while the basic value of *The Prince* is security, "the basic theme" and the "basic value of the *Discourses* is that of liberty" (1978b: 157, 158). But it is not apparent why one could not argue, for example, that the basic theme and value of both is founding and maintaining a stable political order. Nothing is said, for example, that would rule out the hypothesis that the *Discourses* is a call for republican revolution and that the chapter on conspiracies (the longest chapter in the work) could be construed as practical revolutionary advice. There is no dissection of the intricate themes and arguments that run through the work, and there is no careful consideration of why Machiavelli might have chosen Livy's work as a vehicle, or how it is in fact used. Finally, while many of his generalizations and conclusions are commonplace, others are anomalous and unsupported, such as the claim that in the *Discourses* Machiavelli (like Montesquieu!) is not very concerned with the institutional structure of government as a means of insuring virtue in politics (1978b: 171).

These limited and somewhat random observations on Skinner's discussion of Machiavelli are offered only to suggest that few scholars concerned with the intricacies of Machiavelli's work would accept this as an interpretation of the texts in question. It is only fair to repeat that Skinner does not claim to present more than an outline of the texts, but what he offers does not correspond to what his method promises. It would be difficult to accept his discussion as even a definitive prolegomenon to a more dense and systematic textual analysis of *The Prince* and *Discourses*. There are far too many unpacked, and possibly conflicting, generalizations in Skinner's account, too many elements omitted from the analysis, too many interpretative possibilities left unconsidered, and too many gaps in the reconstructed context. Although he offers his discussion as an exemplification of his method, it more clearly exemplifies the problems involved in attempting to relate epistemology to interpretative practice or to judge the latter by the former. What it may exemplify, however, is the characteristic treatment of texts by many intellectual historians.

Conclusion

In the case of Skinner, then, we find an epistemological or hermeneutical argument employed to defend a practical interpretative norm and offered as if it were a method for achieving historicity. Although there are elements that might be construed as relating to a theory of the text and that would provide criteria for a defense and critique of substantive interpretative claims, such elements are truncated, confused with other propositions, and used largely to defend and elaborate a particular hermeneutical argument. My concern has not been so much to criticize the arguments discussed here as to identify and sort out the various types and suggest what in fact is going on when these arguments are presented. Above all, I wish to indicate the rhetorical, strategic, critical, and apologetic roles that epistemology or, in this case, hermeneutics, often plays. Although the philosophical analysis of what constitutes knowing in a particular field may be a possible and autonomous activity, there are strong grounds for suggesting that much of traditional epistemology has been either instrumental or the disembodied residue of instrumentally inspired arguments and that much of contemporary hermeneutics must be viewed in this manner (Gunnell 1981a).

The study of the history of political thought may be facing a crisis, but it is not primarily a theoretical crisis and even less an epistemological crisis. Although a field of study may become absorbed with epistemological issues when its practice falls into a state of crisis, there are no epistemological answers that will solve the problems. A disciplinary matrix is based on more than a set of philosophical precepts and practical norms. Even a theory of the text would not restore to the field the kind of integrity that was provided by the idea of the tradition and the sense of relevance gained by the belief that it was explaining our modern political condition and addressing a crisis of Western thought and action. The history of the history of political theory as a field of study is unintelligible apart from an understanding of the evolution of the concept of the tradition, but that idea may no longer be able to withstand self-conscious scrutiny. Those who identify with the new history may wish to pick up the pieces, both of the subject matter and the discipline. But with the collapse of the paradigm of the tradition, there may be grave questions about the extent it is possible to discover any coherent subject matter and any convincing practical reasons for studying it. The notion that it is possible to reappropriate the classics by a historical warrant and that such a study can be justified, as Skinner argues, by its ability to develop insights into the relationship between political ideology and political action or political theory and political practice seems tenuous. His suggestion that the history of political theory is an important element in the explanation of political behavior is even more shaky. The general project, as well as the distinctions and relationships between such concepts as thought and action, remain nebulous.

The study of the tradition was based on the claim that historical interpretation would produce philosophical insights and practical political explanations, but these interpretations were in fact seldom historical in terms of either purpose or product. Although a more historical approach may locate a text more accurately in its context, it often seems to yield little in the way of textual analysis and philosophical reflection. In view of this, it might be suggested that what is required is sensitive textual analysis coupled with historical awareness and conducted with philosophical and political self-consciousness, but there remain the basic problems of exactly what should be studied, and why. More careful historical research and textual exegesis may produce some significant revisionist interpretations of classic texts and there is no doubt that much of the work of those who may be associated with the new history is directed toward a much wider range of political literature and traditions of political discourse than that which was characteristically the focus of concern in the field. But apart from scholarly antiquarianism, the purpose of the enterprise and its relationship to the wider endeavor of political inquiry is far from clear. Where this leaves us is difficult to say, but it must be understood that rallying around or debating versions of philosophical hermeneutics will not provide a basis for the continuation or reconstruction of the study of the history of political theory.

References

Dunn, John. 1968. The identity of the history of ideas. *Philosophy* 43: 85–116.
Gadamer, H.-G. 1976. *Philosophical hermeneutics.* Berkeley: University of California Press.
Gadamer, H.-G. 1975. *Truth and method.* New York: Seabury Press.
Gunnell, John G. 1981a. Encounters of the third kind: the alienation of theory in American political science. *American Journal of Political Science* 25: 440–461.
Gunnell, John G. 1981b. Political theory and the theory of action. *Western Political Quarterly* 34: 341–358.
Gunnell, John G. 1980. Method, methodology, and the search for traditions in the history of political theory. *Annals of Scholarship* 1: 26–56.
Gunnell, John G. 1979. *Political theory: tradition and interpretation.* Cambridge, MA: Winthrop.
Hirsch, E. D., Jr. 1976. *The aims of interpretation.* Chicago, IL: University of Chicago Press.
Hirsch, E. D., Jr. 1967. *Validity in interpretation.* New Haven, CT: Yale University Press.
Hollis, Martin. 1977. *Models of man.* Cambridge: Cambridge University Press.

Pocock, J. G. A. 1971. *Politics, language and time: essays on political thought and history.* New York: Atheneum.

Ricoeur, Paul. 1976. *Interpretation theory, discourse, and the surplus of meaning.* Fort Worth: Texas Christian University Press.

Schocket, Gordon. 1974. Quentin Skinner's method. *Political Theory* 2: 261–276.

Skinner, Quentin. 1979. The idea of a cultural lexicon. *Essays in Criticism* 29: 205–223.

Skinner, Quentin. 1978a. Action and context. *The Aristotelian Society.* Supplementary vol. 52: 55–69.

Skinner, Quentin. 1978b. *The foundations of modern political thought*, vol. 1. Cambridge: Cambridge University Press.

Skinner, Quentin. 1977. Political language and the explanation of political action. Paper presented at the Annual Meeting of the American Political Science Association, 1977, in Washington, DC.

Skinner, Quentin. 1976. Review of Handbook of Political Science, *vol. 1*, eds. Fred Greenstein and Nelson Polsby. *Political Theory* 3: 385–388.

Skinner, Quentin. 1975–1976. Hermeneutics and the role of history. *New Literary History* 7: 209–232.

Skinner, Quentin. 1974. Some problems in the analysis of political thought and action. *Political Theory* 2: 277–303.

Skinner, Quentin. 1972a. Motives, intentions, and the interpretation of texts. *New literary History* 3: 393–408.

Skinner, Quentin. 1972b. "Social meaning" and the explanation of social action. In Peter Laslett, W. G. Runciman, and Quentin Skinner, eds, *Philosophy, politics and society*, series 4. Oxford: Oxford University Press, pp. 136–157.

Skinner, Quentin. 1971. On performing and explaining linguistic actions. *The Philosophical Quarterly* 21: 1–21.

Skinner, Quentin. 1970. Conventions and the understanding of speech acts. *The Philosophical Quarterly* 20: 118–138.

Skinner, Quentin. 1969. Meaning and understanding in the history of ideas. *History and Theory* 8: 3–53.

Skinner, Quentin. 1966. The limits of historical explanation. *Philosophy* 41: 199–215.

6   Interpretation and the autonomy of concepts (2011)

In the literature of social science in general, and even in political theory where there is greater focus on concepts, there is considerable persistent confusion about the concept of a concept and particularly about the relationship between words and concepts. Even in a work as analytically astute and sensitive to language as Hanna Pitkin's valuable and influential *The Concept of Representation* (1967), the slippage between words and concepts prompts one to ask what constitutes the connection. Pitkin deployed a central organizing metaphor in her discussion of representation:

> We may think of the concept as a rather complicated, convoluted, three dimensional structure in the middle of a dark enclosure. Political theorists give us, as it were, flash-bulb photographs of the structure taken at different angles. But each proceeds to treat this partial view as the complete structure. It is no wonder, then, that various photographs do not coincide, that the theorists' extrapolations from these pictures are in conflict. Yet there is something, there, in the middle of the dark, which all of them are photographing; and the different photographs together can be used to reconstruct it in complete detail.
>
> (pp. 10–11)

In the later edition of the book (1971), Pitkin stated in a footnote that "I now believe, on the basis of reading Wittgenstein, that the metaphor is in some respects profoundly misleading about concepts and language. But on the concept of representation it happens to work fairly well. Since it is central to the structure of this book I have let it stand" (p. 255). It is necessary to understand why Pitkin's metaphor was, as she acknowledged but did not explain, "profoundly misleading" and why Wittgenstein was relevant for rethinking the issue. And, despite her claim to the contrary, I suggest that in some respects the metaphor did not actually work "fairly well," even if it did provide an organizational heuristic.

Pitkin's metaphor was similar to the parable of the blind men seeking to define an elephant in terms of the particular property with which they came in tactile contact. The point of the parable is usually to suggest how things may appear differently when viewed from diverse perspectives, and Pitkin suggested that even though the concept of representation might seem different if pictured from different angles, these perspectives, together, revealed an underlying coherence. In the case of the blind men, however, no combination of definitions based on perceived properties could yield the concept of an elephant, and the story only makes sense because the listener or reader already possesses the concept of the object that the men are attempting to describe. Pitkin put considerable emphasis on the etymology of the word "representation," but although this provides insight into how the word has been used, just as a dictionary does, examining a word does not produce a concept.

If Pitkin had focused on an instance of a particular practice of what is conventionally designated as political representation, such as some aspect of American politics, it might have been possible to look at it from diverse perspectives and gain a more textured account than one "photograph" might produce. Or if she had chosen one concept to which the word "representation" had been typically ascribed, such as the image of the representative as trustee, the analysis might have worked. Her approach, however, was predicated on, or at least encouraged, the assumption that such instances were manifestations of something more universal and fundamental, that is, as her book title indicated, *the* concept of representation. There is, however, no such concept. It is a mistake to take an abstract or generic term such as "representation" and treat it as if it referred to a particular concept. One response to this criticism might be to claim that there are many concepts of representation and that what Pitkin was actually doing was comparing those concepts and attempting to elicit something common from them. But this rendition is also likely to be misleading. Just as there is no one concept to which the word "representation" refers, there are not, strictly speaking, many concepts *of* representation but rather many concepts to which the word "representation" has been applied. We might, confronting a particular political practice interpret it as an instance of a concept, which we label as "representation," but there are a variety of concepts of which that practice might be construed as an instance. These concepts are logically incommensurable, but they are not contradictory because they are specifications of different kinds of things that are not necessarily in conflict with one another, even though they may come into conflict, if there are contending claims about a fact of the matter or what should be the fact of the matter. In the case of Pitkin's analysis, no amount of photographs could bring *the* concept out of the shadows and, as she claimed, make it possible to "reconstruct it in complete detail." There was, so to speak, no "elephant" in the room. What Pitkin was actually exploring were the ways in which the word "representation" had been employed, that is, the different concepts to which the word had been attached and what might be viewed as both different and common among these concepts. This is what she actually accomplished and what made the book so valuable.

Some of the confusion about this matter has emanated from the often referenced argument of W. B. Gallie about "essentially contested concepts"

(1955–56) and from similar assumptions by individuals such as Reinhart Koselleck (1985; 1988). Gallie claimed to be isolating certain concepts, such as democracy, which had a number of common attributes such as the character of being appraisive, internally complex, and capable of different descriptions, which together tended to give rise to disputes about their genuine meaning. Gallie constantly used "term," "word," and "concept" interchangeably, but on the whole, he was really talking about words and the manner in which they were used. There is no such thing as an essentially contested concept, but even if Gallie was actually referring to words, he was wrong in claiming that some words are essentially contested. What are involved in most disputes about the subject of democracy are conflicting claims about to what concept the word "democracy" should refer. Debates about democracy do not, for the most part, emanate from the nature of either a word or a concept even though there are instances in which a failure to distinguish between the word and concept may give rise to controversy. People might argue about the appropriate use of a word – such as, for example, in the case of a debate about whether the American polity is a democracy or a republic, when the parties to the debate do not disagree about the nature of the United States government and are consequently talking about the same concept. But they might, in another instance, agree about the concept of democracy and disagree about whether the United States is an instance. It would be reasonable to say that the use of certain words is *characteristically* contested, but this is often because, as in the case of "democracy," they have historically accrued a great deal of either approbation or disapprobation on which an argument may draw.

Despite all the recent scholarship on conceptual history, there is still considerable incoherence in discussions about words and concepts. This is in part because the interpretation of concepts and the study of conceptual development are often, although not always clearly, tied to ideological agendas. While this does not necessarily nullify their scholarly credibility, it does sometimes create problems. Koselleck's work, for example, like a number of similar projects in the field of political theory, was motivated *by* a critique of modernity and a defense of "the political" or the public realm against society, technology, and Enlightenment values. The failure of the social sciences to be clear about the concept of a concept is, however, in part because there has been little in the way of a satisfactory systematic philosophical treatment on which to draw.

The problem of clarity regarding concepts was evident in Melvin Richter's extensive examination of various forms of *Begriffsgeschichte* (1995) in both Europe and North America. In this discussion, the identity of concepts remained strangely elusive. Despite his concern about transcending past research in the history of ideas in the English-speaking world, as well as trends in the European schools of *Geistesgeschichte* and *Ideengeschichte*, what he viewed as the differences between the old and the new historiography often did not seem decisive. Neither Richter nor the individuals and persuasions that he discussed seemed to advance any very distinct, or distinctive, claim about concepts. Richter noted that "the meaning of concept" can be determined only "within the context of a theory," but while he claimed to describe the "theoretical statements" of a variety of historians, such as Quentin Skinner, what he offered was largely a description of programs and projects in which such statements often seemed conspicuously absent or elliptical. Richter quoted sympathetically someone who suggested that the term "concept" is "useful precisely because of its ambiguity" (p. 21). Such ambiguity, however, has created problems in both Anglo-American and Continental ventures into the history of concepts.

The suggestion that we should approach the issue by reflecting on what we are talking about, when we speak of "acquiring," "having," or "using" a concept, often amounts to a somewhat regressive move that leaves us as puzzled as before about the kind of thing to which the word "concept" refers. MacIntyre, for example, claimed that possessing a concept amounts to behaving, or being able to behave, in a certain way and that conceptual change entails changes in behavior (1966: 2–3). We might very well conclude from this sort of definition that a concept is not so much a kind of thing at all but rather, as Ryle at times claimed, a dispositional or functional category (1949). If this were literally the case, however, it would make little sense to speak of things such as conceptual development or of histories of concepts. What is sometimes reflected in such an image of concepts is the assumption that they are tools or instruments. This image, sometimes derived from remarks of J. L. Austin about "how to do things with words" (1962) and from remarks by Wittgenstein (e.g., 2001: 569), may have much to recommend it, but the equation of concepts with instruments is not sufficient. There are various kinds of instruments and various kinds of usage. What is often assumed in these claims is something that is actually not compatible with Wittgenstein's philosophy, that is, that concepts are instruments for expressing, and indications of, prior mental states. Although behaving in a certain manner might provide criteria for attributing concepts to a person and although, like words, they may be in some sense instruments, we must be able to discriminate concepts as a class of conventional objects and grasp their place in linguistic usage before we can intelligently speak about possessing and using them – and studying them.

It is not a definition of "concept" that is most fundamentally at issue. Definitions are quite infinitely variable depending on the purpose of the definition and what properties or attributes are selected as definitive. Definitions, even of a stipulative kind, assume a prior specification of the thing that is defined. We can only define and describe what we can already identify and specify as a thing of a certain sort, even though a definition may aid someone else in recognizing it. The first question, then, is whether a concept is any kind of distinct or autonomous thing at all. Everyone seems to agree that we possess them and that our thoughts and actions are in some way informed and even governed by them, but they often appear to remain, as Hobbes or

Marx might have said, in the world of spiritual entities, which may in part explain the propensity to reduce them to words, which seem more concrete and objective. Although it is often recognized and emphasized that concepts are not, in the final analysis, the same as words, both social scientists and philosophers seem to have limited success in untangling and relating the two.

Richter noted that historians of concepts usually "distinguish concepts from words. A concept may be designated by more than one word or term ... Yet an individual or group may possess a concept without having a word by which to express it" (1995: 9). Quentin Skinner took strong exception to Raymond Williams's analysis of "keywords" (1976), and one of Skinner's concerns was to distinguish concepts from words. He noted that concepts usually have a corresponding word and vocabulary but that even though an individual may use a word characteristically associated with a concept, it does not necessarily indicate possession of the concept. These claims, on their face, are correct, but they are still ambiguous. Skinner's principal example of the difference between words and concepts was his suggestion that when John Milton claimed that, in his poetry, he wished to do things yet "unattempted," he must have possessed the concept of originality even though the word was not available to him (1989: 7). What Skinner assumed in his example of Milton seemed to be a functional view of concepts. From this perspective, it would be reasonable to say, for example, as some have, that the people who built Stonehenge possessed the concept of a computer, even though we may assume that they did not use the word. The same word can, of course, express different concepts, but it is important to recognize that different words can be spelled or sound the same, that is, a homonym or homophone. The same concept can be expressed by two different words such as the case of "Venus" and the "evening star," both of which refer to an empirically distinguishable planet, but this might not be the case, for example, with "justice" and "equity." We might say that these latter words indicate similar concepts, but they are not necessarily the same concept.

We are often told that concepts are connected to beliefs, which in turn explain action and practices, but again, this approach brings us back to what the "linguistic turn" in social inquiry and intellectual history had sought in some respects to overcome, that is, the focus on a nebulous realm of mental entities or ideas. It is sometimes claimed, for example, that concepts are "constitutive" of and "inform" beliefs and are a "medium of shared understanding," and Skinner consistently identified concepts with "attitudes" and other psychological entities. Despite his emphasis on the public character of language as explicated by individuals such as Austin and Wittgenstein, Skinner still viewed intellectual history as the study of "the history of past thought" and the "history of ideas" (1985: 50). What is lurking behind many claims about concepts is, again, some version of the assumption that concepts express mental predicates. This may be a philosophically defensible position, but it is one to which Wittgenstein was strenuously opposed, and in the literature on concepts and conceptual change, it is seldom actually elaborated or defended. All of this leaves the issue of the exact relationships among words, concepts, mental states, and actions as mysterious as ever, but it is here that we may turn to Wittgenstein for guidance.

Like Austin, Wittgenstein emphasized that words have a "family of meanings," which depend on the concepts to which they refer and the variety of sentences, linguistic performances, language-games, and forms of life in which they are featured (e.g., 2001: 23). What this presupposes is that concepts are conventional objects, but Wittgenstein quite consistently made a strong distinction between words and concepts. His core point was well-summarized when he said that *"when language-games change, then there is a change in concepts, and with the concepts the meaning of words change"* (1969: 65, emphasis added). When scholars write what they claim to be histories of concepts such as liberalism or when someone such as Skinner writes about the history of the state (e.g., 1978), what is actually being recounted is the history of words and the various, and changing, concepts to which those words have been applied. We do not have much trouble grasping what kind of things words are, but describing the nature of a concept seems much more elusive. Words are signs – but, one may ask, signs of what? Although Wittgenstein stressed that philosophical investigations were "conceptual investigations" and that "concepts lead us to make investigations" (1967: 458; 2001: 570), he also noted that "the word 'concept' is by far too vague" (1978: 49). He did not explicitly provide a full-blown answer to the problem, and he may have added to the ambiguity when he suggested that certain concepts could have "blurred edges" and might be "akin" to one another (2001: 71, 76). But when he said that if people did not understand a "concept," he could teach them to use the "words" (2001: 208), he was indicating that words and concepts are not the same thing, even though they are related.

Concepts are not expressions of ideas or representations in the mind, and they are not the linguistic reflections of natural kinds. They are grammatical, but this is not to say that they are unrelated to the "world." Wittgenstein noted that "if things were quite different from what they actually are ... this would make our language-games lose their point" (2001: 142), but he asked, "if the formation of concepts can be explained by facts of nature, should we not be interested, not in grammar, but rather in that nature which is the basis of grammar?" He concluded, however, that:

> our interest certainly includes the correspondence between concepts and very general facts of nature. (Such facts as mostly do not strike us because of their generality.) ... Our interest does not fall back upon these possible causes of the formation of concepts; we are not doing natural science.
>
> (2001: 195)

This was because "the limit of the empirical is – *concept-formation*" (1978: 29). Language and the world are both autonomous, but the world only appears in the concepts embedded in our language or, as Wittgenstein put it, "*essence* is expressed in grammar," which "tells us what kind of object anything is" (2001: 371, 373). "Like everything metaphysical the harmony between thought and reality is to be found in the grammar of the language" (1967: 55). Wittgenstein emphasized that it is in the application of language within human practices that language makes contact with the "world" and that this was also where the "world" finds expression. The best short answer to the question of what constitutes concepts is to say that they are kinds of things designated and discriminated by various forms of linguistic usage. A concept is what Austin referred to as the "sense" of a word.

It is instructive that the word "concept" (*conceptus*) means, literally, the thing conceived, and in pursuing this point, Kuhn's arguments are helpful. The extent of Kuhn's acquaintance with Wittgenstein's work is, despite some compelling similarities (Sharrock and Read, 2002), difficult to ascertain, but the parallels, even textual, between, for example, Kuhn's *The Structure of Scientific Revolutions* (1962) and Wittgenstein's *On Certainty* (1969) are striking, and when approaching Wittgenstein, Kuhn, like Winch, is a significant signpost.

Subsequent to *Structure*, Kuhn attempted to make clearer what he meant by the term "incommensurable," which had been at the core of his argument about paradigms, conceptual change, and scientific revolutions and which had instigated much of the controversy about his account of the history of science (1977; 1993; 2000). He began to move closer to a specific embrace of arguments that seemed to relate to Wittgenstein's philosophy, but this later position was in part a direct response to the arguments of philosophical realists, such as Putnam and Kripke, about the existence, and persistence between theoretical transformations in science, of essential or natural kinds. The heart of Kuhn's argument had involved a competing claim about how changes in scientific concepts constituted changes in the meaning of "world." In the second edition of *Structure*, he had already redefined his somewhat ambiguous use of "paradigm" by equating the term with concrete conceptual "exemplars," which form the basis of a scientific community and "disciplinary matrix." He later focused on what he termed a conventional "lexicon," which was the "module in which members of a speech community, such as a branch of natural science, store the community's "kind-terms" (2000: 315). Such terms were, he claimed, partially defined in contrast with other such terms, but although there might be a certain overlap between lexicons, the evolution of different and succeeding lexicons postulated different universes of fact and evidence, much, he suggested, like the manner in which the biological process of speciation takes place. Consequently, although there were natural kinds, they were relative to the taxonomic systems of scientific lexicons.

Kuhn had been challenged to demonstrate how a historian could write the history of science without assuming a certain basic conceptual continuity of the subject matter. He replied, much in the same vein as Winch, that the historian's interpretive narrative, although employing a language very different from that of the subject matter, must seek to convey the meaning of the kind-terms embraced by scientists at various times but without imposing distorting categories derived from the ontological commitments and language of the interpreter. Interpretation, in the first instance, was not so much a matter of translation as learning and understanding a new language, which might not be fully translatable, and then attempting to reconstruct, that is, represent and communicate, the meaning of that language. There was an important suggestion about the nature of interpretation in his argument, which had actually been more fully developed by Wittgenstein, but Kuhn was in effect saying, much like Winch, that the historian of science and the social scientist were faced with the same task and with the problem of the cognitive differences, and dissonance, between the lexicon of the interpreter and that which constituted the discursive universe of the object of interpretation.

Kuhn's primary point in this case, however, was that different "antecedently available" lexicons in the history of science manifested different and incommensurable concepts to which the word "world" was often generically applied. Each member of a community possessed the same lexical structure that was "constitutive *of possible experience* of the world," even though individuals might not have the same particular experiences. Kuhn also likened this to the difference between the gene pool that defined a species and the particular set of genes that defined an individual. What Kuhn was implicitly addressing was a complex problem often confronted by social scientists. This was the problem of what it means to talk about individuals possessing and *sharing* ideas or concepts. For both Kuhn and Wittgenstein such sharing was basically a function of participating in a particular practice and realm of discourse, not some sort of "downloading" of public domain software. The upshot of Kuhn's argument was, as he had already claimed in earlier work, that the subject of truth claims could not be based on a putatively mind-independent or "'external' world," because the concepts of science were constitutive of what, for that community, was meant *by* the "world." What a scientific revolution involved was a shift between taxonomies of kinds that were not fully translatable from one to the other. Kuhn noted that kinds were usually designated by particular words, especially in modern highly linguistic societies, but his basic point was that these "kind-terms" represented the ontological discriminations constituting the "world" and the basis for attributing the property of "sameness." This is as close as we may get to a description of the concept of a concept.

A concept is the signification of a *kind* of thing and is usually conveyed by words and phrases or equivalent symbols. It is the *sort* of thing to which one is referring. Concepts are, in general, our way of dividing up the world, and in turn, our perceptions of such divisions are constitutive of our concepts. They are not, as Ryle once claimed, merely a "gaseous way" of talking about the meaning of the general terms that we employ in our sentences or the family resemblances we abstract from those sentences. Concepts are conventional entities and thus, by definition, possessed only by language-using and convention-creating creatures. Animals do not possess concepts because, as Wittgenstein said, they "do not talk" (2001: 25, p. 148) and therefore "cannot think" in the sense in which in the case of human beings we primarily refer to thinking (1967: 521–22). It does not make sense to say that animals other than human beings possess concepts even though we often, and quite usefully, anthropomorphize their behavior or *metaphorically*, and functionally, attribute concepts to them. The crucial question of how words are related to concepts can be answered in part by saying that certain, but certainly not all, words refer to concepts, and this is basically equivalent to saying that such words refer to classes of things and are used to talk about particular instances of those things. Where people often go astray, however, is in positing this "thing" as either a mental phenomenon or some material reference behind concepts. Words are usually sufficient for expressing concepts, but they are not always either necessary (e.g., loss of speech capacity does not necessarily entail loss of conceptual ability) or sufficient.

It is important, however, to move beyond Kuhn's focus on exemplars and the theoretical terms of science. Just as concepts specify kinds, there are different *kinds* of concepts, which can be distinguished in terms of their use or the types of claims and language-games in which they are featured. Many of the difficulties in discussions about concepts emanate from a failure to distinguish these types. My concern is not to enter into a full taxonomy of concepts, and I will only discuss three, not necessarily logically comparable, families that I refer to as *theoretical, modal*, and *analytical*.

Theoretical concepts are those of the type on which Kuhn focused. These appear in science or some other relatively determinate linguistic community of first-order discourse in which there are claims about what kinds of things exist and the manner of their behavior. Theoretical concepts are not the exclusive property of any particular practice. Social scientific claims about the nature of social reality are theoretical claims grounded in theoretical concepts, just as is the self-understanding of social actors and their representation of the world. Such concepts constitute the ontologies that define what Wittgenstein referred to as forms of life and a *Weltbild*. Sometimes these display a generic character such as when they refer to a class of particulars (atom, DNA, and so on), but they are no less evident in substantive specifications of instances of these things, that is, in what are commonly designated as facts. Every instance is an instance of some kind of thing, and thus theory and fact are logically identical and only pragmatically distinguishable.

Analytical concepts are those that, on the basis of various criteria, either internal to a domain of discourse or externally generated by an interpreter of that domain, are used to discriminate and classify things that have often already been theoretically constituted. Here we could list stipulative and functional definitions, ideal-types, retrospectively constituted traditions, certain models, and the like. These are often equivalent to what Wittgenstein referred to as a "perspicuous representation" and notations of "family-resemblances." With respect to natural science, for example, we might say that in physics, atoms and molecules, and the distinctions between them, represent theoretical kinds, while the classification of bees is basically analytical. In natural science, however, there are sometimes pointed disputes about the status of certain concepts. For example, in evolutionary biology, there is a significant and persistent controversy about the concept of species, that is, whether it represents a theoretical kind within the context of evolutionary theory or whether it is a taxonomic category. Analytical concepts may be found at all levels of discourse, but they are particularly prevalent in fields such as social science and history, which are confronted with the problem of representing, reconstructing, or interpreting a preconstituted conceptual universe.

Modal concepts represent form rather than substance and include those involved in making various evaluative and prescriptive judgments. They include concepts such as good, beautiful, right, just, rational, probable, hard, high, loud, and so on. Unlike theoretical and analytical concepts, they do not carry with them any necessary ontological commitments and are not confined to a particular practice. Although they have a universal or invariant force or meaning, their criteria of application are relative to particular practices and language-games. It is not their basic force or meaning that is disputed but the appropriateness of their application. The presence of a modal term, such as "just," in a sentence does not even necessarily indicate or dictate that the sentence is, for example, evaluative or normative, but the residual force attaching to "just" is a consequence of its past use in such sentences.

Confusions sometimes arise from the fact that both modal and analytical concepts may mimic or be mistaken for theoretical concepts. The fact that politics is often used as a generic analytical concept has contributed to the myth of "the political." Even though distinctions among these classes of concepts in fields such as natural science may not always be entirely evident or uncontentious, they present greater difficulties in the social sciences because in the latter, concepts are part of the subject matter as well as part of claims about that subject matter. The word "politics" presents a paradigm case of this problem. As I have already noted, there is a prismatic ambiguity attaching to the terms "politics" and "political," which reflects some distinctly different conceptual uses of the terms.

In the first instance, both chronologically and logically, "politics," like for example, "science" and "religion," refers to a conventionally distinct, relatively determinant, historically and culturally situated family of practices and instances of those practices. In this sense, it represents a species of conventional activity that arguably had a beginning, evolution, and dispersion and that has been distinguished by an internal self-understanding of its qualitative features as well as its units and boundaries. In talking about this practice, from a historical or social scientific perspective, we could conceivably use a different word or phrase to refer to it, and even if we refer to it by its indigenous name "politics," it appears in a vocabulary of discourse containing various theoretical and metatheoretical terms that belong to the categories of investigation. E.D. Hirsch was a bit over the top in claiming that it is immoral to interpret a text in a manner that violates the author's intention (1976: 90–91), but as both Winch and Kuhn stressed, if we wish to understand past actions and concepts, it is necessary to be sensitive to their intrinsic discursive meaning. The indigenous meaning of the concept of politics is primary, because the usual reason that we apply the word "politics" more generically and analytically, to refer to instances of things such as power and conflict, is because we often have historically associated those characteristics with the activity of politics. There is a wide range of such properties belonging, or ascribed, to politics that are much more universal than politics itself. Thus we find it easy and tempting to define politics, and cognate terms, analytically in any number of ways, depending on the attributes we may assign to the activity of politics, and for many political theorists "political" functions as a modal term.

Definitions of politics are nearly always at once too broad and too narrow to be sustained as the basis of adequate descriptive and explanatory accounts. The main problem in identifying and understanding politics is not, despite what many political scientists and political theorists have assumed, definitional. The tendency to speak of something as political because it possesses an attribute often associated with politics is no more incorrect than using the language of chess as a metaphor for diplomacy. It is, however, important not to allow slippage between an analytical concept of politics and the use of "politics" to refer to a particular kind of historical practice. There are many well-known examples of conflating the particular and analytical uses of such terms, even in the case of investigators who are committed to "thick descriptions" of social phenomena. There was, for example, the case of anthropologists who believed that magic was, literally, primitive science, or political scientists who maintained that locating something such as relationships of power in a society was equivalent to identifying the existence, and an instance, of politics. There are the problems, then, both of reifying an abstract or analytical concept of politics, albeit maybe one originally derived from observing particular cases, and of extrapolating from the particular to the generic.

In addition to these two senses or concepts that bear the name "politics," there is a third type that should be noted. This is the literal attribution of theoretical status to politics, which is often manifest in the transformation of the adjective "political" into the noun "the political" and which carries with it the implication that politics has some element of essentiality that transcends its conventional forms and transformations and that gives it the status of a natural kind. To assign theoretical status to politics could imply either some reductionist argument such as that which would locate politics biologically or some more transcendent property. But there can be no *theory* of politics in the sense of ontology. This is not simply because of the basic difference between natural and social objects but because politics is only one historical form of social phenomena. There can only be a theory of the *kind* of thing of which politics and other specific human practices are instances.

There are various complex philosophical and ideological motivations behind the emergence of such an essentialist notion of politics, but it is often simply a misbegotten application of an analytical concept, which itself is the extrapolation of a property typically attributed to a historically situated form of political life.

In addressing issues such as how to recover the meaning of texts and how to account for conceptual change in politics and political thought, it is necessary to specify what kind of thing we are talking about, that is, whether it is an analytical concept of politics or a particular and distinct aspect of social or intellectual practice. There is also an important difference between *changes in a concept* and the *change from one concept to another*. Social scientists sometimes speak of how a concept has been, or could be, "stretched," when what they actually mean is that a word may come to refer to a different concept. One could, for example, write a history of Darwin's concept of evolution, that is, a history of its creation, elaboration, deployment, and modification, and we could make arguments about its continuities, and discontinuities, with earlier and subsequent concepts, whether or not the same word was employed. The question of at what point a new concept emerges is important, but it is not a question that can be answered abstractly. But often what is involved is not a change in the concept but the application of the same word to a different concept. What is stretched is often the use of a word to apply to a different concept.

Conceptual revolutions in natural science are not points in the history of a concept but changes from one concept to another in which the word or phrase denoting successive concepts may, or may not, also change. Someone might characterize the mid-twentieth-century geological revolution in plate tectonics as having involved a change in the concept of a continent, but it would be more accurate to say that while the word "continent" persisted, there was a change in the concept to which the word referred – from a kind of thing that was fixed on the earth's crust to an entity that drifted from one place to another. To write the history of the concept would be to write about either changes within the prior geosyncline theory or the emendations to the theory of plate tectonics, while to write the history of the word would be to write about the change in usage between those theories and the different concepts to which it referred. Similarly, although the phrase "human being" existed before and after Darwin, we cannot say that the concept of human being changed but rather that there were two different concepts – one of a special creature and one of a kind of animal. When Darwin arrived at his concept of evolution, he did not at first use the word "evolution" but rather "descent by modification," but both terms referred to a concept that replaced that of special creation.

When Skinner claimed that "there can be no histories of concepts as such" (1988: 283), he might seem to have agreed with my point that in the study of the history of political thought we are usually talking about changes from one concept to another. But he was actually claiming that concepts cannot be isolated from the arguments and linguistic contexts in which they occur. His discussion of the state seemed, however, to have assumed that there was something that persisted between *texts* and argument contexts. Rejecting such a view is not to say that there are no historical connections or similarities between one concept and another but only that they are logically incommensurable. Skinner's claim, however, was that different concepts are not incommensurable, and he assumed that there could not be disagreement and debate unless there was overlap. This, however, was the very point that Kuhn wished to contest. As pointed out earlier, there is a difference between contradiction and theoretical conflict. While there may be conflicts that are the result of contradictions, which entail agreement regarding what kind of thing one is talking about, the kind of conflict manifest in theoretical disputes is quite different. Skinner argued that liberals and Marxists were not debating different concepts of politics but different criteria regarding the range of reference of the term. It would appear that this is really an empirical issue, but it seems more likely that what had been involved were in fact different concepts to which the word "politics" was assigned. Skinner also disagreed with Williams's assumption that the concept of myth underwent a fundamental change from something designated as untrue to something that represented a particular vision of the world. Skinner suggested that what changed was instead a "social or intellectual attitude" about myths (1989: 19). Again, this may be an empirical issue, but probably what changed was the concept, that is, the kind of thing to which "myth" referred, and that the change in attitude followed that conceptual change.

What has been said thus far, however, has focused mostly on the nature and role of concepts within those practices such as science, politics, common sense, and so on, that is, those first-order practices that are conceptually world constitutive. When we confront the case of metapractical inquiry, in fields such as philosophy, the history of political thought, and the social sciences, a different set of issues arises. Here we are confronting the problem of conceptualizing concepts and giving an account of preconstituted practices. This forces us to deal with the problem of interpretation, and the problem of interpreting the concept of interpretation, which in turn raises the further issue of the relationship between what might be distinguished as interpretation and understanding. Although the words "interpretation" and "understanding" are often used to refer to the same concept, there is an important distinction that is sometimes elided. One might be suspicious about Strauss's actual commitment to the precept of "understanding authors as they understood themselves," but it might have been more precise for him to have claimed that we should try to *interpret* them as they *understood* themselves. And when, for example, Winch spoke of "Understanding a Primitive Society," he might also have more felicitously employed the word "interpretation." Although, as already mentioned, some philosophers – such as Davidson, Quine, and from a quite different philosophical perspective, Derrida – explicitly tend to equate understanding and interpreting, there are reasons, such as those Wittgenstein adduced, for challenging such an equation. What are important, however, are not the words but the distinction involved and the relationship between the concepts that are distinguished.

Already in *The Big Typescript*, where much of his final work was adumbrated, Wittgenstein had noted that "an interpretation is a supplementation of the interpreted sign with another sign" and, for example, "in receiving an order we do not normally interpret it – we hear or grasp it," (2005: 16) or understand it. In the *Philosophical Investigations*, he began to sort out more fully the difference between the grammars of "understanding" (*Verstehen*) and "interpretation" (*Deutung*), a difference that may be less obvious in the English language. One thing that he emphasized was that understanding, as well as misunderstanding, like many other mental terms, such as "thinking," "knowing," and "intention," do not refer to some mysterious inner process and cannot be reduced to a physical or psychological event (2001: 196, 209–10, 151, 153–54, 321: p. 155). He noted, for example, that "it is wrong to call understanding a process that accompanies hearing" (p. 163). Equally important, however, was his distinction between understanding as what goes on *within* a practice or language game as opposed to what is involved in philosophy, or any metapractical activity, *giving an account* of what goes on. "Understanding," he claimed, involves the capacity to act in a language and the "mastery of a technique" and requires neither noting something corresponding to it nor a "sketch" (2001: 6, 150, 199, 396). It is not an "act" that one performs or some process that takes place between an order and its execution (431, 433). Understanding a sentence, he suggested, is not unlike understanding a picture or a musical theme, and normally understanding does not require choosing between interpretations (pp. 213, 526–27). When giving someone an order, it is usually sufficient to "give him signs," but if there is misunderstanding, it may be necessary to invoke an "interpretation" (pp. 503–6). Although Wittgenstein acknowledged that the word "understanding" was sometimes used in the sense of substituting one sentence for another, the latter was closer to what he referred to as interpretation (pp. 531–32).

Again, the issue was not what word should be used but distinguishing between two different concepts, which were typically conveyed in the uses of these words. One might argue that Wittgenstein conceived of understanding and interpretation as two aspects of one concept, but on the whole, he treated them as different concepts and distinguished interpretation as a distinctly supervenient action. It would be natural to ask if understanding is a prerequisite for interpreting, and for individuals such as Winch and Kuhn, this would be the case. One might say that the task of the historian or social scientist, as evoked by someone such as Winch or Kuhn, is one of, first, understanding another discursive realm and then, second, interpreting or representing it, but understanding and interpreting are not the same. This was expressed in Wittgenstein's discussion of what it means to follow a rule and how it might seem that whatever one does "is, on some interpretation, in accordance with the rule" and renders its meaning. This view, however, would be closer to something such as Quine's argument about the indeterminacy of translation, but Quine also treated interaction between individuals within a practice as interpretive. Wittgenstein's point was that interpretation is meta-practical. He stressed in the *Investigations* that "any interpretation still hangs in the air along with what it interprets, and cannot give it any support," because interpretations are not, in the first instance, the source of meaning (2001: 198). He went on to discuss how it seemed that "*any* action can be made out to accord with the rule" or conflict with it, but what this really demonstrated was that there "is a way of grasping (*Auffassung*) a rule which is *not* an interpretation*.*" It is instead a matter of acting within a practice and understanding and, consequently, either obeying or disobeying the rule. So even though there might be an inclination to say that "any action according to the rule is an interpretation … we ought to restrict the term 'interpretation' to the substitution of one expression of the rule for another" (p. 201). As Wittgenstein noted, "an *interpretation* is something that is given in signs," and "when I interpret, I step from one level of thought to another" (1967: 229, 234). What an interpretation aims to produce is a "perspicuous representation," a presentation or synopsis (2001: 122), that was the very aim of philosophy – and, it follows, of metapractices as a whole. One of Wittgenstein's most cryptic remarks was that "if a lion could talk, we could not understand him" (2001: 190), maybe because his form of life would be so different, but Wittgenstein might have added that we could *attempt* to interpret him.

This distinction between interpretation and understanding was also closely linked to Wittgenstein's critique of the theory of language that assumed that meaning was a function of naming and ostensive reference. Meaning was, at least in the first instance, a matter of use and understanding within a language-game, because "an ostensive definition can be variously interpreted in every case" (2001: 28). He stressed that "to interpret is to think, to do something; seeing is a state," and understanding is similarly a state. He noted that "it is easy to recognize cases in which we are *interpreting*. When we interpret we form hypotheses" that can be applied to the object of inquiry (p. 181). You "look on the language-game as the *primary* thing. And … you look on a way of regarding the language-game, as interpretation" (p. 656). He conceived of philosophy as a distinctly interpretive practice but one that sometimes went awry "like savages, primitive people, who hear the expressions of civilized men, put a false interpretation on them, and then draw the queerest conclusions from it" (p. 194). This, however, as he suggested in his discussion of Frazer's *Golden Bough*, cuts both ways, because anthropologists studying "savages" were liable to the same mistakes. Sometimes when one hears, for example, an explanation, one may not understand, and this might trigger an interpretation or a variety of interpretations (pp. 210, 215). But, for example, temporarily losing one's train of thought, while speaking from notes and then remembering would not normally involve interpreting or reinterpreting the notes or choosing between interpretations of the situation (pp. 634, 637).

In some of his latest work, Wittgenstein continued to pursue a clarification of the concept of interpretation, particularly in his *Remarks on the Philosophy of Psychology* in which he repeated some of the same points that appeared in the *Investigations*. Returning to his famous example of an ambiguous figure such as the duck/rabbit that had featured so importantly in part II of the *Investigations*, he asked, do I "see" something different or "only interpret what I see in a different way?" He was "inclined" to conclude that in most cases it was an instance of the former, because "interpreting is an action" that would include, for example, descriptions of one's visual experience. "When we interpret, we make a conjecture," while we would not typically speak of seeing as true or false. An interpretation, on the other hand, "becomes an expression of the experience" of seeing. He even allowed for "involuntary interpretation" that "forces itself on us" in certain circumstances, but this seemed very close to the case of "seeing as" or the dawning of "an aspect" where, optically, what is seen remains the same but where there is a change in "conception" whereby one might "clothe" what one sees with an "interpretation" (1980: 1, 8, 9, 20, 22, 31, 33). One can see, hear, and understand a meaning yet "not interpret *it* at all," but in answering a question about it, one "might interpret," which would involve "a thought" and an act of "will." A change of aspect, that is, "seeing as," such as in the case of shifting from specifying a figure as a duck or a rabbit, is very akin to an interpretation, because even though an aspect may "dawn" on one, changing an aspect often involves "more thinking than seeing." It is "to do something." What in this case is seen, however, is not, as some philosophers have contended, some neutral set of lines but the head of an animal. It is this "seeing" an animal, not simply marks on paper, which constitutes the "it" supporting the different aspects or interpretations (1980: 378, 482). In the case of something such as providing an explanation of a movement, however, there is "not a change of aspect, but change of interpretation" (1967: 216). One way to think about the difference between understanding and interpretation is in terms of another analogy that Wittgenstein employed. This was the difference between an eye and the visual field. The eye, like an interpreter, does not participate in the visual field. Although seeing/understanding are not interpretations, the two are not unrelated. It was in his discussion of "two uses of the word 'see'" that Wittgenstein first introduced the concept of "'noticing an aspect.'" Here he demonstrated how an ambiguous figure illustrated in a book may be seen differently depending on how "the text supplies the interpretation of the illustration." Because "we can also *see* the illustration now as one thing now as another," we are apt to "interpret it, and *see* it as *we interpret* it," but "seeing an object according to an *interpretation*" does not mean that it is "forced into a form it did not really fit." What is seen and the representation of what is seen are not "alike," but "they are intimately connected" (2001: 165, 169).

In discussing interpretation, it is difficult to avoid confronting the concept of a context. Whether positively or negatively assessed, Wittgenstein's focus on meaning as use, the manner in which words gain meaning by their role in sentences and speech acts and the place that these acts have in language-games and forms of life have all contributed to making him a candidate for the title of "arch contextualist" – and relativist. But the details and implications of his contextualism require considerable unpacking. Wittgenstein noted that "a multitude of familiar paths lead off" from hearing or seeing any set of words, and consequently it becomes necessary to "invent a context for it" or "guess" at one if we do not immediately understand it. The latter, however, is an interpretive act (2001: 525, 652). He argued that words do not intrinsically carry with them a certain explanatory "atmosphere" (*Geist*), and "thus the atmosphere [*Atmosphäre*] – that is inseparable from its object – is not like an 'aura'" but rather the "special circumstances" in which it exists (pp. 155–56). He noted that "the description of an atmosphere is a special application of language, for special purposes" and that "one can construct an atmosphere to attach to anything," but it may not necessarily have much to do with the actual situation of the object (pp. 607, 609). Wittgenstein emphasized that linguistic meaning is largely a function of the "wider context" (*Zusammenhang*) of an utterance (e.g. 686) and that actions, facial expressions, observations, and intentions all gain significance in terms of their surroundings (*Umbegung*) and circumstances (*Umständen*) (pp. 539, 583). Even the solution of mathematical problems depended on the context of their formulation (p. 334). Neither tone of voice nor state of mind is an answer to the meaning of an expression (pp. 160–61). For example, the "dawning of an aspect is not a property of the object, but an internal relation between it and other objects" that is manifest in "seeing the sign in this context," because words must "belong to a language and to a context, in order really to be the expression of the thought" (pp. 180, 185).

Wittgenstein noted that there were "*countless* kinds" of sentences, and "this multiplicity is not something fixed," because they come and go in infinite variety as changes take place in the "activities" and in the "language-games" and "forms of life" with which practices and discursive regimes are associated (2001: 23–24). All that can be said of linguistic performances in this respect can be said of actions and events as a whole that have material or behavioral conditions and a comparable grammatical, syntactical, and performative context. He once noted that "the common behavior [goings-on] of mankind is the system of reference by means of which we interpret an unknown language" (206). Although this statement has been given a number of different interpretations, including the suggestion that he was referring to some set of biological universals, it seems credible to extrapolate from the "context" of his statement that he was referring to his claim that in the case of human action, "intention is embedded in its situation, in customs and institutions" (p. 337). As he said later:

> How could human behavior be described? Surely only by sketching the actions of a variety of humans as they are all mixed up together. What determines our judgment, our concepts and reactions, is not what *one* man is doing *now*, an individual action, but the whole hurly-burly of human actions, the background against which we see any action.
>
> (1967: 567)

Wittgenstein cautioned, however, that while an object in part gains its identity in terms of its context, interpreters can become so caught up in their fascination with a context and its explanatory power that they lose sight of the object of inquiry. "People who are constantly asking 'why' are like tourists who stand in front of a building reading Baedeker and are so busy reading the history of its construction, etc., that they are prevented from *seeing* the building" (1984: 40). This problem has certainly been present in the work of certain intellectual historians.

If we wish to think about metapractices and the nature of interpretation, it is meaningful to explore, at least briefly, Wittgenstein's account of philosophy. When Winch, in his essay on "Understanding a Primitive Society," attempted to exemplify what his idea of a social science would entail in the practice of inquiry, he did not mention that Wittgenstein had said at one point that "savages have games ... for which there are no written rules. Now let's imagine the activity of an explorer traveling throughout the countries of these peoples and setting up lists of rules for their games. This is completely analogous to what the philosopher does" (2005: 313). This should leave little doubt about the epistemological parallel between philosophy and social science. Wittgenstein pointedly denied that "philosophy is ethnology," but he claimed that it was essential to "look at things from an ethnological point of view," which "means that we are taking up a position outside, an interpretive position, so as to be able to see things *more objectively* (2005: 37). Although much of Wittgenstein's work was taken up with a therapeutic analysis of issues in philosophy itself, he did not conceive of philosophy as simply self-reflection, but he noted that in the first instance "work in philosophy – like work in architecture in many respects, is really more a working on oneself. On one's own interpretation. On one's way of seeing things" (1984: 16). Philosophy was unique in that there was no philosophy of philosophy that constituted a separate practice or metaphilosophy, or as Wittgenstein put it, no "second-order philosophy" (2001: 121), but this was because it was itself a metapractical activity. Philosophy was forced, in part, to think about itself, because it was necessary to think about its relationship to the discursive universe that was its object of inquiry.

Although in some sense it may be meaningful to speak about how natural scientists think about their activity and its relationship to their subject matter, they do not, literally, have a relationship to their subject matter apart from how that relationship is conceived internally within the practice of science. Nature is never alien to natural science. If we attempt to stand back and talk about the relationship between science and nature, we have no basis, independent of science or some alternative first-order discourse, for specifying the nature of nature. Certainly natural scientists, in addition to what we might think of as requisite self-awareness, might and can step outside of science in order to reflect on the practice of science, but the practice of science does not require such reflection, which might even be detrimental. In the case of natural science, knowing about the practice of science is not, any more than in the relationship between folk music and ethnomusicology, the key to knowing how to do it. But even if, as Wittgenstein claimed, philosophy involved working on oneself and it was first necessary for the philosopher to "cure many intellectual diseases in himself" (1984: 44), philosophizing was directed outward toward another discursive universe. The question was, to whom and in what manner?

Philosophy, as in the case of Wittgenstein's own work, was clearly addressed to the community of philosophers, and here there was no doubt that the goal was therapeutic – "to shew the fly the way out of the fly-bottle," free people from the pictures that held them captive (2001: 119, 309), to "pass from a piece of disguised nonsense to something that is patent nonsense" and even to change a pupils "taste" and *"way of looking at things"* (1984: 17; 2001: 309, 464). This might involve considerable destruction and seem to leave behind only "rubble," but the goal was clarity. Since what was at the root of many philosophical problems were the entanglements of everyday language, and since philosophical ideas seeped into that language, there was no lack of intercourse between philosophy and other practices or an absence of functional similarities, but this did not mean that there was no distinction between philosophy and other practices. He famously noted that the "philosopher is not a citizen of any community of ideas" (1967: 455) and that "philosophy may in no way interfere with the actual use of language; it can in the end only describe it. For it cannot give it [such as the practice of mathematics] any foundation either. It leaves everything as it is" (2001: 124).

As I noted earlier, this idea of philosophy leaving "everything as it is" has been one of the mostly contentiously interpreted of Wittgenstein's statements. What this statement implied was that both philosophy and its subject matter were autonomous, but this did not mean unrelated or lacking potential for mutual interaction. Political theorists continue to be uneasy with the notion that politics and political theory are two different things and claim that even if they belong to different discursive realms, there is a "fine line" between the two. But there is also a "fine line" between, for example, parasites and their hosts and between skin and flesh, but we should not confuse the two. It is difficult to find a metaphor that captures the nature of metapractices. Although in one sense they are parasitic in that the very idea of a metapractice makes no sense in the absence of a host, they do not necessarily injure or gain sustenance from the host. They might then be considered epiphytic, but they are really *sui generis*. Wittgenstein said that a philosophical claim did not, as such, change its object of inquiry but "simply puts everything before us" (2001: 126). His point was that the relationship was contingent. Unlike conceptual or theoretical moves *within* a practice, such as natural science, whereby the conception of the subject matter, and the use of language, could be either transformed or given a foundation, philosophical investigations, that is, "grammatical" or "conceptual investigations" of other linguistic domains, do not necessarily have such effect. Whether they might or should was an open question about which Wittgenstein, with respect to his own case, was somewhat ambivalent (2001: 90; 1967: 458).

In one respect, his hopes for his work seemed modest. It was not "impossible that it should ... bring light into one brain or another – but, of course, it is not likely." And he did not want to "spare other people the trouble of thinking" but instead to speak to the philosopher "who can think himself" and to "stimulate someone to thoughts of their own" even if to an outsider the activity might seem "insane" (2001: x; 1969: 50, 467). "My ideal is a certain coolness. A temple providing a setting for the passions without meddling with them" and since "you cannot lead people to what is good; you can only lead them to some place or other. The good is outside the space of facts" (1984: 2–3). Late in life he suggested that a philosopher might demand:

> "Look at things like this!" – but in the first place that doesn't ensure that people will look at things like that, and in the second place his admonition may come altogether too late; it's possible, moreover, that such an admonition can achieve nothing in any case and that the impetus for such a change in the way things are perceived has to originate somewhere else entirely ... Nothing seems to me less likely than that a scientist or mathematician who reads me should be seriously influenced in the way he works ... I ought never to hope for more than the most indirect influence.
> (1984: 62)

The point is not that one necessarily should adopt what might seem to be Wittgenstein's somewhat ascetic and aesthetic attitude but rather that philosophy and all of what I refer to as metapractices, whatever their cognitive stance, have a practical relationship to their subject matter that can be neither avoided nor settled unilaterally. It is, however, an issue that whatever the attitude adopted must be confronted. Whatever methods and aims of inquiry are embraced, social science is an interpretive and reconstructive practice. What may seem paradoxical in this regard is that Wittgenstein's later philosophy was a rejection of representational philosophy, that is, both those philosophies that claim that language represents, or is an expression of, prior thoughts or ideas and those philosophies that claim that language represents or is grounded on some transcendent ineffable reality. But philosophy was nevertheless in the business of representing in that it was dedicated to giving an account of a conceptually preconstituted realm of conventional objects. The essential business of metapractical investigation is representational in the most literal sense that its object of inquiry is not internally generated but stands apart just as much as the landscape is different from what is represented by the landscape painter. Wittgenstein used the term "explanation" (*Erklärung*) in a variety of familiar ways – often with respect to explaining the meaning or uses of a word (e.g., 2001: 71, 87, 533), but he stressed that such philosophical or grammatical explanation was a matter of "describing" the use of signs rather than explaining in the sense of positing something deeper or establishing through "experiment" a "causal connection" (pp. 126, 169, 496). He consistently rejected the idea that he was doing anything like natural science but rather was conducting something like a "natural history of human beings" in the sense of describing the variety of conventional performances but with the *caveat* that it diverged from certain other forms of natural history in that his method might involve the need to "invent fictitious natural history for our purposes" (2001: 25, 415: para. 195). What Wittgenstein was driving at when he claimed that he was not "doing natural science," and maintaining that his "considerations could not be scientific ones" or concerned with "empirical problems" and with "*explanation*" in the sense of advancing a "theory," was a certain kind of distinction indicating that what characterizes natural history, as opposed to natural science, is that it is more observational and taxonomic than experimental. To the extent that philosophy is explanatory, it is in the sense that it involves "description" and is interpretive, holistic, nonreductive, and ecological. It does not treat its immediate subject matter as epiphenomenal and seek an ideal that transcends particularity. He often spoke of what he did as "explaining" meaning, and since he seldom used the word "theory," not much should be made of his putative rejection of theorizing. When he did talk about theory, it was, as already noted, usually with respect to theories in natural science or with respect to general philosophical theories such as realism and idealism that were at the very core of his rebellion within the field of philosophy (2001: 81, 89, 109, 195, 392). It would, as I have stressed, be odd to suggest that Wittgenstein did not offer a theory, quite in the sense that we might think about a theory in natural science, of the phenomena that constituted the subject matter of philosophy, that is, of language, concepts, conventions, and the like. It was his account of this kind of stuff that demanded an interpretive method, if we want to understand such a method, the best place to start is in terms of Wittgenstein's account of a perspicuous representation or presentation (*übersichtliche Darstellung*).

In talking about the idea of a social science, Winch gave more emphasis to Weber than to any other social theorist, and there is a remarkable similarity between Weber's account of ideal types and Wittgenstein's philosophical "method of representation" (2001: 50). Wittgenstein might be construed as identifying something approximating Weber's image of ideal types when he spoke of the manner in which philosophy might approach its conventionally constituted subject matter. Wittgenstein suggested that what was required in giving an account of a *Lebensform* and *Weltbildt* that is, what Weber had referred to as cultural objects, was a "perspicuous representation" or "sketches of a landscape" that "produces just that understanding which consists in 'seeing connections.'" He asked if this was a *Weltanschauung*, and although he did not directly answer the question, he seemed to conclude, like Weber, that it was not (at least in the sense that Spengler had used the term) but that it was nevertheless necessarily rooted in a philosophy or world view. The kind of representation that he sought would be accomplished by "inventing *intermediate cases*" that determined "the way we look at things." The subject matter consisted of "language-games" embedded in various social practices and forms of life, but he recommended, and saw the necessity of creating, second-order language-games that would be "*set* up as *objects of comparison*" and that were "meant to throw light on the *facts* ... by way not only of similarities, but also dissimilarities." Here one might generalize in the sense of seeking "family resemblances" but not succumb to the kind of "craving for generality" that characterized so much of philosophy and modern thought in general. Such a model would, again, be, "an object of comparison ... a measuring rod; not as a preconceived idea to which reality *must* correspond" (2001: 67, 122, 130, 131). What Weber criticized was the projection of an ideal or prototype onto the world of social action, when the purpose should have been to employ the ideal as a pragmatic device for interpreting that world. And this same idea was at the heart of the great transformation in Wittgenstein's philosophical approach when he turned away from the method of the *Tractatus*. Even his new view of language as rule governed was less an empirical claim about how language functioned than an ideal type designed to illuminate how it functioned. He was ambivalent about Spengler because although Spengler saw the necessity for ideal typification, he, like Goethe, believed that the ideal must be behind what it typified. The mistake of Spengler was still that of confusing the prototype with reality.

It would be difficult to imagine a better account of the kind of thing that Weber talked about as an ideal type. Such typifications were central to the activity of interpretation. Interpretation involved seeing something but, in addition, seeing it in a certain way and thus the necessity to first "*see*" something and then "*interpret*" it" (Wittgenstein, 2001: 193). When Weber talked about the need to impose social scientific concepts on phenomena during the course of inquiry, he was not, in the end, suggesting that this was like the manner in which natural facts gained their identity in terms of the concepts that composed a scientific theory. That was one kind of "seeing," but there is another kind, which is characteristic of interpretation. Both Weber and Wittgenstein were talking about what it was "to see an object according to an *interpretation*" which presupposed a prior identity of the phenomena. In natural science, we just *see* a fact, but in social science, as both Weber and Oakeshott stressed, we interpret and thus characterize a preconstituted fact *as* a "this" or a "that" identified in the language and description of social science.

This is the hallmark, and paradox, of a metapractice, and it is what binds political theory to the rest of social science. Metapractices, however, despite the intrinsic commonalities of their condition, are also shaped within their cultural contexts, and to understand the peculiarities of political theory, it is necessary not only to locate it within the history of American political science but also to view it within the even broader setting of the relationship between politics and the American scholar.

References

Austin, John L. 1962. *How to do things with words.* Cambridge, MA: Harvard University Press.

Gallie, W. B. 1955–56. Essentially contested concepts. *Proceedings of the Aristotelian Society* 56: 167–198.

Hirsch, E. D. 1976. *The aims of interpretation*. Chicago, IL: University of Chicago Press.

Koselleck, Reinhart. 1985. *Futures past: on the semantics of historical time*. Cambridge, MA: MIT Press.

Koselleck, Reinhart. 1988. *Critique and crisis: enlightenment and the pathogenesis of modern society*. Cambridge, MA: MIT Press.

Kuhn, Thomas. 1962. *The structure of scientific revolutions*. Chicago, IL: University of Chicago Press.

Kuhn, Thomas. 1977. *The essential tension*. Chicago, IL: University Chicago Press.

Kuhn, Thomas. 1993. Afterwords. In *Thomas Kuhn and the nature of science*, ed. Paul Horwich. Cambridge, MA: MIT Press.

Kuhn, Thomas. 2000. *The road since structure*. Chicago, IL: University of Chicago Press.

MacIntyre, Alasdair. 1966. *A short history of ethics*. New York: Macmillan.

Pitkin, Hanna. 1967. *The concept of representation*. Berkeley: University of California Press.

Richter, Melvin. 1995. *The history of political and social concepts: a critical introduction*. Oxford: Oxford University Press.

Ryle, Gilbert. 1949. *The concept of mind*. London: Hutchinson.

Sharrock, Wes, and Rupert Read. 2002. *Kuhn*. Malden, MA: Polity.

Skinner, Quentin. 1969. Meaning and understanding in the history of ideas. *History and Theory* 8: 3–53.

Skinner, Quentin. 1978. *The foundations of modern political thought*. New York: Cambridge University Press.

Skinner, Quentin. 1985. What is intellectual history? *History Today* 35: 50–52.

Skinner, Quentin. 1988. Reply to my critics. In *Meaning and context: Quentin Skinner and his critics*, ed. James Tully. Princeton, NJ: Princeton University Press.

Skinner, Quentin. 1989. Language and political change. In *Political innovation and conceptual change*, ed. Terence Ball, James Farr, and Russell L. Hanson. New York: Cambridge University Press.

Williams, Raymond. 1976. *Keywords: a vocabulary of culture and society*. London: Fontana.

Winch, Peter. 1970. Understanding a primitive society. In *Rationality*, ed. Bryan Wilson. Oxford: Oxford Univ. Press. First published in *American Philosophical Quarterly* I (1964).

Wittgenstein, Ludwig. 1967. *Zettel*. Berkeley: University of California Press.

Wittgenstein, Ludwig. 1969. *On certainty*. Oxford: Blackwell.

Wittgenstein, Ludwig. 1978. *Remarks on the foundations of mathematics*. Cambridge, MA: MIT Press.

Wittgenstein, Ludwig. 1980. *Remarks on the philosophy of psychology*. Oxford: Blackwell.

Wittgenstein, Ludwig. 1984. *Culture and value*. Chicago, IL: University of Chicago Press.

Wittgenstein, Ludwig. 1993. *Philosophical occasions: 1912–1951*. Indianapolis, IN: Hackett.

Wittgenstein, Ludwig. 2001. *Philosophical investigations*. Oxford: Blackwell.

Wittgenstein, Ludwig. 2005. *The big typescript*. Oxford: Blackwell.

Part III

Theorists, philosophers, and political life

7   Why there cannot be a theory of politics (1997)

The concept of a general theory of politics emanates from diverse perspectives. One distinct source has been, and continues to be, political science's dream in its boldest moments, such as the height of the behavioral era or more recent hopes associated with rational choice analysis, of finding one dominant unifying conceptual structure for explaining political phenomena. Such a conceptual structure would, in turn, it was claimed, yield nomothetic empirical knowledge of politics. In more modest moods, the goal of the discipline has been to achieve a measure of theoretical unity either through plural, but converging, analytical frameworks or through cumulative empirical generalizations. Equally persistent, however, has been a quite different, and often oppositional, quest for a universal theory of politics or "the political." Hannah Arendt, Leo Strauss, Sheldon Wolin, and others were committed to recovering and articulating a more qualitative sense of the essence and preeminence of political life.

My concern is neither to revisit these arguments nor to examine in detail contemporary varieties of these general positions. Rather, I will challenge the basic assumption that there can be a general theory of politics. Although I will attempt to unpack some of the complexities inherent in this argument, the core claim is that politics is a particular historical configuration of conventional or symbolic phenomena and cannot, in itself, be the subject of theoretical statements – either empirical or normative. Conventions are manifest in and constitutive of instances of action and speech, including practices such as politics, but only conventions as such can be a theoretical object. An elaboration of a general theory of conventions and human action is beyond the scope of this chapter.[1] My principal concern is to clarify what we can, and should, mean when we talk about theory in political inquiry. I do, however, discuss one principal source of the uneasiness that attends the idea of accepting politics as merely a realm of historical particularities or conventional tokens. This is the problem of the practical relationship between social science and politics.

My basic thesis is closely tied to two other propositions: that there is a logical symmetry between theory and fact, and that there is a logical asymmetry between social and natural science. Stated abstractly, these are hardly novel claims, particularly in the intellectual ambience of post-positivism, but in the course of explicating them, I will attempt both to add weight to the general claims and to distinguish sharply my formulation from the manner in which they have most often been framed and defended. As an entry into this discussion, I begin with a selective reprise of a certain line of argument in the philosophy of social science. I focus on the work of Peter Winch in part because his position is still often not clearly understood and in part because his work exemplifies many of the issues and problems that I wish to confront.

I

More than a generation ago, Winch argued that there could not be *theories* of social phenomena. His point was that only natural phenomena, with their inherent regularities, were susceptible to general causal law-like explanations. When social science is conceived in terms of the methodology of natural science, it is, he claimed, "misbegotten." Social science properly understood, he suggested, is really a mode of philosophy or fundamentally like philosophy. Winch defined philosophy as concerned with conceptual analysis, and he argued that the task of social science is, similarly, to understand the concepts that inform conventional or "rule-governed" and "meaningful" social action. Furthermore, since social science must also specify "what is involved in the concept of a social phenomenon" and must be concerned with "giving an account of social phenomena in general," it could be said that "many of the more important *theoretical* issues which have been raised in those studies belong to philosophy rather than to science and are, therefore, to be settled by *a priori* conceptual analysis rather than empirical research."[2]

This was, for some, a confusing set of claims, since the concerns of philosophy and social science as institutionalized practices are considerably different. Winch's equation between philosophy and social science was, however, part of a rhetorical strategy designed to justify a new version of the old argument that social science and natural science were "logically incompatible."[3] Before pursuing this issue, however, there are several other features of Winch's work that I will bring into focus.

First of all, while harking back to arguments such as that of Max Weber regarding the ultimately historical or idiographic nature of social scientific explanation and the need for an internal or subjective understanding of social action, Winch's position was explicitly grounded in Ludwig Wittgenstein's account of language and action. One of the principal advances in this formulation, focused on the public character of conventional activity, was to escape the difficulties associated with the image of intuitive interpretation that had characterized the claims of individuals such as R. G. Collingwood as well as certain German idealist accounts of the human sciences.[4] Second, despite Winch's stress on the special attributes of social phenomena that demand a methodology different from that of the natural sciences, his work was basically a metatheoretical challenge to positivist conceptions of the nature of social scientific explanation. Although predicated on a general image of social reality, it was most essentially an exercise in the philosophy of social science. Winch's book, then, cannot be construed as fulfilling his own demand for a full account of the nature of social phenomena, that is, a thorough explication of the "notion of a form of life as such" which he referred to as a "theoretical" issue. Third, despite the fact that Winch's argument was directed against the dominant positivist philosophy of social science, and such ancillary doctrines as that of the methodological unity of science, it was still mortgaged to that philosophy. All of the images of natural science Winch used as a contrast model in defining social scientific inquiry were drawn from the positivist account of the logic and epistemology of natural science.

Fourth, an important part of Winch's analysis was to demonstrate what I will refer to as the second-order character of social inquiry. Just as philosophy is concerned, for example, with how the first-order practice of natural science conceives of reality and the acquisition of knowledge, social science must elucidate the assumptions about reality and knowledge in various kinds of social activity. The subject matter of social science is, in Winch's words, another "discursive" activity. Finally, his account also implicitly raised the issue of the *practical* as well as the *cognitive* relationship between first and second-order practices. He rejected both the "master-scientist" image of philosophy that had been so central to the field and that would be challenged even more pointedly by later critics, such as Richard Rorty,[5] but he also took pains to disassociate himself from an "underlabourer" view of philosophy *and*, by implication, of social science, which suggested a lack of interaction between the practice of understanding "human conduct" and the practices that were the object of that understanding.[6] Winch's formulation, then, left a fundamental ambiguity about the practical relationship of second-order discourses to their subject matter. This ambiguity would be seized upon by critics of a more rationalist bent who, from various ideological perspectives, sought support for a distinctly judgmental and interventionist image of social science and political theory, one that went beyond mere "understanding" and what they believed were the relativist premises and implications of Winch's position.[7]

Many similar arguments about the autonomy of social scientific inquiry, from both the perspective of Continental philosophy, such as phenomenology, and post-Wittgensteinian analytical philosophy, appeared in the next few years.[8] Charles Taylor, for example, published what would become a classic essay about the interpretive or hermeneutical character of social science which, he claimed, distinguished it from natural science's approach to the explanation of "brute data."[9] Like Winch's, Taylor's analysis remained bound within the horizon of positivism in terms of his description of the form of explanation, and relationship between theory and fact, that characterized the practice of natural science. Furthermore, although Taylor had a great deal to say about the "textual" nature of social phenomena and the particular mode of inquiry that this required, what he, like Winch, offered was primarily an alternative to the positivist philosophical image of social scientific inquiry. His analogy between texts and social action, as well as the theoretical grounds of their similarity, were thinly developed. Taylor did, however, have more to say about the *uses* of social science. His argument was informed by a notion of social science as a reflective critical endeavor directed toward social enlightenment.

While these anti-positivist philosophers of social science stressed the conceptual and conventional character of social reality, their principal concern was to challenge the idea of the unity of science and to demonstrate that the study of social phenomena required a methodology different from that of natural science. Their arguments about the nature and autonomy of social inquiry amounted, then, to philosophical reconstructions of the logic of social science, and they remained beholden to positivist accounts of natural science. Although their work contained theoretical intimations, they did not make good on their promissory note to provide what Winch had called a "theoretical" account of "social phenomena in general." There was, in effect, an inversion of epistemology and theory, since substantive conceptions of social reality were introduced largely in support of claims about the nature of social scientific inquiry. Finally, although they focused on the issue of the cognitive relationship of social science to its subject-matter, they did not, despite the pointed and diverse positions taken by individuals such as Taylor and Michael Oakeshott, confront adequately the issue of the practical relationship. This latter issue, however, has historically both driven the search for a theory of politics and drawn social science into the orbit of the philosophy of science.

II

The positivist philosophy of natural science not only remains embedded in the practice and self-image of much of social science but continues to constrain attempts to analyze the differences and similarities between natural and social science. In much of the literature of Critical Theory, for example, from Max Horkheimer to Jürgen Habermas, a crucial theme has been the distinction between social and natural science, but the latter has been represented in positivist terms. There is also a widespread and more general assumption that the language of the philosophy of science and its account of science is congruent with the structure of scientific practice. This has been perpetuated in the post-positivist period by attempts to redescribe, or even conduct, social science in terms of post-positivist accounts of social scientific explanation.

This is only one manifestation of a yet larger problem. Political and social theory has, in a number of ways, become unreflectively indentured to philosophy. In no case is this more true than with respect to the concept of theory. It is very difficult when discussing the concept of theory in natural science not to resort to some philosophical rendition, or a remnant thereof, and this syndrome has spilled over into the social sciences. This is because "theory" is primarily a metatheoretical term and concept. Apart from rare exceptions, such as theoretical physics, it only has systematic meaning in the practice of talking *about* science – that is, in the philosophy of science. Neither the language of science nor scientific practice, for the most part, manifests any such internally discriminated sphere. Part of the reason that social science and political theory are so obsessed with the issue of theory, that is, with what it is, how to make it, and how to deploy it, is because philosophy has for so long conveyed the message that theory is a key component of science. This may be meaningful as a metatheoretical claim, but it has little to do with charting, or constituting, the actual activity of science.

The initiating issue in the philosophy of science at its late nineteenth-century inception, which has most fundamentally shaped its discursive development to this day, is that of the nature of theory. But, as a general problem, this is a philosophical rather than a scientific issue. Although there have also been parallel arguments in philosophy about the nature of scientific facts, this concept, like theory, has no distinct counterpart in the language and practice of natural science. The terms may appear in various contexts in scientific discourse, but the activity of science is organized around specific empirical claims of varying degrees of generality and not around a metalanguage for talking about classes of claims such as theory and fact, and the relationship between these classes.

Within the practice of natural science, theory sometimes refers simply to grand ideas or cosmological claims such as that about the "big bang." Often it indicates generally accepted ideas – such as atomic theory, the theory of relativity, and the theory of evolution. Sometimes, on the contrary, it refers to hypothesis and conjecture – unconfirmed claims. Occasionally it alludes to the, either circumstantially or intrinsically, un-observable dimensions of physical phenomena. Finally, it is sometimes used to designate particular potentially falsifiable empirical claims such as the "theories" about how the Grand Canyon was formed. Philosophical concepts of theory, and debates about the definition of "theory," have little or no significance within the practice of natural science. In social science, however, much greater significance, and contentiousness, surrounds the concept of theory, its identity, what possesses this status, its role in inquiry, and how it relates to facts. Much of this discussion, however, is primarily the residue of philosophical issues and burdened with the baggage attaching to those issues. Is it possible, then, to say anything, of general social scientific relevance, about a theory of politics – or about why there cannot be a theory of politics – without simply legislating the meaning of "theory"?

The plural meaning of "theory" in natural science does, indirectly, indicate a dimension of the discourse of natural science that social science might well emulate but which has been obscured by the dark glass of philosophically mediated images. What is common to many of the diverse uses of the term "theory" in natural science is the assumption that theories are existence claims. This is also close to the classical meaning of the root concept – *theoria*, which was always explicated in terms of an oracular metaphor indicating, whatever the realm of reality, the apprehension of something concrete and existential. It also conveyed a sense of identity between the act of seeing and the object that was seen. By the eighteenth and nineteenth centuries, however, there had been a fundamental transformation in the concept of theory as it took on the connotation of speculation about a separate factual or phenomenal reality and was viewed as a conceptual framework for organizing observations.

The late nineteenth-century crisis of physics, and the conclusion that Newtonian mechanics was *only* a theory, sealed the philosophical fate of the concept and insured its subservience to the idea of a distinct and given order of facts as the beginning, end, and ground of science, and as the source of both the meaning and validity of a superstructure of theoretical terms and claims. What is often not understood, however, is that the philosophy of logical positivism, which codified this view, as well as much of later empiricism was, despite its rejection of metaphysics, informed by idealist philosophy. This was the case both with respect to the notion of theory as a mental construct for organizing perception and with respect to the assumption that factual reality was conveyed by, and ultimately amounted to, propositions based on observations reducible to sensory experience. This entailed a rejection of what might be called theoretical realism, or the assumption that theories are themselves basic existence claims, and the adaption of a variety of instrumentalist accounts of theory. Theory was conceived as a conceptual tool for generalizing about, and economically structuring and explaining, epistemologically and ontologically independent observable facts.

During the twentieth century, instrumentalism as a theory of theory swept the social sciences. It prevailed in part because it was propagated by the positivists and logical empiricists who dominated the philosophy of science. But the attraction of instrumentalism also had its roots in the history of the social sciences. These disciplines sprang from practical concerns and were conceived as instruments of social change. Practical instrumentalism and cognitive instrumentalism were mutually reinforcing. Finally, the instrumentalist interpretation made the goal of emulating natural science seem more plausible. If theories, despite their somewhat depreciated epistemological status, were a hallmark of advanced science but in the end somewhat arbitrary schemes and devices for dealing with given facts, science seemed within the reach of everyone. There has been a long history of cognitive instrumentalism in social science, but more recent classic statements of the instrumentalist account of theory have been articulated by a wide range of individuals including Milton Friedman, Talcott Parsons, Anthony Downs, and a variety of behavioral political scientists.[10]

Instrumentalism remains the pervasive image of theory in the practice of social science. However, it is a particularly pernicious formulation. In addition to its problems as a philosophical account of theory, it subverts what I have distinguished as theory and theorizing within the activity of social science. This is the class of claims, within any practice of knowledge, that addresses and answers, explicitly or implicitly, the issue of what kinds of things exist and the manner of their existence. A theory is what may be called an empirical ontology. Theories are neither conceptual constructions that explain facts nor generalizations from facts. They are the claims that tell us what there is to be explained – or described and evaluated. Facts are simply particularized theories, and theories are generalized facts. Both theories and facts are specified by the criteria of justified belief operative in a particular disciplinary matrix and community of inquiry.[11]

If we bracket the wide variety of things that are usually called theory in social science, theory, in the sense that I have used the term, is nevertheless always present. The facts discriminated and described by social science, upon which various conceptual schemes and models are imposed, are informed by theories of social reality, but these theories are usually submerged, unreflective, and unexplicated. Such persuasions as rational choice analysis and the "new institutionalism," for example, both imply theories, albeit quite different, of human action and social conventions in general, but they are seldom specified or defended. Both are essentially frameworks for analyzing patterns of behavior, but the concept of behavior as such tends to remain theoretically opaque.

III

Two explicit, but quite different, attempts to elaborate a theory of action, and conventionality, are represented in the 1951 work of Parsons and Shils and the 1984 treatise by Habermas.[12] The former was largely an attempt to combine behaviorist psychology and positivist philosophy. The latter was certainly more complex, but suffered from a persistent inversion of epistemology and theory. Habermas tailored his analysis of action to justify his image of a critical social science and to support a claim about universal grounds of normative judgment. Quentin Skinner's work represents yet another example of a move toward theory which falters as theory becomes subservient to the defense of a particular epistemology of historical understanding and textual interpretation.[13] Anthony Giddens has attempted to reconcile notions of agency and structure and to develop a general theory of action, but, on close inspection, his construction is largely a composite of various metatheoretical claims about the nature of social scientific explanation.[14]

Whether they focus on language, action, speech, or texts, what Winch, Taylor, Habermas, Skinner, Giddens, and many others have in common is the claim that social reality is conventional and that this entails a special logic and idiom of inquiry. Yet the theory of conventions remains obscure and incomplete, in part because of their focus on distinguishing social science from natural science. There are grounds for reconsidering this matter, and at least one reason to embrace natural science as a model – but not because of some philosophical image of natural science or some philosophical dogma about the unity of scientific explanation. Rather, the natural sciences represent what I will call determinate practices of knowledge. Such practices are fundamentally identified by the fact that they are predicated on explicit theories or basic substantive reality claims. There may be a number of reasons why theory in social science cannot, or is unlikely to be, as paradigmatic and hegemonic as in natural science, but if there is to be any validity accorded to postpositive philosophies of social science that stress understanding conventional objects, they must be theoretically redeemed. Yet despite the functional parallel between theory in natural and social science, that is, the need in both cases for an account of the kind of phenomena which they address, it is still necessary to differentiate logically between these classes of enterprise.

We often bark up the wrong gum tree when we pursue the issue of what distinguishes natural science from social science. From one perspective, it is, or should be, the same thing that distinguishes one natural science from another – the theoretical, and factual, domain that defines its units and boundaries. Yet there remains a nagging, and reasonable, belief that the social sciences are somehow generically different from the natural sciences. I will insist that they are, but not exactly for the reasons that have been traditionally invoked, even though I will argue that the distinction does turn on the conventionality of social phenomena.

The answer is certainly not that the natural sciences deal with a special kind of facts that can be discriminated by attributes such as hard, objective, observable, unchanging, or brutish. All facts, as such, whether social or natural, are logically equal. Facts are neither things nor a class of things but rather a class of propositions. Winch, Taylor, and others were really saying that there is a fundamental difference in the manner of cognition; that there is something about natural phenomena that is distinct and separate from their *explanation* or the claims of a knower, while *understanding* social phenomena involves achieving a certain sort of identity with, or sharing of, the ideas and intentions behind behavior. Winch even hinted that the full understanding of a human practice might entail at least vicarious participation.

These arguments were on the right track with respect to their focus on the conventional character of social phenomena, but their image of the cognitive relationship between social science and its object led them to draw incorrect conclusions. To the extent that it makes sense to talk about some general basic difference in kind between natural and social phenomena, and to draw out the cognitive entailments of the conventionality of the latter, the genre of arguments advanced by individuals such as Taylor has seriously misconstrued, if not transposed, the character of this difference.

IV

The world, the order of reality, explained by natural science is not a world that is in some prior fashion experientially given. It is, in a radical sense, constituted by the theories and facts of science; it is a discursive residue of scientific practice. We may speak metaphorically about natural science explaining or interpreting nature, but while we may find it soothing to believe, metaphysically, in the autonomy of nature, we know it only through the language of science or some other logically comparable realm of discourse (religion, common sense, etc.). The field of geology is a paradigm case. When basic geological theories change, it is not only the earth that changes but the history of the earth – a history that can be nothing other than a retrospective projection or extrapolation of those theories. In an intellectual climate influenced by postmodernism, it may be more tempting than ever to suggest that the meaning of texts and other conventional objects is a function of their interpretation and the theories of which, and by which, the interpreter is possessed. There is an important element of truth in this claim, but it is not the element that has usually been extracted.

What distinguishes natural science, and a number of other knowledge practices that I will designate as consisting of primarily *first-order* discourses, is that while their accounts of their subject matter may change internally or compete with one another externally, it makes no sense to ask about the identity of the phenomena apart from the theoretical constructions that are constitutive of such phenomena. There is no theoretically neutral world or a language in which to convey it. The world is not a piece of common currency that can be cashed in at any knowledge bank. As Nelson Goodman put it, "the uniformity of nature which we marvel at or the unreliability we protest belongs to a world of our own making."[15]

The social sciences and philosophy, however, belong to the category of *second-order* discourses. They are activities that study other activities. They are supervenient practices that cognitively confront a subject matter that is discursively preconstituted and preinterpreted. This world of human convention is "given" in a manner in which the natural world is not. The world of particular social practices encountered by social science is not theoretically constructed by social science. Since the meaning of that world, both its present and the past, may seem to be infinitely contested in second-order inquiry, it is tempting to suggest that the meaning of social phenomena is always relative to an interpretation of them. Similarly, many are wont to say that there is no literal or final meaning of a text, since meaning is a function of the authority of interpretive communities.[16] This kind of claim has merit, but it requires unpacking and examination, and there is an important sense in which this is less true of social science than of natural science.

When talking about the interpretation of a text, it is important to distinguish, although few discussions do, between interpretation *within* a practice and interpretation *between* practices. While it would be perfectly reasonable to claim, for example, that the meaning of a scientific treatise is a function of the interpretation that scientists ascribe to it, it is much more difficult to make the claim that the meaning of such a text, or the meaning of a social practice, is a function of external or second-order interpretations. Texts as well as configurations of social phenomena have a certain basic conceptual autonomy. Their meaning is not, in the first instance, a product of external interpretation any more than the meaning of scientific discourse is a product of the philosophy of science. Indigenous interpretations may, however, be challenged by second-order discourses.

The "world" which traditional philosophical epistemology has so long sought to vouchsafe by transcending particular historical first-order constructions is, indeed, as Goodman and Rorty have suggested, a world with which we can dispense. As Goodman noted:

> While we may speak of determining what versions are right as learning about the "world," the world supposedly being that which all right versions describe, all we learn about the world is contained in these right versions of it; and while the underlying world, bereft of these, need not be denied to those who love it, it is perhaps on the whole a world well lost.[17]

We cannot, however, reduce the conventional worlds of social phenomena to the constructions of social science. Even though social science's adoption of theoretical instrumentalism and the idea of the dichotomy of theory and fact was philosophically vulnerable, it may have reflected an intuitive awareness that there is a significant sense in which social science theories are imposed on the facts or, more accurately, that there is a confrontation between two realms of theory and fact represented in second- and first-order discourses. There is, then, in principle, and almost necessarily, a cognitive conflict between social science and its subject matter which does not exist in the case of natural science. There is a conflict of cognitive authorities concerning the issue of appearance and reality and such matters as the identity of the subject matter.

At this point we can begin to see the fundamental difference between natural and social science, and the implications of the conventionality of social phenomena. The difference is not rooted in the distinctiveness of some form of cognition such as "understanding." The concept of understanding or interpretation as a mode of knowing implies the autonomy and separate identity of the object. "Interpretation" derives from the Latin root *interpres* which means negotiator, and interpretation is, quite literally, the negotiation of meaning. It involves a dialectical relationship between two social constructions – that of the social scientist and that of the social actor. The distinctiveness of social science is, then, a matter of the relationship between second- and first-order discourses. But the relationship of social science to its subject matter is not only cognitive. It is, at least potentially, also practical.

There is a fundamental will to power built into all metapractices and metadiscourses with respect to their relationship to their object of inquiry. A claim to cognitive authority is almost inseparable from a claim to practical authority, and a claim to practical authority inevitably rests on cognitive grounds. Since metapractices, such as social science, usually lack authority within the sphere of their subject matter, their claim to practical authority must often rest on cognitive grounds, on the idea of theoretical intervention. It is from this concern that the search for a theory of politics has historically emanated.

V

Although there is a great deal of philosophical discussion about the problem of "theory and practice," there are definite limits to what can be said generically about the relationship between what I prefer to call second- and first-order discourses. Second-order practices – such as social science, the philosophy of science, and epistemology in general – were originally discourses of legitimation and critique within the practices from which they became detached and which became their object of knowledge. Their histories, as separate institutionalized enterprises, could be construed as a story of successive strategies for reassimilation into the practices that constitute the object and the recovery of authority. In the case of the philosophy of science, the normative cast of the language may represent little more than a vestigial hope that it can speak to scientific practice. The same congenital and persistent urge to meld theory and practice has more distinctively shaped the discursive development of social science and its tributaries such as political theory.[18]

The problem of theory and practice is ultimately a practical problem to which there is neither a theoretical nor metatheoretical solution. It is a historical question which can be addressed only by looking at the careers of philosophy, social science, and other metapractices. There are, however, certain general features and problems that characteristically attach to these practices, and this brings us back to social science's relationship to philosophy – a relationship that often borders on unreflective obsequiousness. How do we explain this subservience? The natural sciences are not so constrained, and are, at most, vaguely aware of philosophical dicta. It may be in part a matter of disciplinary insecurity, and it may be in part a consequence of the fact that the social sciences were to some extent creations of philosophical discourse. But the subservience has still deeper roots.

The social sciences have frequently turned to philosophy in their search for authority – particularly to establish a scientific identity and cognitive legitimacy. This was not simply a matter of intellectual credibility but of practical purchase. Knowledge was the only basis of a claim on practice. But the social sciences have also been drawn to philosophy because they share with it the general structural dilemma of second-order practices with respect to their relationship to their subject matter. One manifestation of this dilemma, in both philosophy and social science, is the pervasive concern with relativism, which is basically a displacement of the theory/practice problem that haunts all metatheoretical practices.[19] In the cases of both the philosophy of science and political theory, for example, the issue of relativism has significantly structured the discourse.

Relativism is usually presented as primarily a problem in the first-order practices of science, politics, or morals – an immanent and imminent danger that criteria of practical judgment may break down. But what usually precipitates the concern is the work of someone like Thomas Kuhn or Rorty who disclaims the ability of philosophy to supply transcendental grounds of scientific truth. Philosophers claim that such arguments undermine scientific truth, and political theorists warn of the dissolution of society. Karl Popper, for example, suggests that such arguments threaten the integrity and progress of science. Although some, Allan Bloom for example, claim that relativism has actually infected politics, they also claim that the carrier of the disease is philosophy. In each case, however, the practical efficacy attributed to academic philosophy and social science – both to destroy and save its object of analysis – quite belies its actual power and role.

Relativism is an endemic anxiety of second-order discourses, because it is the dark side of rationalism, the abyss that seems to be opened by the loss of a belief in transcendental truth. But rationalism, or epistemological foundationalism, of some sort, is the primary basis on which a second-order activity has, in principle and practice, sought to trump the account of reality and the criteria of judgment in first-order activities. Relativism is, however, not a genuine practical issue except in the sense that the image of a cognitive state of nature may always haunt a practice of knowledge or a community of values. And it is also a pseudo-philosophical problem, since it is really a manifestation of the issue of the relationship between the orders of discourse. Relativism can be sustained as a genuine issue only if we can accept seriously the project of philosophical foundationalism. It is only against the background of this Quixotic epistemological quest that the problem arises. Those who are criticized as relativists usually do not deny the idea of rationality and objectivity in particular practices but rather deny the ability of philosophy to specify criteria that transcend a theoretical context. The issue of relativism, however, involves not only the problem of the universality of knowledge claims but that of the universality and nature of the object of knowledge. And this brings us back to the initiating claim of this chapter – that there cannot be a theory of politics.

VI

While there are many who, from the standpoint of early post-positivistic philosophy of social science, join in the assertion that politics is not amenable to nomothetic causal explanations, the claim that there cannot be a theory about politics in some other universal manner is less palatable. Many believe that without the idea that political theory as a practice can say something deeper and more general about politics, than what is represented in various historical conventional manifestations, the authority of theoretical practice – of second-order discourse – is weakened. Its claim to a privileged position with respect to its subject matter is ultimately based on its putative access to some form of epistemic authority, and this is, and always has been, the ultimate impetus behind the search for a theory of politics. If, however, theories are understood as ontological claims about what kinds of things exist and the manner of their existence, then there cannot be a theory of politics – either descriptive or normative – any more, or less, than there could be a theory of natural science, Christianity, art, or other first-order practices.

Politics is a historical form of human convention. We can theorize about conventions but not about their particular manifestations, just as we can have theories of atomic structure but not of particular chunks of matter. To say, however, that social science confronts a conventional or discursive world is not to close the issue of what this means theoretically. Conventions may be, and have been, construed as appearance or reality – as phenomena or epiphenomena. In the case of Marxist theory, for example, conventions are the basis of particular explanations, but they are in turn predicated on deeper material structural forms and dynamics. For a wide range of post-positivist philosophers of social science, on the other hand, conventions are the manifestation of ideas, beliefs, and other mental predicates. If, however, there is nothing ontologically or theoretically deeper than convention and discursive practices, this has important implications for political analysis.

Politics is conventional by any criteria; the issue is whether it is *merely* conventional or whether it is a fundamental and necessary form of conventionality. We might say that for Aristotle and Hegel, for example, it is a fundamental and necessary form. Much of contemporary political theory has also sought some such status for politics. The recent Carl Schmitt revival, among both the Left and Right, is in part fueled by this ontological temptation to seek the grail of "the Political." Another recent example of the attempt to give politics theoretical status is the Derridian post-Marxism of Ernesto Laclau and Chantal Mouffe.[20] While the practical concerns of the discipline of political science may have been sublimated and overshadowed by its scientific aspirations, scientism in political science was originally rooted in practical concerns and in the belief that only cognitive authority could lead to, or influence, political authority.

Much of the search for a theory of politics springs from the same concerns that have made relativism an obsession in political theory – the problem of the authority of second-order discourses. Establishing an ontology of politics, a transcendental theory of the political, is very much tied to the issue of the identity of political theory and its practical relationship to politics. Many believe it is difficult to make normative claims regarding politics without transcendental support. This was in part what was involved in political science's search for the State in the nineteenth century; it was also manifest in later formulations such as the political system. Yet all such attempts to find a political essence, either scientifically or philosophically, and arrive at a definition of politics that is more than stipulative or descriptive prove problematical.

The concept of politics belongs to a genre of concepts with a fundamental ambiguity. To say, as some have, that they are "essentially contested" is not quite correct, but they are used in different and contested ways. There is a tendency to define politics by extrapolating attributes from the typical practices of politics – such as conflict, power, and interest – or to define politics functionally – such as the authoritative allocation of values. The next step is often to suggest that, consequently, politics is necessary and ubiquitous. From this perspective, it is reasonable to say that politics is universal, but this is really to say very little. Such definitions are at once too broad and too narrow, and to claim anything universal about politics on this basis is merely tautological.

There can only be a theory of politics in the derivative sense that politics is an instance of human conventions which, in turn, are a theoretical object, just as in geology there cannot really be a theory about the formation of the Grand Canyon except as a historical instance of a theory of the structure of the earth. No matter what we may wish politics might be, and no matter what some may claim that it has been, it is, in fact, the historical particularities associated with town meetings, city councils, corrupt campaigns, and myriad other sub-forms tied together less by a model imposed by the social scientist than by traditions and the self-understandings of social actors. This is not to say that social science cannot redescribe or retheorize politics; it necessarily does so at least in the limited sense that the language and theories of social science are not those of society. But this returns us once more to the fact that the issue at stake is not just that of a cognitive relationship but a practical one.

Not only has politics been construed by political theorists in a variety of ways that may not have much to do with actual political practice, but the activity of political theory has also been romantically depicted. Despite the images of it conjured up in the present or imposed upon the past – whether as the potential agent of human emancipation or as a source of general laws of political behavior – the activity of political theory is in reality a highly professionalized academic sub-field in the context of the modern university. What the practical relationship between political science and politics actually has been, is, and might be is an interesting question but one seldom confronted anymore by the mainstream discipline. Political theorists are still much absorbed with the issue of theory and practice,[21] but they rarely engage it in any historically situated manner. Instead, we are presented with philosophical images of politics and political theory and abstract statements of the relationship between them.[22] Tracy Strong, for example, editor of the journal *Political Theory*, stated that "I take politics to be that form of human activity which constitutes the most general response to the simultaneous asking of the two questions, 'who am I?' and 'who are we?'" He then defined "political theory" as "a self-conscious community of discourse about politics."[23] This is much like defining science as the attempt to understand the world and the philosophy of science as discourse about that endeavor. It tells us little about the actual practice of either and distracts us from thinking about the real relationship between them.

Only if we return to politics as an actual situated historical object and to the deeper theoretical issue of conventionality and human action, of which politics is a manifestation, can we begin to confront meaningfully the cognitive and practical dimensions of the relationship between political theory and politics. This would entail, on the one hand, political science at least relinquishing images of theory derived from an obsolescent philosophy of science and turning its attention toward the issue of the basic character of social phenomena, and, on the other hand, political theory engaging politics in its particularity rather as a philosophical abstraction. At such a point, political science and political theory might once again have an intellectual rather than simply a professional connection.

Notes

1 See John G. Gunnell, "Political Inquiry and the Concept of Action: A Phenomenological Analysts," in *Phenomenology and the Social Sciences*, ed. Maurice Natanson (Evanston, IL: Northwestern University Press, 1973); "Political Theory and the Theory of Action," *Western Political Quarterly*, 34 (September 1981); "Politics and the Theory of the Conventional Object," in *Between Philosophy and Politics: The Alienation of Political Theory* (Amherst: University of Massachusetts Press, 1986), Ch. 6.

2 Peter Winch, *The Idea of a Social Science and its Relationship to Philosophy* (London: Routledge and Kegan Paul, 1958), pp. 15–18, 40–43 (emphasis added).

3 Winch, *The Idea of a Social Science*, p. 73.

4 Most notably Wilhelm Dilthey.

5 Richard Rorty, *Philosophy and the Mirror of Nature* (Princeton, NJ: Princeton University Press, 1979).

6 See, for example, Michael Oakeshott, *On Human Conduct* (Oxford: Clarendon Press, 1975).

7 See, for example, Richard Bernstein, *The Restructuring of Social and Political Theory* (New York: Harcourt Brace Jovanovich, 1976).

8 For representative selections, see Fred Dallmayr and Thomas A. McCarthy, eds, *Understanding and Social Inquiry* (Notre Dame, IN; University of Notre Dame Press, 1977).

9 Charles Taylor, "Interpretation and the Sciences of Man," *Review of Metaphysics*, 25 (September 1971).

10 See Gunnell, *Between Philosophy and Politics*, Ch. 2, for a discussion of instrumentalism in political theory and in the philosophy of science.

11 For a fuller discussion, see John G. Gunnell, "Realizing Theory: The Philosophy of Science Revisited," *Journal of Politics*, 57 (November 1995).

12 Talcott Parsons and Edward A. Shils, eds, *Toward a General Theory of Action* (Glencoe, IL: Free Press, 1949); Jürgen Habermas, *The Theory of Communicative Action*, Vol. 1, *Reason and the Rationalization of Society* (Boston, MA: Beacon Press, 1984).

13 James Tully, *Meaning and Context: Quentin Skinner and His Critics* (Princeton, NJ: Princeton University Press, 1988); John G. Gunnell, "Interpretation and the History of Political Theory: Apology and Epistemology," *American Political Science Review*, 76 (June 1982).

14 Anthony Giddens, *New Rules of Sociological Method* (New York: Basic Books, 1976); *The Constitution of Society: Outline of the Theory of Structuration* (Berkeley: University of California Press, 1984).

15 Nelson Goodman, *Ways of World Making* (Indianapolis, IN: Hackett, 1978), p. 10.

16 Stanley Fish, *Is There a Text in this Class? The Authority of Interpretive Communities* (Cambridge, MA: Harvard University Press, 1988).

17 Nelson Goodman, "The Way the World Is," in *Problems and Projects* (Indianapolis, IN: Hackett, 1972). Also see Richard Rorty, "The World Well Lost," *Journal of Philosophy*, 69 (1972).
18 For a discussion of the intellectual history of academic political theory in the United States, see John G. Gunnell. *The Descent of Political Theory: The Genealogy of an American Vocation* (Chicago, IL: University of Chicago Press, 1993).
19 John G. Gunnell, "Relativism: The Return of the Repressed," *Political Theory*, 21 (November 1993).
20 Ernesto Laclau and Chantal Mouffe, *Hegemony and Socialist Strategy: Towards a Radical Democratic Politics* (London: Verso, 1996); Ernesto Laclau, *New Reflections on the Revolution of Our Time* (London: Verso, 1990).
21 Ian Shapiro and Judith Wagner DeCew, eds, *Theory and Practice: Nomos XXXVII* (New York: New York University Press, 1995).
22 See Jeffrey Isaac, "The Strange Silence of Political Theory," *Political Theory*, 23 (1995).
23 Tracy Strong, *The Idea of Political Theory: Reflections on the Self in Political Time and Space* (Notre Dame, IN: University of Notre Dame Press, 1990), 3–4.

8   Speaking politically (1998)

Once we cut through all the abstract discussion of the relationship between theory and practice, the intellectual agony surrounding the problem of relativism, and the displays of epistemological *machismo*, we encounter a real dilemma and one that has attended the historical career of social science and other academic metapractices. Most university humanists, social theorists, and political theorists, at least in their professional capacity, have little direct cognitive and practical contact with the particularities of politics; yet while engaged in the performances associated with their normal academic pursuits, many wish to affect politics, or even be understood as participating in it. This dilemma springs in part from the very nature of metapractices and the basic character of their relationship to their subject matter, but what is most crucial is the historical and existential context. Although the dilemma can be construed as a generic aspect of the relationship of intellectuals to politics, from Plato to the present, it has been specific to the social sciences since their institutionalization in the nineteenth century. The issue is largely one rooted in and defined by the genealogy of these disciplines (Gunnell, 1993) and in the contemporary relationship between the university and public life (Freeland, 1992; Geiger, 1993). The paradox of the social sciences has been that they arose from reform movements and moral philosophy, and while social scientists believed that the university offered scientific legitimation for claims that would have practical purchase, it largely, in the end, insulated these disciplines from public life and partisan politics (Gunnell, 2000). The residual image of "social science as public philosophy" is still very much alive, as indicated in work such as that by Robert Bellah and the other authors of *Habits of the Heart* (1996), but it is an image that must be historically and analytically scrutinized.

I

Maybe the most striking differences between the philosophers to whom Socrates referred and those in our own time are that, for the most part, the latter, even in their youth, were not involved with politics and that, in ancient Greece, philosophy was not an institutionalized professional activity. At least in the United States, not only are the boundaries between academic and public discourse quite distinct but the career paths that bring individuals to these respective spheres are largely separate. And increasingly, in a world marked by professionalization and specialization as well as by the demise of such diversions as general military service, scholars often have not significantly experienced any way of life other than that of the academy. They are not, and seldom resemble, Gramscian organic intellectuals, and neither can they be cast in the image of the amateur public figure that Ralph Waldo Emerson referred to as the American scholar. Despite a great deal of discussion about the relationship between intellectuals and politics or public life (e.g., Fink, Leonard, and Reed, 1996; Eyerman, 1994; Boggs, 1993; Lemert, 1991; Robbins, 1990; Johnson, 1988; Bauman, 1987), specific consideration of the academic intellectual has been minimal. The academic intellectual, then, is not a "mere" writer but rather a writer of a particular kind in particular circumstances. There are many American scholars but few American public intellectuals, even though scholars often mimic the voice of such intellectuals.

There is, as I have stressed, an important sense in which it is in the very nature of metapractices to seek authority and to seek it in epistemic terms. This is evident, for example, in all the classic texts of political theory, but there are some distinct differences between the spirit of many of these works and the modern academic theorist. While it is tempting, and common, to characterize the classic literature as foundationalist, the claim of reason that it advanced was usually consciously rhetorical and often ironic. What these texts reveal is an awareness that the issue of theory and practice is indeed a practical issue and that the claim to epistemic privilege is not only tenuous but without demonstrable grounds. What emerges most clearly, from Plato to Marx, is the realization that what characterizes human beings is that they are naturally unnatural and that their world is ultimately held together by convention and agreement – however obtained (Gunnell, 1979). Contemporary academic foundationalism is of a different order. It has not only taken seriously the rhetoric of epistemic privilege but often pursued it exclusive of the circumstances in which it has been asserted. Despite the inherent pull toward foundationalist formulations, however, it is neither natural, in the sense of necessary, nor, in any obvious way, prudent for metapractices to follow this path. In the contemporary world, the rhetoric of foundationalism is no longer very convincing, and taking foundationalism seriously only inhibits thinking contextually.

Although Max Weber's essays on the vocations of science and politics have usually been construed as, for better or worse, encouraging a separation between social science and politics, the actual motive, as for others such as Mannheim, was to find a way to connect them (Gunnell, 1993). The paradox was that given the character of the twentieth-century university and in a pluralistic society, the only authority that social science could claim was the authority of science, which was gained through a claim to objectivity and to knowledge that stood outside the realm of politics. The Weberian paradox has been at the very core of the history of the social sciences, and although Weber never offered any very clear answer to the problem of exactly how social science was to advance its claims in the world of politics, the general answer, that is, to achieve proximity through distance, has been consistent. Even positivism, which has been understood as eschewing value judgments, was rooted, in both philosophy and social science, in a search for the social uses of knowledge.

It might be argued that there is a way in which positivism was correct about the fact/value dichotomy. It was correct in recognizing and stressing the logical distinction between two kinds of statements. Where it went wrong was, first, in assuming that one kind of statement was inherently cognitively privileged, and, second, in assuming that the basic distinction was categorically exhaustive with respect to what can be done with words. Those who attacked the positivist distinction on the basis that there inevitably were value words that crept into ostensibly empirical claims and that there was always a normative slant inherent in any such claim bought into both the positivist assumption that particular atomistic words were the fundamental carriers of meaning and the assumption that the dichotomy was the fundamental issue for joining the conversation. But there was also another insight that was implicit in the positivist agenda – even if incorrectly pursued. Positivists claimed, for example, that in the case of social science there could be credible descriptive and explanatory statements but that value claims were not really capable of adjudication.

If we think about social science in terms of its place in the realm of second-order discourse, there is something to be said for this position. The descriptive and explanatory claims of a second-order discourse about a first-order activity are probably more supportable than normative injunctions. We might be able to make a better case for a description of American politics that goes beyond what political actors may perceive than a case for the ability of social science to devise values and performances to which such actors should subscribe. This is true in much the same sense that second-order analysts might be better able to describe and explain what is going on in the game of baseball than to prescribe strategies and plays or even make a case for why one should play that game as opposed to another. That social scientists should have something of normative significance to say about politics is no more a given than that sportscasters should be heeded by baseball players or actors by theater critics. The essential import of this chapter is not that the academic intellectual does not, cannot, or should not affect politics, but I challenge some prevailing and persistent assumptions about each of these matters and urge a more realistic assessment.

Many political theorists and philosophers propagate an image of themselves as public moralists, and while I do not wish to suggest that academics retreat from normative claims, I question the belief that metapractical adherents to a number of persuasions, ranging from natural law to neoMarxist critical theory, possess, or should possess, any inherent ethical authority and even the assumption that their influence in public life would necessarily be salutary. While there is, as I have already stressed, at least a latent claim to first-order authority on the part of most metapractices, there are, for example, few, either in philosophy or science, who would overtly argue that philosophical discourse actually does, or should, play a significant role in scientific practice. It would be unlikely that anyone would suggest that philosophers of science are, in any significant manner, participants in science or could be construed, in the course of their normal activity, as "speaking scientifically." As with so many metapractices, whatever practical connection to their subject matter may have once existed has long since become attenuated, and what remains is largely discursive traces. What is it, then, about politics that engenders the assumption that a variety of metapractices, which present themselves as in some way attending to this sphere, have something to say to it or actually perform in it? What is the basis of the claim that such metapractitioners as social scientists, historians, philosophers, political theorists, and even literary critics; are, in some general manner, acting in or on politics or should do so?

These metapractitioners have tended to adopt a dualistic, and sometimes contradictory, strategy: on the one hand, claiming that the vocations of political theory and politics can be assimilated and, on the other, asserting that the former is both distinct and epistemically privileged. ... This simultaneous search for identity and difference is an endemic feature of those practices of knowledge that study other forms of human activity, and it is rooted in both cognitive and practical motives. Immanuel Kant's defense of the preeminence of theory, and philosophy, more than two hundred years ago may be the paradigm case. There can be little doubt about the immediate impetus. He was apprehensive both about the status and role of philosophy vis-à-vis other fields and about its relationship to political authority or what he designated, respectively, and prejudicially, as the realm of truth and theory vis-à-vis power and practice. Statesmen, and other practitioners, he claimed, were:

> of one mind in going after the *academician*, who concerns himself with theory *on* their behalf and for their good; but since they imagine themselves to understand this better than he, they desire *to* banish him to his academy ... as a pedant, who, unfit for practice, only stands in the way of experienced wisdom.
>
> (1983: 62–63)

Like many after him, Kant set out to demonstrate that although theory and practice represent different activities, there is a kind of functional unity as well as an intrinsic basis for the priority of the former and its relevance to the latter. Kant's assumption was that theories, or rules and principles, were indigenous to practice, and thus theory and practice were, in effect, one; at the same time, theory, as an activity, merited a privileged position.

Metapractitioners today still employ such idioms as "speaking truth to power" and "theory and practice" that rhetorically obscure some of the most fundamental questions about the relationship between metapractices and their object. There is, first, a propensity to blur the line between academic and public discourse. The boundary separating these realms may not always be clear, rigid, or impermeable, but neither is it merely analytical. Derrida, for example, claims that "every philosophical colloquium necessarily has a political significance" and that the "essence of the philosophical" and the "essence of the political" are "always entwined" and joined by an "a priori link" (1982: 13). It is precisely such unsupported assertions and semantic erasures that spawn an obfuscating rhetoric that perpetuates the failure to come to grips with the actual relationship between academic and public discourse. As Richard Rorty has noted, the impact of Jacques Derrida on the American left has, despite all the intimations about a critical philosophy, been in the direction of disengagement. Despite all the talk about deconstructive reading, there simply is no *political* notion of how to resist (1994: 117). Although claims about political theory as a form of political discourse or phrases such as the "politics of interpretation" (Mitchell, 1983) may, in some instances, be illuminating, they often reflect conceptual strategies for displacing or repressing the issue of the actual relationship of metapractices to their object of inquiry.

It is sometimes suggested that political theory is simply an abstract and reflective form of political discourse; that politics is ultimately a linguistic practice and therefore not really unlike academic metapolitics and its confrontation with texts; that in a world of ultimate textuality, the master of texts is the consummate political actor; that human affairs are, at least in the modern world, a holistic entity and that, as George Orwell noted, "in our age there is no such thing as 'keeping out of politics'. All issues are political issues" (1968: 137); that since there is no clear boundary between the academy and politics, academic practice, through cultural dispersion, educational osmosis, and various other avenues, inevitably has political consequences; that a cultural object like politics gains identity only in relation to other cultural objects, and thus neither disciplines nor their subject matters can be viewed in isolation; and that academic analysis and prescription with respect to public issues such as feminism, abortion, and gay rights are themselves a kind, or dimension, of political practice. While all of these propositions may have some general merit and while each may be true in some set of historical circumstances, they often are advanced less as arguments than as pleas for an excuse not to confront the real issue of the relationship between the academy and politics. The assumption seems to be that to admit difference is to deny contact, but as I argued earlier, it is impossible to speak cogently of relationships without assigning criteria of difference to the things in question.

There might seem to be some intuitive basis for suggesting that a field such as political theory or political science, which is specifically concerned with political phenomena, can be construed as a means or form of political action. Furthermore, politics is, after all, a relatively familiar activity and one that is often encompassed by the same culture to which the metapractitioner belongs. Under these circumstances, problems of practical and cognitive distance seem mitigated. We might, however, be less inclined to think, for example, of the anthropologist studying cannibals as participating in cannibalism (Gunnell 2000), and we would also probably not be likely to say that a sociologist studying the family is engaging in family life. Suggestions of an identity between politics and political *theory* often seem, in the end, to have little more than a lexical basis. One common conception of theory and practice is to conceive of both as contained within, as elements of, a particular field or activity. Literary critics, for example, speak about the theory and practice of literary interpretation. Here theory is understood as a set of principles of inquiry, or an epistemology, and as something that can both guide the practice of interpretation and serve as a basis for judging it. This notion of theory and practice is often extended, sometimes consciously and sometimes unreflectively, to the relationship between metapractices and their object. Even the concept of theory as an internal guide to practice is dubious, but the extension of this concept to the relationship between second- and first-order practices, and the claim of epistemic and, consequently, practical authority on the part of the former, are misleading.

The assumption that a field such as academic political theory is in some way relevant to, or may have an effect on, politics is often based less on evidence than aspiration. When the same claims are made for literary criticism, and this enterprise is advanced as a critical social practice, credulity seems even more strained. But as university practices, one activity has probably as great, or small, a claim as the other. Asking whether political theory has a closer tie to politics than literary criticism is something like asking which liberal arts major is the best preparation for law school. They are both academic enterprises that are subject to the contextual and internal restraints and possibilities of such pursuits. But since claims about political theory as a means to or form of political action are so familiar, it is interesting to look at an extended argument for literary interpretation as "politics by other means" and "itself a way of changing the world" (Mitchell, 1983: 1, 5).

Frank Lentricchia, like Christopher Norris, Terry Eagleton (1976; 1983), and others, has argued strongly for the idea of literary criticism, and university education, as not only *means* of social change but *modes* of social action. He asks if it is possible to "do radical work *as* a literary intellectual," that is, a person "who works mainly on texts and produces texts." He concludes that scholars, "in their work in and on culture, involve themselves inescapably in the political work of social change and social conservation." Lentricchia claims that the role of the "university humanist ... as a social and political actor has been cynically underrated and ignored." He refers not to an academician who engages in supplementary extrinsic political activity but rather the person whose work "is carried on at the specific institutional site where he finds himself and on the terms of his own expertise, on the terms inherent to his own functioning as an intellectual." Lentricchia argues that "our potentially most powerful political work as university humanists must be carried out in what we do, what we are trained for":

I would go so far as to say that those of us in the university who conceive of our political work ... not as activity intrinsic, specific to our intellectuality (our work as medieval historians, for example) are being crushed by feelings of guilt and occupational alienation. We have let our beliefs and our discourse be invaded by the eviscerating notion that politics is something that somehow goes on somewhere else, in the "outside" world, as the saying goes, and that the work of culture that goes on "inside" the university is somehow apolitical – and that this is a good thing.

(1983: 1–7)

Appropriating, but reversing the meaning of, Marx's aphorism, Lentricchia claims that "the point is not only to interpret texts, but in so interpreting them, change society" and the structure of power through the transformation of culture. By doing what they quintessentially do, academicians, he argues, can play, or play upon, politics. Theory in literary criticism is advanced as a form of rhetoric and persuasion and a vehicle for a radical and "oppositional critic, seeking to amplify and strategically position the marginalized voices of the ruled, exploited, oppressed, and excluded" and to create a new "community." In the end, "all literary power is social power" (1983: 10–12, 15, 19).

This vision is often less audaciously articulated, but it is widespread even if pointedly rejected by others. Harold Bloom, for example, maintains that "criticism is not a program for social betterment, not an engine for social change" (1993: 205), and Fish has offered an extended response to arguments such as those of Lentricchia. He argues that while some wish to "blur the boundaries between academic subjects or between the academy and the world," interdisciplinarity does not produce a more total vision of society, and, at least in the United States, the very condition of being an academician is to "remain distanced from any effort to work changes in society" (Fish 1995: viii, 1). His assessment is that the rewards and demands that govern the life of the contemporary academic professional are such that "the relationship between art and the production of civic virtue is thin to the point of vanishing," that "artistic freedom has been purchased at the expense of artistic efficacy," and that "if you want to send a message that will be heard outside the academy, get out of it" (pp. 2, 32, 36). It is necessary, he claims, to distinguish between actual politics and the "general (and trivial), sense in which everything is political" and to realize that changes in the language and issues defined by academic practice do not "make it into an instrument of political action" (pp. 45, 97).

Fish's scenario may, typically, be rhetorically overdrawn, but it is less extravagant than many of the claims presented by those he criticizes. My claim, again, is not that, in either principle or practice, metapractices have no first-order consequences, but rather that one cannot assume that they do or should have such consequences. There may be, or have been, instances in which something approaching Lentricchia's image may come close to corresponding with the historical situation, but most of those who embrace genetically the notion that there is an identity between textual analysis and politics offer little in the way of evidence. They rarely fully explore the analytical dimensions of the relationship, let alone examine the actual institutional and historical setting and the operative connections among the orders of discourse. Arguments for both identity and privilege have begun to surface in a number of areas such as cultural studies and the new historicism. Oppositional literary theories are presented as forms of social criticism and "cultural politics" (Brantlinger, 1990; Agger, 1992; Grossberg, Nelson, and Treichler, 1992). This kind of imagery encourages a neglect of the actual configuration of discursive practices and of the relationships among them, but often the assumption is that the recognition of boundaries is implicitly to defend the insulation of "theory" from "practice." "Practice," however, tends, in these discussions, to lose any substantive reference.

Neither I, nor, I think, Fish would claim that an activity and body of academic literature such as feminist theory is not relevant to politics and has not had a political impact. The issue is exactly what impact it has had and whether one can extrapolate from such a case to generalizations about the academy and politics. Patrice McDermott, for example, argues that "feminist academic journals have played a central role in breaking the boundaries between politics and scholarship" (1994: 12), but her study of such journals does not explore and assess their impact on feminist politics. Feminist theory is somewhat unique in that it *represents* what might be construed as a political constituency, but there is a question of what is meant by representation. It is reasonable to say that feminist theory refers to and sometimes addresses an identifiable political or social movement. It has, for the most part, however, not been chosen as a representative any more than Marxist critical theory has been chosen by the unemancipated writ large. The idea of representation is unilateral. In the case of feminist theory, there may be a certain form of identity between the theorist and her subject matter, but this case also presents a salient example of the paradox of the academic intellectual. As McDermott puts it, feminist theory exemplifies the problem of "ironic reflexivity," that is, the attempt to meet the demands of academic "detachment" while being "passionately engaged," but the tension is yet deeper. It is not only a matter of attempting to meet such general formal academic standards as objectivity, which are actually often not pressed very strictly, but the more subtle demands of speaking in the idiom of various philosophical authorities who informally govern academic discourse but who often both render it inaccessible to the very constituency that one hopes to address and persistently draw discussion away from the particularities that initiated concern.

I have, to this point, been focusing primarily on the situation and internal characteristics of metapractices, but an important part of what is at issue is the character of their subject matter – or at least their perception of it. One reason that politics has so often been abstracted and romanticized by metapractices such as political theory is that its actual manifestations have been perceived and encountered, in a variety of ways, as pathological, banal, dangerous, and mundane. Politics, it seems, has required discursive purification and sublimation before it could be approached. As in the case of the philosophy of science's reconstruction of science, politics, in the literature of metapractices, often emerges as a philosophical object that is only vaguely, if at all, related to the various actual conventional phenomena manifest in campaigns, city councils, school boards, town meetings, legislatures, and numerous other venues. The "practice" to and about which "theory" speaks is largely a metapractical caricature or an abstraction.

It is symptomatic that a volume devoted to a consideration of "social science as moral inquiry" (Haan et al., 1983) essentially ignores the concrete practical dimensions of the relationship between the academy and public life. More recently, in a series of essays in a *Nomos* volume on "theory and practice" (Shapiro and DeCew, 1995), philosophers and political theorists embrace positions such as "critical race theory," argue that Rawls's conception of justice as fairness demands the use of solar technology, assess the quality of life in developing countries, and make a variety of other claims about practical matters, but there is no discussion of exactly how such philosophical analysis bears on the practices and issues toward which it is supposedly directed. "Theory" is used generically to encompass everyone from Aristotle to Rawls, and "practice" appears as an abstract and equally undifferentiated datum. There is scant attention either to the situation of the academician, who for the most part, either explicitly or implicitly, is the principal reference for "theory," or to the historical and concrete manifestations and permutations of politics. As the literary critic Edward Said has suggested, there tends to be:

> a complete divorce between the academy and the world. The American academic in particular has a unique kind of arrogance, a presumption that he or she can talk about these general issues without any form of commitment to any social or political institution except the academy and the furthering of a certain career.
>
> (1993: 119)

Metapractical talk *about* politics is quite different from talking *to* and *in* politics, yet the assumption persists that, as one contributor to the *Nomos* volume put it, "political theory is simply conscientious civic conversation without a deadline" (Shapiro and DeCew, 1995: 148). There is characteristically a failure to recognize that the "theory/practice problem" is less a universal with various manifestations than a category for subsuming historically situated issues that have a certain family resemblance. Political and social theorists may conjure up all sorts of philosophical grounds for the claim that metapractices should be heard and heeded in the world of first-order activities such as politics, but there is wide resistance to a concrete, historical, and contextualized examination of the moral relevance of social science and its practical relationship to its object of analysis. One reason the social sciences, as a whole, have not adequately confronted this issue is, as I have stressed throughout this volume, their peculiar and perennial involvement with philosophy. The social sciences have become too philosophically encumbered.

It is perhaps understandable that a professional philosopher might claim, for example, that "the philosophy of the social sciences ... is the indispensable starting-point for all social science" (Trigg 1985: 205), but why this should be the tacit or explicit premise of so many social scientists requires some explanation, particularly since few philosophers find much virtue in social science (see, however, Bunge 1996). During the past century, the philosophical validation of science has really amounted to a validation of philosophy, and we might assume that philosophy will continue to valorize whatever first-order enterprises it takes to be authoritative. Social science, however, has seldom been the subject of such validation. Part of the explanation is historical. From the beginning, philosophy, particularly in Germany and England, struggled to defend itself against what it perceived as incursions from the specialized empirical human sciences, and the residue of this concern is still evident in many dimensions of contemporary philosophy. But social science, as is so evident in a work such as that of Winch as well as various humanistic critiques of the enterprise, is a competing metapractice. The social sciences have, strangely, seldom recognized their historical, if not natural, enemy. It is something of a paradox that their endemic condition of cognitive insecurity and practical guilt has led them to seek identity and authority in philosophy. The search for philosophical justification has, however, produced both theoretical atrophication and a failure to come to grips with the practical issue of the relationship between academic and public discourse.

I have pointed to the persistent inversion of theory and epistemology, the manner in which self-reflection in social science has taken place through the medium of an alien discursive screen, how philosophical doctrines have often become the premises of the practice of social scientific inquiry, and the extent to which social science finds itself attached to the destiny of ideas that may be intrinsically problematical. Am I saying, then, that social science does not need philosophy or that it should practice philosophical abstinence? This is too large and complex a question for any general response. My concern has been less to offer blanket judgments and prescriptions than to detail past problems and to signal persistent and characteristic concrete dangers. I would caution, yet once more, against construing my strictures regarding philosophy as tantamount to a call for reflective abnegation. My references to philosophy are specific and not a wholesale assault on this universe of discourse, but the problem is less with philosophy per se than with its use and abuse by social science. With respect to the relationship between natural science and the philosophy of science, my assumption and claim is that it has been an attenuated one. Often what philosophers meant by science was a logical construct that had little to do with actual scientific practice, and natural scientists, for the most part, have had little knowledge of, and have seldom been touched by, philosophy. Despite the pretensions of a philosopher such as Popper to have been a participant at crucial junctures in the development of modern science and to have grasped the essential contours of scientific rationality, the history of contemporary natural science has been little affected by the philosophy of science. There may have been some instances, such as in the cases of Heisenberg and Einstein, where the interaction of philosophy and science has been both significant and felicitous, and even though my hypothesis regarding this matter is largely a null one, the issue deserves careful exploration. The traditionally closer relationship between social science and philosophy might lead one to suspect that there have been instances in which contact with philosophy has propelled the social sciences in fruitful directions, and this, too, is a matter open to argument and investigation.

Nothing I have said about the dangers of intercourse with philosophy should be construed as an attempt to deny social science a rhetoric of inquiry and an epistemological vindication of its theories and methods. It is unlikely, for a number of closely related reasons, that the pluralistic universe of social science, as well as specialized subfields such as political theory, will become more intellectually homogeneous or paradigmatic. First, the conventional and historical character of the subject matter is characterized by diversity, change, and ideology that are reflected in the world of inquiry. Second, there are internal rivalries among the social sciences for cognitive and practical authority as well as external challenges to their status that limit their capacity to become theoretically hegemonic. Third, such internal factors as the historical peculiarities of professional structure inhibit consolidation. Fourth, the endemic practical concerns of social science engender differences based on the purposes of inquiry and the normative concerns often attached to these purposes; fifth, justifying their cognitive authority – both to their subject matter and to other metapractices – is a persistent problem. Finally, these fields cannot, by their very nature as metapractices, detach themselves from the general problem of their relationship to their subject matter. For all of these reasons, social science will, unlike the natural sciences, continue to be involved with a rhetoric of inquiry that will inevitably find inspiration and sustenance in external authorities such as philosophy.

There is, however, always a danger of becoming a prisoner of one's own rhetoric and allowing that rhetoric to govern or even displace what it justifies, and much of the criticism that I have advanced revolves around this problem. While the purpose of a rhetoric of inquiry has often been to secure the cognitive autonomy and identity of social science and to advance its practical aspirations, it has, paradoxically, tended to divert attention away from such matters and function more to advance the fortune of professional enclaves and reinforce existing persuasions. There have been few instances when someone has been converted from one social scientific paradigm to another through the force of argument rather than professional pragmatics, and the rhetoric of inquiry has had little external impact on first-order discourses and the practical relationship of social science to its object of inquiry. Rhetorics of inquiry, however, and the philosophies that inform them, are matters of fundamental choice that have implications for the conduct of metapractices.

While most images of critical theory have been predicated on some version of rationalism or foundationalism, it is now common to find a basis for critical metapractice in deconstructionism and the work of individuals such as Derrida. Such a move indicates, in part, that the issue is less foundationalism per se than a philosophical justification of the cognitive authority of metapractices. While Habermas and others maintain that postmodernism is an instance of a wider crisis of reason, precipitated by Gadamer, Rorty, Lyotard, and others (e.g., Habermas, 1987), that denies the possibility of philosophical privilege and undermines the idea of critical theory, postmodernism is sometimes invoked as a kind of reverse transcendentalism. Rather than empowering, for example, political theory with privileged access to knowledge, the claims to truth in the practices it studies are devalued so that both seem to occupy the same playing field. Theory seems to retain an attenuated but still superior reflective position even in Rorty's image of an "edifying" philosophy that would join in the "conversation of mankind."

Antifoundationalist tendencies in contemporary philosophy, such as the work of Rorty, have caused strong reactions simply, in part, because of their challenge to traditional philosophical practice. But this alone is not sufficient to explain the controversy that has arisen and its impact on other second-order fields such as social science. Although social scientific disciplines have suffered an identity crisis in the wake of the critique of specific philosophical doctrines to which they had subscribed, such as positivism and other forms of foundationalism, the deeper issue raised by postpositivism and antifoundationalism involves the nature of the relationship between second- and first-order discourses. It has precipitated a crisis in the general claim to authority on the part of all metapractical discourses. But while one strategy has been to shore up rationalism and attack "relativism," another has been to find ways within newer philosophical persuasions to assert philosophical privilege and to seek assimilation to their object of inquiry. While the traditional claim to authority of social science was based on postulating knowledge above power, much of poststructuralism and postmodernism seeks to demonstrate both that knowledge is power and that language and discourse, the province of philosophy, are at the core of power relationships. While the attack on traditional epistemology has challenged the authority of philosophy, political theory has turned to seeking grounds of normativity within the heart of the contemporary antifoundationalist challenge.

Although I have identified strongly with antifoundational arguments in philosophy, it is not because I wish to join many of the controversies in which these claims are usually featured – such as whether foundationalism or antifoundationalism offers the better basis for a critical social science or whether there are connections between such philosophical positions and certain ideological dispositions. I have argued that much of antifoundationalism, and what is often called relativism, is not just another philosophical stance but an argument against a whole conception of philosophy and an argument that forces a reevaluation of basic assumptions about the orders of discourse. I take the core of antifoundationalism not only as raising serious questions about much of the enterprise of modern philosophy and the "epistemological quest" but, more important, as indicating that metapractices have no inherent cognitive authority over their subject matter, that epistemology is not a substitute for theory, and that the practical role of social science is not a function of metatheoretical potency.

The fundamental claim of antifoundationalism, as implied by Winch and Kuhn and forcefully advanced by individuals such as Rorty and Cavell, is that traditional epistemology has been a misguided attempt to speak genetically about the criteria of knowledge. These arguments, however, must be recognized as largely a gloss on Wittgenstein. What has defined the epistemological quest, and continues to shape much of philosophical discourse, is a classic case of alienation, that is, the abstraction and projection of natural or ordinary certainty beyond a theoretical and practical context and then its reification as a realm of transcendental knowledge that is advanced against an equally alienated skepticism. This philosophical theology, as we experience it today, began with Kant and was perpetuated by individuals such as Frege and Husserl, and it set the tone of modern philosophy. What the epistemologist has sought is a transcontextual supradiscursive basis for underwriting or undermining substantive first-order claims to knowledge, but what has been achieved is only a fetish incapable, in the end, of creating or dissolving doubt. But it is a fetish to which social scientists and social theorists have been attracted long after much of philosophy has forgotten what it originally represented. If the transcendental illusion were merely an aberration of professional philosophy, it would be simply an intradiscipilinary curiosity. This is sometimes the manner in which it appears in the work of Cavell and Rorty, who often seem to have little sense of the effect of the siren call of epistemology in the odyssey of fields such as social science.

Rorty originally suggested that the epistemologist's overtures have been "shrugged off by those who wanted an ideology or self-image" (1979: 5), but the response to his work by social theorists, on both the left and right, should by now have disabused him of this idea. His claim that "there is no wholesale, epistemological way to direct, or criticize, or underwrite, the course of inquiry" (1982: 162) has, along with similar claims associated with postmodernism, traumatized social theorists of various persuasions. While the intense reaction to Rorty's pragmatic liberalism is in part a consequence of the discursive heritage of this concept in the history of social science, it is more generally a manifestation of the degree to which the identity and claim to authority of social science has been predicated on various forms of philosophical foundationalism. The concern of some with what is taken to be Rorty's conservatism, or the conservative implications of his work, as well as the worry about the socially destructive impact of his relativism, derives from the assumption that a different attitude toward epistemology would have different practical import with respect to both ideology and the authority of metapractices. Although questions of epistemology, narrowly conceived, revolve around the status of knowledge, what propels the obsession with epistemology in second-order practices is often less a cognitive than a practical concern. From Aristotle's idea of political science to Marx's notion of praxis, there has been a recognition of the peculiar character of second-order claims, and this is still reflected in contemporary social science.

When Aristotle spoke of political science as a practical, rather than a theoretical, science, he meant, first, that it was *about* a conventional or practical world. Even more explicit was his claim that it was a practical science in that it had an end in action and was directed toward a world created and changed through human agency, it was practical in intention and purpose, and its object was the subject of, and subject to, human artifice. His point was not that political science was lacking theoretical grounds, that it did not possess a theoretical understanding or a detached perspective and language, or that it was merely instrumental. It was rather that there was something about the character of its claims that rendered them less than meaningful if detached from a practical context of human action. When designating political science as practical, Aristotle did not mean that, like the knowledge and art of the statesman, it was embedded in practice but quite the opposite. Although in some sense it might be based on, or a distillation of, the practitioner's moral and factual knowledge as well as knowledge of *how* to do certain things and although it might have utility for practice and be directed toward practice, it was distinctly still knowledge *about* politics. Yet it professed to say something authoritative – descriptive, explanatory, evaluative, prescriptive – with respect to politics. This entailed potentially, and maybe necessarily, a clash of authorities – the authority of knowledge about politics versus the authority of politics. It also involved the question of how these universes of discourse were and could be related – both in principle and with respect to the limitations and possibilities of specific historical instances.

What Aristotle meant when calling political science practical was not only that it had an end in action and a practical purpose but that unless it in some way became part of practice, it had a diminished status as knowledge. Part of the sense of urgency that we might discern in many of the texts that have come to compose the classic canon of political theory derives from the assumption that what is advanced as knowledge is lacking full significance if not instituted or in some way made practically effective. Consequently, the focus was often on the vehicle of theoretical intervention. The very idea of pure practical knowledge has an oxymoronic aura, while the notion of practical pure knowledge does not seem as strange even if it implies the problem of how to translate from one sphere to another. While knowledge of natural things is ultimately validated by the conventional acceptance of claims about the existence, and manner of existence, of the objects in question, there is an important sense in which knowledge about politics, which is itself a conventional object, is validated only through institution. There is a way in which it is not knowledge of anything unless put into practice or unless practice descriptively and prescriptively conforms to it. All this is true of practical knowledge that is most essentially practical in that it is exemplified in practice, but there is a special poignancy and sense of paradox attached to those claims that are "practical" in the Aristotelian sense, that are advanced by an external activity. They are claims to practical authority on the basis of something outside of practice. The question is what kind of authority outside a practice can command the attention of practice?

It is this conflict between knowledge "about" and knowledge "in" that has given unity and continuity to the venerable discussions of "theory and practice." The second-order/first-order discourse relationship is the "truth" of the "theory/practice" problem. Second-order discourses are, by their nature, derivative, with respect to both their origins and current practice, and although various species of second-order activities, and different manifestations of each, have their own particular history of their relationship to their subject matter, the fundamental problematic has been generic and constant. Part of that problematic has been to justify their existence and their authority to speak to and about their subject matter – in both principle and practice. Most second-order discourses such as the philosophy of science, ethics, and social science continue to reflect their genesis. Even though they are institutionally and discursively distanced from the practices from which they sprung, they conduct themselves, in many respects, as if they were still involved in, or significantly interacting with, those practices, but when the problem of the practical relationship between metapractical discourses and their object is approached as an epistemological issue, what continues to be missing is any direct confrontation with the practical issue of the relationship between social science and politics. Even when it is confronted, however, the discussion has, in a peculiar way, become decentered.

II

In the mid-1990s, a political theorist challenged his colleagues by asking why, as obsessed as many were with issues surrounding liberalism and democracy, they had failed to address events and ideas associated with the 1989 revolution in Eastern Europe when the "walls of communism came tumbling down." Jeffrey Isaac argued that "American political theory responded to this situation with a deafening silence" that amounted to a "shocking indictment" of the field (1995). While political theory, he noted, is quick to embrace every new intellectual or philosophical fad, the "reticence" to comment on, or even "interpret," such "current events" seemed odd in the case of a profession that claims to be the "heir" of Plato, Machiavelli, Locke, Kant, Tocqueville, Paine, Hegel, and Marx. Were these events, he asked, too recent, too foreign, too lacking in theoretical and historical significance? Isaac concluded that such explanations were not sufficient and that the most fundamental sources of political theory's alienation from politics were its professionalization, its focus on the classic canon, an absorption with "metatheoretical" issues and an "aversion" to "first-order" inquiry, and the peculiarly American character and setting of the enterprise. While this general diagnosis, which closely mirrored arguments that I had earlier presented at some length (Gunnell, 1979; 1986; 1993), pointed to continuing problems with the enterprise of political theory, it did not confront certain underlying issues that were also elided by most of the symposiasts and others who responded to Isaac's critique. Some begrudgingly admitted that political theory must do better, but much of the commentary defended the current practice of political theory and suggested that by being "untimely" it was more relevant than many realize (Connolly, 1995) and that there were dangers involved in premature ejaculation (Gillespie, 1995). One later response claimed that the integrity of political theory is compromised "if it becomes trapped by responding to events" (Brown, 1997: 2), and another suggested that the real problem is less with political theory than with the conditions of the modern world in which "political theory is so difficult" (Wolin, 1997: 1).

What Isaac's criticism indirectly points to is the disjunction between what political theorists do and what they claim to do. There is certainly no lack of pretension to public relevance. The fundamental issue, however, is not how political theorists responded to the events in Eastern Europe. Isaac's complaint could as easily have been directed toward political theory's estrangement from the particularities of politics in the United States, and the problem has hardly been limited to the last quarter of the twentieth century. The basic problem is what political theory and other academic metapractices *could* and *should* be doing, and have done, with respect to engaging politics. Isaac's claim that the failure of political theorists to "address" and make "intelligible" the events of 1989 amounted to a "serious ethical abdication" is premised on the assumption that political theory has some particular ability, obligation, and authority to perform in this manner. Isaac pointedly criticized what I have called the "myth of the tradition," that is, the assumption that contemporary academic political theory belongs to a lineage that includes the classic canon (Gunnell, 1979; 1986). And he also noted, as I have stressed, that the image of political theory as a "vocation" separate from political science, evoked by Sheldon Wolin and others, signified more the emergence of a professional academic identity than the recovery of an epic past (Gunnell, 1993). Yet heroic images of academic political theory as the descendant of the "great tradition" still resonate in Isaac's critique and distract attention from what kind of an enterprise is represented in the contemporary discipline and the context in which it actually exists.

Why, one might ask, should political theory, or a variety of other forms of university scholarship, have something empirically and normatively significant to say about current events and on what basis can philosophers and political theorists make authoritative judgments about such matters? These activities certainly have no priestly or other form of institutional relationship to their subject matter. While we might reasonably expect relevant commentary from, for example, journalists or even mainstream political scientists who study particular areas such as Eastern Europe, it is less clear why we should attribute this role, in any general manner, to academic political theorists and political philosophers. In most instances, neither graduate training nor the typical modes of professional research prepare them for such a task. Isaac seemed to assume that political theorists should and can play a role as public ethicists, and what his challenge to the field prompts is a consideration of this assumption, which both he and many of those he criticizes hold in common.

One of the difficulties in confronting the issue of the relationship between the academy and politics derives from the prismatic ambiguity attaching to the term *politics* and its cognates. The facets of meaning that give shape to the concept of politics often support rhetorical and distorting refractions, since the concept refers not only to a historically and culturally circumscribed activity but often to the study of that activity as well. Many academic university programs in political science officially call themselves departments of government or politics, and there are historical reasons for this that involve establishing a sense of identity with their subject matter. Because we have become familiar with such designations, we forget that this practice is logically equivalent, for example, to philosophers of science constituting themselves as a department of science. This abstruseness attaching to the term *politics* allows, either purposively or unselfconsciously, the propagation of a sense of both assimilation and authority. It is easy to be seduced into believing that by talking *about* politics, one is in some manner engaged *in* politics, that such commentary is at least a virtual politics if not a more reflective dimension, or even microcosm, of political life. And it is common to assume that arrogating politics as an object of inquiry carries with it some natural authority to evaluate and prescribe with respect to it.

While there may be, for example, despite the alliterative and semantic resemblance, little likelihood of confusing anthropology with anthropophagy, or even sociology with society, political theory has often been understood, popularly as well as professionally, as something in politics as well as commentary about politics and thus as in some way bridging the orders of discourse. This has been the case in the history of academic political theory, and the general assumption is still evident. For example, in a recent article in the *New Yorker* magazine comparing the actions of President Clinton with the ideas of Oakeshott, the author suggested that "these days, political philosophy exists in two varieties – as a specialized subject taught in universities and as a thing that every politician just has." He noted that "sometimes the academic and the popular senses of the term meet up, so that what the professors teach and what the politicians talk about resemble each other, and sometimes they don't" (Gopnik, 1996: 194). There may well be reasons both politicians and academicians might wish to play on either the differences or similarities between these spheres, but the real issue is exactly how and if they in fact "meet up."

Often lurking behind, or coupled with, notions about an underlying affinity between politics and political theory is the image of culture and society as a seamless web in which every strand ultimately resonates when another is tweaked. This image is now bolstered by references to "intertextuality" and the assumption that a "mere writer" must necessarily have an impact on, or in effect participate in, the social practices addressed. Richard Harvey Brown, for example, argues that social science is necessarily a mode of "civic discourse" that, in its positivistic form, has, albeit often inadvertently, abetted repressive social forces characteristic of the bureaucracy and market. He urges a change in ideology and methodology that would provide a more rhetorical focus and "transform the human sciences into a fully democratic civic discourse" and provide an "agency for the empowerment of citizens" (1989: ix; 1987). Probably many would agree with the sentiment expressed in such a position. There can be little doubt that in various ways the practices of social science have an impact on other dimensions of society, and few would quarrel with the notion that it would be salutary to enhance the democratic character of any social practice. The difficulty with arguments such as that of Brown is that they do not directly address such crucial issues as exactly how this internal transformation is to be effected, how social science actually intersects with politics and various social structures, and why professed practitioners of a democratic social science should be invested with the influence and authority that is presumed. Skepticism about such images need not imply that there cannot be situations in which they are relevant but only that they have limits as general accounts of the relationship between particular forms of human conduct and the metapractices that study them.

Another crucial ambiguity attaching to "politics" and "political," however, ... involves the difference between the functional, generic, and stipulative uses of these words, on the one hand, and their particularistic or historical referential role, on the other hand. Although there is nothing invidious in this distinction, a problem arises when it is not recognized or when it is strategically obscured. It is neither incorrect nor surprising that activities manifesting certain functional characteristics such as power or struggle are referred to as politics. There are, however, many well-known examples of conflating the particular and generic uses of "politics" – such as when images abstracted from the structure and processes of political practice in the United States were employed by political scientists as a basis for analyzing and describing the "politics" of third-world countries. There are the problems both of reifying an abstract or analytical definition of politics, albeit maybe one originally derived from observing particular cases, and of extrapolating from the particular to the generic. Similar conceptual problems emerge in discussions about political theorists and historians as political actors, the politics of interpretation, political theory as a form of political practice, and the like. These are, if taken literally, category mistakes, and it is necessary to heed the subtle dangers of conceptual slippage.

III

The relationship between politics and disciplined, or disciplinized, political science and political theory, from the last quarter of the nineteenth century to the present, is a matter that does not lend itself easily to analysis in terms of abstract philosophical pronouncements about theory and practice. What is, in the end, most fundamentally at issue, as I suggested earlier, is the relationship between the university and politics. What can be said, in general, may amount to little more than noting that quite a bit of politics seeps into the university but very little of the university leaks out into politics. Much of what we may see in the academy as representing social and political forces in society is less the catalyst of such forces than a reaction to them. How, exactly, the relationship between the academy and politics plays out, however, has much to do with the situation of the modern university in particular societies. We often fail to recognize how much contemporary political theory bears the genetic imprint of its nineteenth-century origins and subsequent evolution. Social science originated as a surrogate for religion and moral philosophy, and the implantation of German philosophy complemented and accentuated this perspective. No matter how much the demography of the field has changed, it still reflects the Protestant evangelical spirit from which much of it originally sprung as well as several complementary infusions from German philosophy. What political theorists have failed to figure out, however, is exactly how this academic community with its vast production of claims about public morality has, could have, and deserves practical significance.

The political theorist Michael Walzer, for example, has advanced the idea of the theorist as a "connected critic" who, while seeking necessary "critical distance," enters the "mainstream" and pursues criticism as "interpretation" and "opposition" and seeks to mediate between "specialists and commoners" or "elite and mass" (1987: 1988). Yet none of Walzer's many historical examples, from the Hebrew prophets to Michel Foucault, touch directly upon the circumstances of contemporary institutionalized academic metapractices. Charles Lindblom, the dean of American policy analysts, has grappled intensively with the problems of whether social science can provide "usable knowledge" (Cohen and Lindblom, 1979) and of how social scientific inquiry can contribute to social change (Lindblom, 1990), that is, with the issue of relating knowing about to knowing how, but in the end, the matter seems to come down to the place of the university in contemporary society.

Russell Jacoby has advanced the thesis that the American university has come to function as a sort of "brain drain" that has attracted but also absorbed and neutralized the potential public intellectual, particularly on the left (1988). This is a provocative claim, but it is based on a romanticized image of the past existence and impact of public intellectuals in American political life. Thomas Bender, for example, has more carefully explored the impact of the modern university on certain dimensions of the participation of academics in public life (1993). While there may be something to the notion that academic discourse is a kind of surrogate politics, those attracted to the university were seldom those who really had a stomach for political life and dirty hands. Jacoby's more recent analysis, in the *Chronicle of Higher*

Education, probably hits closer to the mark. He suggests that the university is at once politicized and apolitical (1996). Academicians take positions on a variety of political and moral issues but in a universe, and language, that are quite disconnected from practical politics; instead a kind of virtual politics is represented in academic discussions of public issues. Just as scientific issues resonate in the philosophy of science, political issues are reflected in the discourse of social science, but neither the philosophy of science nor social science has much impact on its subject matter.

There are spheres of academic discourse that would seem to have distinct external constituencies, and some may believe that this is evidence of a connection between virtual and real politics. I would suggest that it is evidence of a connection but not the kind that many would suggest. It is evidence that the academy tends to reflect what is already happening in society, that it is reactive, not that its intellectual concerns lead political life. We might very well ask what political movement ever originated within the American university, and at the same time, we might speculate about how much the university is responsible for the lack of both conservatism and socialism in the United States. The question then becomes one of whether the virtual politics of the academy reverberates back on what initially inspired it. One can reasonably assume that there are many ways in which it does, but the empirical questions of how and how much and the normative question of the extent to which this is good for either politics or the academy are not easy to answer. The dream that scholarly activity is a form of, or a route to, speaking politically in America is deeply rooted in the history of the academy, but it is largely an academic fantasy.

We may learn something from the example of someone such as Said, who is, by anyone's standards, both a scholarly virtuoso and a public intellectual – if not a political actor. He notes that even though he is professionally "certified" only to teach literature, he is moved by political "causes and ideas" that relate to the "values and principles" in which he personally believes. But with respect to the latter, he considers himself "a rank amateur," and as much as he makes "a conscious effort to acquire a new and wider audience for these views," they represent arguments that he would "never present inside a classroom" (1994). The academy, he claims, "is *not* a place to resolve sociopolitical tensions" but to "understand them" (1993: 122). We may feel no need to subscribe to such neo-Weberian asceticism, but we should be able to sense the resonance of the deeply embedded belief that only by holding our academic and political commitments apart can we be efficacious in either domain. Said, much like Noam Chomsky, seeks neither political credit for his academic status nor academic recognition for his political views. Many would see these individuals as exemplars because they are in some measure politically effective academicians, but whatever symbiosis we may believe that we discern between their vocation and avocation, their political work is carried on quite separate from their academic work and they possess skills that are hardly the product of their academic training. To the typical academic, Fish offers the challenge, "Were you to wake up one morning and say to yourself, 'I think I'll become a public intellectual', there would be no roadway or sequence of steps whose negotiation would lead to the implementation of your new resolve" (1995: 117). Since to be a public intellectual requires at least a hope for public attention, "academics, by definition, are not candidates for the role of public intellectual" (pp. 117–18).

Allan Bloom's claim, and lament, that leftist ideology has taken over the university is strangely complementary to Jacoby's position. Bloom assumed that the university was less the prison of ideas than a staging zone for political education (1988). Probably either position would be difficult to sustain empirically, but Jacoby probably has a better grasp of the place of the university in contemporary American society. Despite abstractly voiced concerns about, and attestations to, relevance, most scholarly activity is generated and propelled by academic concerns and professionalism. Much of political theory, characterized by a self-image that seems quite unrelated to its actual practice and condition, bespeaks, however, of a wider syndrome.

A dominant theme in many humanistic social scientific fields is that they are, in one way or another, a form of political action or that they can exercise significant influence on public life. While most of these claims are advanced by individuals who fancy themselves radical and oppositional thinkers, conservatives such as Bloom, Roger Kimball (1990), Dinesh D'Sousa (1991), Martin Anderson (1992), and Lynne Cheney (1995) protest the influence of these individuals in the American academy and warn of their corrosive impact on public life and morals. The question is whether they do have any such influence. "Have hordes of tenured radicals, the flotsam and jetsam of the counterculture 1960s, who failed to take over the government, reappeared two decades later to take over the English departments and to threaten Western culture from inside its former citadels of defense?" (Edmundsen, 1993: 3). The truth of the matter is that many of such an ideological bent have so reappeared, but they are not even a threat to the academy, let alone civilization. Despite radical rhetoric, they rarely do anything to change or democratize the very habitat in which they reside. What the commentators on both the left and right, those who see academic pronouncements as a form of political action and those who fear those pronouncements, have in common, however, is the belief that what takes place in the university really has consequences. Specifying, or determining, the exact nature of these consequences is another matter.

Claims about the alienation of the academy from politics are answered in a number of ways, as in the case of the responses to Jacoby in the wake of his comments in the *Chronicle*, but they often do not squarely confront the issue. One response is to point to what is sometimes called the "crossover" phenomenon, that is, instances of academics entering political life or politicians moving to the academy, but this response fails to take account of what the metapractical dream has been all about, that is, to have authority over practice without joining it. And "crossover" has other difficulties attached to it.

While examples may seem intuitively significant – Woodrow Wilson, Henry Kissinger, and Hubert Humphrey moving in one direction and Jimmy Carter and others in the other direction – these are exceptions that do not prove the rule. What these classic cases, as well as instances of Straussians joining the Reagan and Bush team or the influence of communitarian liberals and academic advocates of strong democracy in the Clinton White House, tell us about the general relationship between political theory and politics is difficult to say. To some extent they indicate that these realms are actually quite disparate and that what is involved is more a choice between vocations than articulation. But what Shadia Drury's study of Leo Strauss's influence on the American right suggests is that it is a unique case (1997). It is fascinating in part because it is so unusual, not because it represents the manner in which the ideas and students of political theorists are characteristically involved in politics. And even though we might wish to think that this is an example of theory leading practice, it may represent more an instance of practice using theory, even though it is often difficult to disentangle reasons and rationalizations.

Another line of argument is based on the "trickle-down" hypothesis that the university can, and does, play, through education and other processes of cultural diffusion, a major role in shaping the public consciousness. Some also subscribe to the view that there are many individual theorists who are actually talking about politics and confronting pressing political problems, both by dealing with the philosophical dimension of these issues and by speaking to and for various concrete and sometimes marginalized constituencies. And there is the further claim that many do not give only at the office but take their work home and, through their individual efforts, carry it into the relevant communities. While these are interesting theses, they remain largely at the level of professional folklore. To the extent that they can be demonstrated, they may indicate something about a few individuals but do not tell us very much about the general structural relationship between political theory and politics. There is, however, a more significant point. In instances as diverse as nineteenth-century social science, various images of political science as policy analysis, critical theory, David Easton's announcement of a postbehavioral revolution, and Wolin's account of political theory as a vocation, the vision involved transcending the vagaries and unpredictability of individual action and establishing a professional cadre as an institutional social force that would carry authority and inform practice on a systematic basis.

Although, at least intellectually, if not professionally, political science and political theory had begun to go their separate ways by the early 1970s, both the mainstream discipline, represented by Easton's image of a "new revolution in political science" (Easton, 1969), and theoretical dissidents, embracing Wolin's call to the vocation of political theory (1969), continued to grapple with the issue of the relationship between political theory and politics. Both Easton and Wolin made pleas for relevance, but neither Easton's call for the reconstruction of political science as public policy analysis nor Wolin's idea of political theory as a form of political education managed to transcend the tensions of the past. Easton's hope for a national federation of social science advisers was never realized, and Wolin's attempt, through the short-lived vehicle of *democracy*, to translate the academic idiom into the language of politics is an instructive example of the difficulties involved. But both of these visions raise issues long latent in the history of the social sciences. These include not only the general problem of the relationship between academic and political discourse but the compatibility of democracy and the claims of political theory.

One issue that received short shrift in Isaac's critique, and in the responses to his argument, was a consideration of whether political theory actually had anything to say about the events of 1989. I happened to be in Berlin, at an academic conference dealing with the historical origins of modern social science, the day that the "wall" came down. It was a profoundly moving event, and as usual, theorists were in awe at being so proximate to actual politics. What was most striking, however, was the general lack of any sense of the imminence of the event and the inability to provide more than the most mundane explanation of its occurrence. As people simultaneously danced on the wall and chipped away at it, several of us crossed, unhindered, into East Berlin. I asked an East German border guard, who was standing at attention in the middle of the bridge while being showered with rose petals and champagne, what he thought of it all. His answer was much the same as that of my colleagues: "*Rationalität hat geseigt.*"

Finally, and maybe most important, there is the often neglected issue of justifying the very idea of theoretical intervention when there is a simultaneous commitment to democracy. This theme of the tension between science and democracy has been prominent, for example, in every attempt to recount the history of American political science (Smith, 1997). There is a presumption that although such intervention may be difficult to achieve, it is, in principle, desirable, but the problem is not simply one of the conflict between science and democracy with respect to demands and commitments. The claim of second-order epistemic privilege is not easily reconciled with an image of democratic deliberation. And one can easily construe the history of political philosophy as affirming Hannah Arendt's observation that truth and politics are ultimately incompatible (1968). Two centuries of discussions of this matter with respect to the role of social science leave little doubt about the elitist attitudes of those who claim superiority for metapractical judgments. There is also a paradox attending many of those individuals that cry out from within the walls of the university for nothing less than the emancipation of humankind. Often their voices are situated in structures that are far from democratic. The academy and academic disciplines are often not models of democratic society. Academic freedom is freedom that is, in all senses of the word, academic. There is a folk music parody of the song "My Way" that is titled "Their Way" and relates the story of typical academic success from cowering student to oppressive full professor. It is instructive to remember that there are very few highly visible academic oppositional thinkers, on any part of the ideological spectrum, who have not, in the end, done it "their way." If academic intellectuals wish to democratize the world, they might well begin with the university.

It is easy to speak abstractly about the political responsibility of intellectuals, and there are probably few who would disagree with the general claim that those who, by the very vocation in which they are engaged, are devoted to the pursuit of truth and self-consciously concerned with standards of validity have a special responsibility to evoke these values in a wider public sphere (Maclean, Montefiore, and Winch 1990). But such a position does not answer a number of pragmatic questions regarding such matters as the capacity of academic intellectuals to engage in political discourse, the extent to which they, any more than other citizens, are ideologically untainted and neutral seekers of truth and right, and the degree to which they are in a position to exercise this responsibility. It is, in the end, difficult to say what ethical imperatives should govern academic practices with respect to their relationship to politics as well as what constitutes authenticity in this relationship.

Much of what I have said will inevitably be read by many as, at best, urging academic asceticism. The spirit that animates my basic argument, however, is closer to what I take Wittgenstein to have meant when he said that "philosophy may in no way interfere with the actual use of language; it can in the end only describe it. It cannot give it any foundation either. It leaves everything as it is" (1953: 124). The point is not, I think, that describing, interpreting, explaining, evaluating, and other forms of metapractical discourse may not, cannot, or should not have an effect on their object but rather that they are different from the practices they talk about and are contingently related to them. Maybe the greatest ethical lapse among metapractices is not the failure to speak to or about certain events or address various moral issues but rather the refusal to come to terms with the actual situation and character of the academic enterprise. Despite what someone such as Lentricchia may suggest, Marx's point was that philosophy *qua* philosophy, that is, as a second-order practice, cannot change the world. The answer is not the production of ever more finely grained epistemology and metaphysics – and maybe not even substantive, good reasons couched in academic discourse. In the end, the actions that we deplore are defeated by acting otherwise and, in various ways, convincing others to do the same, and the academy is only one circumscribed arena for such pursuits, There is a persistent, but often unreflective, assumption that academicians, by simply doing what comes naturally, that is, practicing academic virtuosity, are somehow necessarily acting in other spheres – politics, moral discourse, or the pursuit of human emancipation. The danger of such false consciousness is something that is ever present in the very nature of metapractices. They both long to return to their origins and yearn for authority over the universe from which they sprung. Much of the talk about philosophers and political theorists speaking politically represents little more than the discursive residue of unrequited hope.

References

Agger, Ben. 1992. *Cultural Studies as Critical Theory.* Washington, DC: Palmer Press.

Anderson, Martin. 1992. *Impostors in the Temple: The Decline of the American University.* New York: Simon and Schuster.

Arendt, Hannah. 1968. *Between Past and Future.* New York: Viking.

Bauman, Zygmunt. 1987. *Legislators and Interpreters.* Ithaca, NY: Cornell University Press.

Bellah, Robert, et al. 1996. *Habits of the Heart.* Berkeley: University of California Press.

Bender, Thomas, 1993. *Intellectuals and Public Life.* Baltimore, MD: Johns Hopkins University Press.

Bloom, Allan. 1988. *The Closing of the American Mind.* New York: Simon and Schuster.

Bloom, Harold. 1993. In Edmundsen, *Wild Orchids and Trotsky.*

Boggs, Carl. 1993. *Intellectuals and the Crisis of Modernity.* Albany: State University of New York Press.

Brantlinger, Patrick. 1990. *Crusoe's Footprints: Cultural Studies in Britain and America.* London: Routledge.

Brown, Richard Harvey. 1987. *Society as Text.* Chicago, IL: University of Chicago Press.

Brown, Richard Harvey 1989. *Social Science as Civic Discourse.* Chicago, IL: University of Chicago Press.

Brown, Wendy. 1997. "The Time of the Political." *Theory and Event* 1.

Bunge, Mario. 1996. *Finding Philosophy in Social Science.* New Haven, CT: Yale University Press.

Cheney, Lynne. 1995. *Telling the Truth.* New York: Simon and Schuster.

Cohen, David, and Charles Lindblom. 1979. *Usable Knowledge.* New Haven, CT: Yale University Press.

Connolly, William. 1995. "The Uncertain Condition of the Critical Intellectual." *Political Theory* 23.

Derrida, Jacques. 1982. *Margins of Philosophy.* Chicago, IL: University of Chicago Press.

Drury, Shadia. 1997. *Leo Strauss and the American Right.* New York: St Martin's Press.

D'Sousa, Dinesh. 1991. *Illiberal Education.* New York: Free Press.

Eagleton, Terry. 1976. *Criticism and Ideology: A Study in Marxist Literary Theory.* London: Verso.

Eagleton, Terry 1983. *Literary Theory: An Introduction.* Minneapolis: University of Minnesota Press.

Easton, David. 1969. "The New Revolution in Political Science." *American Political Science Review* 63.

Edmundsen, Mark, ed. 1993. *Wild Orchids and Trotsky.* New York: Penguin.

Eyerman, Ron. 1994. *Between Culture and Politics.* Cambridge: Polity Press.

Fink, Leon, Stephen Leonard, and Donald Reid, eds. 1996. *Intellectuals and Public Life.* Ithaca, NY: Cornell University Press.

Fish, Stanley. 1995. *Professional Correctness.* Oxford: Oxford University Press.

Freeland, Richard. 1992. *Academia's Golden Age: Universities in Massachusetts 1945-1970.* New York: Oxford University Press.

Geiger, Roger. 1993. *Research and Relevant Knowledge: American Research Universities Since World War II*. New York: Oxford University Press.

Gillespie, Michael. 1995. "Beyond East and West." *Political Theory* 23.

Gopnik, Adam. 1996. "Man Without a Plan." *New Yorker*, October.

Grossberg, Lawrence, Cary Nelson, and Paula A. Treichler. 1992. *Cultural Studies*. New York: Routledge.

Gunnell, John. 1979. *Political Theory: Tradition and Interpretation*. Cambridge, MA: Winthrop.

Gunnell, John. 1986. *Between Philosophy and Politics: The Alienation of Political Theory*. Amherst: University of Massachusetts Press.

Gunnell, John. 1993. *The Descent of Political Theory: The Genealogy of an American Vocation*. Chicago, IL: University of Chicago Press.

Gunnell, John. 1997. "Paradoxos Theoretikos." In *Contemporary Empirical Political Theory*, ed. Kristen Monroe. Berkeley: University of California Press.

Gunnell, John. 2000. "Political Theory as a Metapractice." In *Political Theory and Partisan Politics*, ed. Edward Portis, Adolph Gunderson, and Ruth Shivery. Albany: State University of New York Press.

Haan, Norma et al., eds. 1983. *Social Science as Moral Inquiry*. New York: Columbia University Press.

Habermas, Jürgen. 1987. *The Philosophical Discourse of Modernity*. Cambridge, MA: MIT Press.

Isaac, Jeffrey. 1995. "The Strange Science of Political Theory." *Political Theory* 23.

Jacoby, Russell. 1988. *The Last Intellectuals*. New York: Basic Books.

Jacoby, Russell. 1996. "America's Professoriate: Politicized, Yet Apolitical." *Chronicle of Higher Education*, April 12.

Johnson, Paul. 1988. *Intellectuals*. New York: Harper and Row.

Kant, Immanuel. 1983. *Perpetual Peace and Other Essays on Politics, History, and Morals*, trans. Ted Humphrey. Indianapolis, IN: Hackett.

Kimball, Roger. 1990. *Tenured Radicals: How Politics Has Corrupted Our Higher Education*. New York: Harper and Row.

Lemert, Charles C., ed. 1991. *Intellectuals and Politics*. Newbury Park, Calif.: Sage.

Lentricchia, Frank. 1983. *Criticism and Social Change*. Chicago, IL: University of Chicago Press.

Lindblom, Charles. 1990. *Inquiry and Change*. New Haven, CT: Yale University Press.

Maclean, Ian, Alan Montefiore, and Peter Winch, eds. 1990. *The Political Responsibility of Intellectuals*. Cambridge: Cambridge University Press.

McDermott, Patrice. 1994. *Politics and Scholarship*. Urbana: Illinois University Press.

Mitchell, W. J. T., ed. 1983. *The Politics of Interpretation*. Chicago, IL: University of Chicago Press.

Orwell, George. 1968. *The Collected Essays, Journalism, and Letters of George Orwell*. Vol. 4, *In Front of Your Nose*. New York: Harcourt, Brace and World.

Robbins, Bruce, ed. 1990. *Intellectuals: Aesthetics, Politics, Academics*. Minneapolis: University of Minnesota Press.

Rorty, Richard. 1979. *Philosophy and the Mirror of Nature*. Princeton, NJ: Princeton University Press.

Rorty, Richard 1982. *The Consequences of Pragmatism*. Minneapolis: University of Minnesota Press.

Rorty, Richard 1994. "After Philosophy, Democracy." In *The American Philosopher*, ed. Giovanna Borradori. Chicago, IL: University of Chicago Press.

Said, Edward. 1993. In Edmundsen, *Wild Orchids and Trotsky.*
Said, Edward. 1994. *Representations of the Intellectual.* New York: Pantheon.
Shapiro, Ian, and Judith Wagner DeCew, eds. 1995. *Theory and Practice: Nomos XXXVII.* New York: New York University Press.
Smith, Rogers M. 1997. "Still Blowing in the Wind: The American Quest for a Scientific Study of Politics." *Daedalus* 126.
Trigg, Roger. 1985. *Understanding Social Science.* Oxford: Basil Blackwell.
Walzer, Michael. 1987. *Interpretation and Social Criticism.* Cambridge: Cambridge University Press.
Walzer, Michael. 1988. *The Company of Critics.* New York: Basic Books.
Wittgenstein, Ludwig. 1953. *Philosophical Investigations.* New York: Macmillan.
Wolin, Sheldon. 1969. "Political Theory as a Vocation." *American Political Science Review* 63.
Wolin, Sheldon 1997. "What Time Is It?" *Theory and Event* 1.

9 Reading Max Weber
Leo Strauss and Eric Voegelin (2004)

> It is itself entirely a question of practical judgment and cannot therefore be definitively resolved.
>
> Max Weber

What Max Weber was referring to in this quotation was the problem of the relationship between social science and politics, but his claim that the matter was not susceptible to a philosophical solution was a conclusion that a wide range of thinkers could not accept. The extent to which Weber became an object of criticism for many political theorists has often been noted, but there has been little close scrutiny of these critiques. Although much of the discussion of Weber's work revolved around his plea for scientific objectivity and a separation of facts and values, the underlying issues were far more complex. I have elsewhere discussed the place of Weber's work in the 'Weimar conversation,' and especially the essays on the vocations of science and politics, as well as the projection of that conversation, by émigré scholars, into the American context,[1] but it is worth examining in more textual detail some paradigmatic examples of that projection and the confrontation with Weber. The complex exchanges of teaching and learning between émigré scholars and their American hosts were complicated by contests among the émigrés about their own legacy, and Americans were left to make what they could out of these contests.

I

For many of the scholars who emigrated to the United States, Weber was, as he was for Karl Mannheim, the pivotal social thinker of the twentieth century, but when the émigré scholars began to address issues in political theory in terms of an analysis and critique of Max Weber, most Americans had little sense of either Weber's work and its context or why he was singled out for emphasis. The Americanization of political science after the First World War, and the dominance of what may loosely be termed the pragmatist perspective during the interwar period, had contributed not only to a submergence of issues regarding political principles but to a certain hostility to the very idea of principles which, until the end of the 1930s, were associated with various forms of ideological rigidity and political absolutism.

Weber's stress on the heterogeneity of facts and values resonated with behavioralists in American political science who had adopted the language of logical empiricism in the philosophy of science, itself, ironically, largely the importation of émigré scholars, but since there was in fact no actual philosophical connection between this literature and Weber's formulations, the behavioralists' general approval gave them no insight into the contest over the Weber legacy. The issue of values and their justification was closely tied to the problem of theory and practice for many of the émigrés, as well as for those who had responded to Weber in the Weimar context, but Americans had themselves been closely attuned to the questions about the relationship between social science and politics. Yet why Weber should be considered so central to this discussion by émigrés was far from evident to most American political scientists, even though for half a century American social scientists had embraced what, functionally, might be designated as Weber's strategy for bringing social science to bear on politics. The scattered exposure of American political scientists to his work had been only tangential and indirect, but presuppositions that bore a strong resemblance to Weber's arguments were more deeply sedimented in the discourse of American political and social science than most of its practitioners realized.

First, American political scientists, in the late nineteenth and early twentieth centuries, had also endorsed a separation between science and politics, and between facts and values, but, as with Weber, they had done this with a view to getting them back together in a wider context, as a matter of theory as well as practice. They had decided, much like Weber, that, in a socially plural society and in a situation in which the university's place as a repository of scientific authority depended on its increasing specialization and in which the political field was ideologically diverse, the only way for the academy to gain practical purchase was, ironically, by distancing itself from political issues and achieving cognitive authority in terms of a position of scientific nonpartisanship.[2] Exactly how such authority, even if achieved, was to be exercised, remained, as it did for Weber, an intractable problem.

Second, with the rise and practical recognition of informal political processes and the consequent decline of the nineteenth-century theory of the state as a basis for demarcating a natural substantive domain of the 'political' that gave disciplinary identity to political studies, it became increasingly necessary to delineate that subject domain and identity, both methodologically and analytically. For individuals such as Arthur Bentley, who had been influenced by Simmel and Dilthey during his studies in Germany, the intellectual resources and justification for this task, as with Weber, were distinctly neo-Kantian, but they were related also to some strikingly similar ideas of American pragmatists. Despite his emphasis on the group theory of politics, Bentley's philosophical interests did not make converts among political scientists, and he was 'rediscovered' only in the late 1940s, after the émigrés had done much of their work. Although the émigrés lacked curiosity about the history of American social science, they recognized the parallel between their concerns and the practice of political science; and the choice of Weber for emphasis was not simply a continuation of the Weimar conversation without regard to the new context.

II

For Leo Strauss and Eric Voegelin, Weber represented the dangers of neo-Kantianism in social theory, and this philosophical perspective, they believed, had created both a cognitive and practical crisis. The cognitive crisis derived in part from the status of philosophy once it had become reduced to epistemology and retreated from speaking in a first-order manner about reality. In the case of the social sciences, philosophy was demoted to a third-order status, such as speaking about the conceptual foundations of these disciplines, and this had the practical effect of reducing the authority of philosophy in both the university and public policy. For these individuals, Weberian neo-Kantianism spelled the loss of a substantive normative and empirical vision on which to predicate political philosophy, and it seemed to carry with it the practical danger that such philosophy would lose its capacity to speak to and influence politics. The problem of relativism, which was at the heart of the commentaries of both Strauss and Voegelin, has never been primarily a problem about the dissolution of grounds of judgment in the first-order worlds of politics, science, or moral life, but rather a problem of vouchsafing the authority of knowledge in second-order enterprises. [3]

Despite some significant differences between those usually designated as neo-Kantians – such as Wilhelm Dilthey, Hermann Cohen, Hans Vaihinger, Wilhelm Windelband, Ferdinand Tönnies, Heinrich Rickert, and Georg Simmel – there was, at least, a family resemblance among them. These individuals, situated in a post-Hegelian intellectual universe, rejected the idea of any intrinsic and universal meaning of history or intelligible structure of society. Dilthey found meaning *in* particular events and in human actions and believed that this meaning could be recovered hermeneutically, but there was no longer a belief in the comprehension of the whole scope of human history and society. For the neo-Kantians, the purpose of philosophy was to provide an epistemological elucidation of, and foundation for, empirical inquiry. The specialized empirical sciences were viewed as the principal mediators of reality and its infinite variety, and the task of philosophy was to illuminate their presuppositions. In effect, epistemology, which had once functioned as a kind of rhetoric of inquiry in defense of first-order claims against internal rivals and external authorities, was becoming a separate field and was taking over the core province of philosophy once occupied by metaphysics.

While Strauss and Voegelin considered Nietzsche to be a primary expression and author of a general crisis of western culture, they conceded him a latent respect that they did not grant other figures that they associated with modernity. Nietzsche, they believed, at least called attention to the nihilism implicit in the situation, and he never relinquished the idea that a grand philosophy could create value and change the world rather than being simply a handmaiden of the empirical sciences. In somewhat the same way, these émigré political theorists viewed Weber as symptomatic of the modern crisis but also as forcing a confrontation with it because of his fearless and self-aware deployment of the neo-Kantian approach.

When it came to questions of epistemology and methodology, that is, issues regarding the foundations of knowledge and the mode of its acquisition, the neo-Kantians had rejected any kind of representational philosophy that posited an identity between concepts and reality. Phenomenology, naive realism, and other essentialist formulations were set aside. The concept of reality functioned as a kind of ideal or limiting concept, and although they might say that reality was infinite, this was less an ontological claim than an expression of the endless ways in which it could be experienced and conceptualized. The form of reality was conceived as always constructed and independent of the objectivity of any *Ding an sich*, Weber, applying Rickert's critique, attacked both the classical economists and the Historical School for their attempts to seek general laws and for their confusion of abstractions with reality and its individual heterogeneous character. He argued that the concepts that ordered experience might sometimes be formed with forethought and systematically deployed, notably in the sciences, as opposed to the relatively unreflective formulations of everyday life, but he viewed all concepts alike as responses to practical concerns and interests.[4]

Despite this instrumental image of the origin of knowledge, Weber argued, like other neo-Kantians, that while all knowledge claims could be judged in terms of their logical validity and other standards of verification, each discipline constructed its own conceptual universe on the basis of its values and perspectives, with no predetermined domains rooted in a preconstituted reality. Weber echoed the old claim that the goal of science was causal knowledge of reality, but for him this remained an ideal in the Kantian sense, regulatory but unachievable, since all science was grounded in abstraction and perspectival thinking. The criteria might in some general sense be the usefulness of concepts, but there was no general standard of utility that exceeded the problems, values, and concerns of the practitioner of the specific science. The extent to which Weber consistently conformed to the general philosophy of such neo-Kantians as Rickert remains controversial, but Strauss and Voegelin did not doubt that this was the context to which his work belonged.

In successive Walgreen Lectures at the University of Chicago, in 1949 and 1951, Eric Voegelin and Leo Strauss selected Weber as the most important modern figure in their respective critiques of the loss of philosophical standards of valuation and the failures of contemporary political science. Like émigré social scientists who sought to use Weber to mediate their entry into 'mainstream' American social science discourse, they drew on encounters with Weber's many-layered thought, and fame, to make quite a different bid to be heard among students of politics. The commonplace tendency of equating critical émigré political thought with leftist programs badly misjudges the complex situation. The concerns of the émigrés about the status of philosophy and the problem of theory and practice transcended ideological differences. These lectures represented the apex of the émigré critique of political theory in the United States, as well as being the most fundamental statements of two intellectual programs that would play a major role in American political science and political theory during the next generation. In both cases, the authors began by confronting the work of Max Weber.

My concern in this chapter is neither to support Weber's position nor to advance the cause of his critics. Both Weber and his critics stood, by today's standards and from my perspective, on very shaky philosophical grounds. What is interesting is the extent to which these critiques of Weber bring to the surface issues that would in many ways define the émigré confrontation with American social science.

III

Although Strauss and Voegelin were ostensibly defending the possibility of transcendental judgment in human affairs, they were also, more fundamentally, pursuing arguments for the priority of academic philosophy over empirical social science and for the capacity of second-order discourses such as philosophy and a coordinated social science to trump, both theoretically and practically, the perceptions and claims of first-order discourses such as politics, or a political science subservient to its factual appearances and practicalities.

Strauss began *Natural Right and History*[5] by focusing on historicism and how it had undercut the possibility of political philosophy, but before he actually took up his discussion of how this modern temporalizing of all knowledge was linked to the distinction between facts and values, uniquely associated for him with Weber, he claimed that the 'crisis of modern natural right' and the decline of political theory were rooted in a *practical* problem. The problem was that 'philosophy as such had become thoroughly politicized.' While it had once been 'pure,' it had, since the seventeenth century, increasingly become 'a weapon, and hence an instrument,' and the result was that the difference between 'intellectuals and philosophers,' or what had once been understood as the difference between 'gentlemen and philosophers,' as well as the difference between 'sophists or rhetoricians and philosophers' had disappeared (p. 34). This complaint actually resembled Weber's concern about the lack of a distinction between science and politics, so Strauss's basic quarrel with Weber must be located other than in the line drawn between theory and practice. Strauss maintained, moreover, that the practice of both philosophy and political philosophy entailed apprehending fundamental and universal problems and alternatives that transcended historical horizons. Yet in this respect, as well, he did not present himself as directly in conflict with Weber, who had claimed that science could produce universally valid results. Strauss further maintained, not unlike Weber, that such knowledge was, in itself, of no practical value and that the whole purpose of science and philosophy was to be in a position to serve the 'ultimate goal of wise action' for which there was 'no final solution.' If, then, Strauss's basic divergence from Weber was not with respect to the separation of science and politics, the universality of knowledge, and the practical purpose of social science, what was the issue?

According to Strauss, what endangered political philosophy was not just historicism, relativism, and positivism, which had combined to produce the belief that the definition of what is right changes as historical circumstances change. Nor was the problem simply that this view crept into and subverted political life. What was most dangerous was the modern assumption that there existed 'a variety of unchangeable principles of right and goodness which conflict with one another, and none of which can be proved to be superior to the others.' This was distinctly the Weimar problem, which was marked by a diversity of ideologies and philosophical perspectives, and for Strauss it was also the congenital problem of American liberalism. Here, Strauss argued, was where Weber came in, and this was what led Strauss to say that no one had thought more deeply about the 'basic problem of social science' than Weber and that 'whatever may have been his errors, he is the greatest social scientist of our century' (pp. 35–36). Weber, like Nietzsche, led us to the brink of the abyss and made us peer into it.

Strauss maintained that Weber ultimately went against the Historical School in Germany, with which he had originally been involved, not because it rejected 'natural,' that is, 'universal and objective,' norms but because, like nineteenth-century positivists and unlike the thoroughgoing historicists, it believed in universals, demonstrable laws of historical development as well as the objectivity of values in a particular cultural setting. There were two basic reasons, Strauss suggested, why Weber did not fully succumb to historicism when he rejected this last vestige of the idea of ultimate meaning in history. First, there was his 'devotion to the idea of an empirical social science as it prevailed in his generation,' that is, one that was independent of *Weltanschauungen* and valid for all times and places and based on the assumption that facts and causes could be scientifically determined. Historically and socially relative for Weber were, however, the values and interests that directed science, the attending conceptual schemes it employed, the significance attributed to scientific findings, and even the belief in science itself as valuable. Second, Strauss claimed that, although Weber maintained that there was an 'indefinitely large variety' of concrete and historical value ideas, he believed that they contained 'elements of a trans-historical character' and that 'ultimate values are as timeless as the principles of logic.' It was, ironically, according to Strauss, Weber's particular notion of 'timeless values' that was 'the basis of his rejection of natural right' (p. 39). 'Timeless values' were plural not singular in the world of politics; and social science as a distinct vocation and order of discourse was ultimately unable to choose among them.

This proposition, Strauss claimed, was closely tied to Weber's insistence on the distinction between values and facts.

Strauss argued that at the heart of Weber's position was his claim that 'facts and values are absolutely heterogeneous' and that there is a fundamental opposition between 'Is and Ought.' It was this proposition that both dictated the 'ethically neutral character of social science' and prohibited it from answering value questions. Values entered the picture in terms of providing perspectives and criteria of selection in science and with respect to the manner in which science and its analyses of facts and causes could be employed to illuminate the practical consequences of various value choices. Strauss claimed that if there were 'genuine knowledge' of the 'Ought,' Weber would be wrong and there would not be a cognitive opposition between fact and value and such a practical distance between social science and politics. Since 'social science is meant to be practical,' it would then be in a position to be a 'truly policy-making' science. What ultimately troubled Strauss, I would contend, was Weber's weak claim to epistemic privilege for social science. All that science could do, according to Weber, was to 'clarify' values and leave the practical choice between them up to 'free, non-rational decision' (pp. 39–42) beyond social science's sphere of authority.

Although Weber may have implied that the scientific clarification of values and their consequences would, in principle, substantially constrain practical choice, choice was still ultimately ungrounded. Strauss argued that this position regarding the theoretical equality of all ideals and preferences 'necessarily leads to nihilism' or the idea that any value preference is, by ultimate standards, as good as any other. He even suggested that the practical implications of this epistemic perspective ultimately led to Hitler. At this point, however, one must ask how, in Strauss's view, does a philosophical stance such as this relate to National Socialism? Or how does philosophical nihilism, even if correctly diagnosed, produce practical nihilism? For Strauss, it was not 'the treason of the intellectuals' (Benda), the ideological opinion-makers in practical politics, who were committed to ultimate values, but the treason of philosophers that set the scene for the emergence of the kind of 'liberal relativism' that took over political practice and allowed one set of 'timeless values' to gain ascendancy. It was the collapse of a vision of privilege among philosophers that precipitated the problem. Although Strauss noted that Weber stressed the need for an ethic of responsibility and for intellectual honesty, he provided no foundation for such attitudes. Although this might be considered a 'noble nihilism,' there was, in the end, no real ground on which to distinguish it from 'base' nihilism (p. 48).

Strauss insisted that it was actually impossible to separate fact and value, and science and politics, because evaluative language and criteria were inevitably involved in any statement of fact. Strauss's famous example was the poverty of any description of a concentration camp that eschewed a word such as 'cruel.' What Strauss was most concerned with, however, was less the logical status of the positivist claim that it was possible to achieve scientific objectivity by doing away with evaluative language than the manner in which it tended to propagate an image of social science as confined to a 'purely historical or "interpretive" approach.' 'The social scientist,' he continued, 'would have to bow without a murmur to the self-interpretation of his subjects.' It was this objection that Strauss shared with a number of Weimar thinkers and their progeny, often of a quite different ideological disposition, such as Jürgen Habermas.

Tacitly alluding to Mannheim as a follower of Weber, Strauss noted that there existed a 'sociology of knowledge' that maintained that any belief can qualify as knowledge, but, he argued, this position created the 'danger of falling victim to every deception and self-deception of the people that one is studying; it penalizes *every* critical attitude; taken by itself, it deprives social science of every possible value' (p. 55). Although such a project was 'merely preparatory or ancillary' to critical judgment, Strauss maintained, there was a legitimate motive for 'understanding people in the way in which they understood themselves,' anticipating his later well-known rule for the study of the history of political philosophy. Weber, he contended, failed to grasp the demands of such authentic interpretation. Despite his insistence that social science was an interpretive endeavor, Strauss argued, Weber employed abstract conceptual schemes and ideal types that in fact precluded an understanding of actors and authors as they had understood themselves. What ultimately 'endangers objectivity,' however, was the rejection of value judgments on the part of an interpretive science. 'In the first place, it prevents one from calling a spade a spade. In the second place, it endangers the kind of objectivity which legitimately requires the forgoing of evaluation, namely, the objectivity of interpretation.' Strauss argued that if one believed that objective value judgments are impossible, then much of past thought is rendered as a delusion and cannot be understood on its own terms (pp. 57, 61). Above all, however, a merely interpretive social science carries no social authority – a claim that would define not only Strauss's position but that of most forms of critical theory.

Strauss concluded that Weber failed to demonstrate that there is no rational way for choosing between ultimate values by the application of philosophical criteria. All he really demonstrated was that 'the conflict between ethics and politics is insoluble' and perennial. Strauss believed that this divide was in the nature of things and defined the human condition. Yet, according to Strauss, Weber simply failed to provide adequate support for the side of ethics in this struggle. What lay behind Weber's position, Strauss contended, was the assumption of 'power politics' and the belief that 'conflict' rather than 'peace' was the natural condition of humanity. This, he argued, had been a core idea of modern political thought since the time of Machiavelli and Hobbes, and it had led, and would lead, to political extremism.

In Strauss's view, Weber rightly saw science as a path to clarity and understanding, but historicism, along with a neo-Kantian rejection of the idea that a natural apprehension of reality is the foundation of science, held him back and made him unable to acknowledge the possibility that science could attain ultimate truth and choose between conflicting claims to timeless truth. If science did not have faith in its own ability to do this, it could hardly convince others. Strauss argued that, in order to overcome the limitations of Weber's perspective and gain a grasp of natural right, it was necessary to return to teachings that he ascribed conjointly but incommensurably to classical philosophy and the Bible. This was the path that Strauss mapped out in *Natural Right and History* and which would inform his entire influential body of work.

IV

While for Strauss historicism was the principal sign of the supposed decadence of modern thought, and positivism a tributary, Eric Voegelin claimed that nineteenth-century positivism was both the prime expression and cause of the theoretical 'derailment' that defined the modern crisis of the West. The contemporary political crisis, however, had the salutary effect, he contended, of awakening a concern with a theory of politics. Theoretical consciousness slumbered during periods of comparative stability when there was 'a contraction of political science to a description of existing institutions and the apology of their principles, that is, a degradation of political science to a handmaiden of the powers that be.' Voegelin argued that this was the condition into which social science had fallen in Germany and, now, in the United States. The task envisioned in *The New Science of Politics*[6] was a 'recovery from the destruction of science which characterized the positivist era and a restoration' of theoretical science through a 'return to the consciousness of principles' that could be the basis of a critical and politically engaged social science (pp. 1–2). As in the case of Strauss, it was this restoration of philosophy and its epistemic authority that was the goal of Voegelin and the objective of his critical focus on Weber.

While positivism demanded adherence to the logic and method of the natural sciences and assumed that methods were the 'criterion of theoretical relevance in general,' Voegelin argued that this 'perverts the meaning of science,' whose authentic search for truth differs, methodologically, among the distinct spheres of inquiry. In political science, the appropriate approach was 'metaphysical speculation and theological symbolism' rather than the 'accumulation of irrelevant facts' on the basis of defective theoretical principles. The latter attitude had culminated in 'the attempt at making political science (and the social sciences in general) "objective" through a methodological exclusion of "value judgments",' predicated on a dichotomy between fact and value and the assumption that only statements of fact could be scientific and objective, while metaphysics, ethics, politics, and the like were deemed unscientific and subjective.

Despite the destructive work of these 'methodologists,' they had, at least, been concerned with maintaining the critical function of history and social science, thus keeping it from falling into 'disrepute.' This had a 'wholesome effect of theoretical purification,' but it went too far. By setting aside classical and Christian philosophy, it amounted to a 'confession that a science of human and social order did not exist.' Values became 'unquestioned axioms and hypotheses' which informed the scientific 'explanation of facts,' and the implication was that there were as many sciences as there were ideologies and periods of history. The result was the 'sinking of historical and political science into a morass of relativism.' Here entered the 'person of Max Weber' with whom this development 'ran to the end of its immanent logic' and who stood 'between the end and a new beginning' (pp. 4–6, 9–14).

Voegelin noted that for Weber a value-free science involved generalization through the use of ideal types and the search for causal relations. The basic purpose, however, was to enable someone, such as a politician, to calculate the probable consequences of certain value choices and actions. In this respect, Weber sought 'clarity about the world' in which he passionately participated as well as a way to transmit that clarity to others, and, in Voegelin's view, he was 'headed again on the road toward essence' and the 'search for truth.' His journey, however, was cut short by his assumption that the values, which were the 'ordering ideas of political action,' were ultimately based on a variety of '"demonic" decisions' that lay beyond rational discussion and the critical intervention of science and philosophy. For Voegelin, as for Strauss, Weber simply did not provide a sufficiently convincing case for politics to listen to science. Although his search for consequences indicated an awakening of the notion of 'responsibility' amidst the 'demonic disorder' of the age, this was not enough. His work, however, did imply something more. If not, Voegelin asserted, its 'grandeur' might be called into question and it would amount to little more than a kind of existentialism. Voegelin contended that Weber actually 'went much further' than it might seem on the surface.

According to Voegelin, Weber's whole conception of science 'assumed a social relation between the scientist and the politician, activated in the institution of a university, where the scientist as teacher will inform his students' about 'political reality' and thus change their perceptions and choices. Consequently, values, in a practical sense, that is, in the world of politics, might not be so 'demonically fixed' after all, and a teacher might be effective at least by 'indirection' or by evoking 'shame,' even if the student ultimately fell back on the 'ethics of intention.' This indicated that 'the rational conflict with the unquestionable [ideological] values of political intellectuals was inherent in his enterprise of an objective science of politics' and that 'the original conception of a value-free science was dissolving.' Weber recognized that the plurality of values in politics augured 'relativism' and that 'political science would be degraded to an apology for the dubious fancies of political intellectuals.'

Weber's escape, Voegelin claimed, was not only his image of the critical function of social science but his view of principles as facts in human history, as in the case of the Protestant ethic. He 'introduced them by the back door' by demonstrating that 'verities about order were factors in the order of reality' that could not be reduced to material circumstances, even though the time had not yet come when one could say that materialism was not a theory but a 'falsification of history' that only an 'ignoramus' would choose (pp. 14–19). For Voegelin, however, the failing of Weber was the weakness of his image of the social scientist's capacity for adjudicating among claims to ultimate values and thereby its weakness as an avenue of theoretical intervention into the world of politics.

Although, Voegelin argued, the whole idea of a value-free social science was at the 'point of disintegration' and a notion of a different kind of objective science was beginning to come into focus, Weber found himself unable to take the 'decisive step.' Despite his studies of religion, which pointedly omitted pre-Reformation Christianity, he did not admit the idea of 'a rational science of human and social order and especially natural law' which he could also have observed in Greek philosophy. To treat these as merely value choices would have required showing that the claims were unfounded, and this would have, in turn, forced him to become a metaphysician himself. In the end, what his position amounted to was an 'abolition of values' by reducing them to facts even though the particular values that he chose to study indicated his own sense of their cultural importance and his 'sensitiveness for excellence.' He was moving toward a restoration of science but was held back by his acceptance of the 'positivist taboo on metaphysics.' His image of 'rational action' and his belief that history was in the grip of increasing rationalization was in one sense the last vestige of Comte's philosophy, but there was a 'new tone' in that he saw it less as progress than disenchantment and de-divinization. This signaled 'his brotherhood in the sufferings of Nietzsche,' but he did not follow the latter into 'tragic revolt.' Weber actually 'saw the promised land but was not permitted to enter it,' yet in his work, in effect, 'positivism had come to an end, and the lines on which the restoration of political science would have to move became visible.' Weber's attribution of irrationality to religion and metaphysics was ripe for reversal and for a demonstration that the rationality of the modern age was in fact the real manifestation of irrationalism (pp. 21–22).

V

What again deserves emphasis is how much these accounts of Weber shared with theorists who embraced a very different philosophical and ideological perspective, such as those associated with the Frankfurt School. What overrode the differences among many of the émigrés was their common concern with establishing the cognitive authority of second-order discourse and vouchsafing its practical significance. For example, despite his ultimate disagreement with Weber, Strauss's insistence on the difference between philosophers and intellectuals was in many respects quite similar to that which Weber had advanced in his essays on the vocations of science and politics, as well as the impetus behind his methodological essays on objectivity and the heterogeneity of faces and values. So, one might again ask, what exactly, in the end, prompted Strauss and Voegelin to choose Weber as the archetypal social scientist?

Part of the issue was that Weber had, in his own life, consistently 'crossed the line' and played the roles of both political actor and 'scientist,' but one of Weber's principal concerns, as in the case of Strauss and Voegelin, was to find a way to mediate between scholarship and politics and to make the former authoritative in that relationship, through the medium of the university. Weber's distinctions between both science and politics and fact and value were parts of an attempt to undercut the political stance of his opponents as well as to separate them from a position of social influence, but his distinction was, paradoxically, in the service of getting politics and science back together on a sounder basis than that which had characterized the previous generation. Since what also agitated Strauss and Voegelin was the ascendancy of social science in the university and the displacement of philosophy, Weber was in effect a direct rival in the sphere of the intellect. There was also an ideological divide. For both Strauss and Voegelin, Weber was in many respects 'the quintessential liberal' whose philosophical doctrines and political practices, they imagined, opened the way to Hitler. The most important dimension of the tension, however, derived from their concern that the kind of intellectual authority posited by Weber was too flaccid. Weber had both limited faith in the capacity of scholars to convince people of the ability of philosophy to achieve transcendent truth and severe doubts about the possibility of the practical effects of philosophical doctrines, at least in his time. What most distinctly drew these critics to Weber was not some abstract issue regarding philosophical truth and the separation of facts and values but rather the practical issue of the relationship between social science and politics.

Since much of what Strauss and Voegelin had to say about Weber was based on his methodological essays, it is important to understand the character of these essays, written in the decade between 1904 and 1913, and exactly what Weber was doing when he wrote them. Despite analyses such as those of Strauss and Voegelin which characterize Weber as absorbed with methodological issues, he was hardly, by nature or trade, a methodologist and epistemologist. And to suggest, as Sheldon Wolin has, that his methodological work was a displacement of political passion is simply to misconstrue his biography.[7] These essays constituted a rhetoric of inquiry, justifying both his substantive research and its relationship to public life. Weber was very aware of this legitimating function, but while many of the neo-Kantian philosophers embraced this *ex post facto* role of metatheory and saw their task as explaining how knowledge in the empirical sciences is possible, Weber hardly viewed this as his mission. It was in the context of the *Methodenstreit* and *Werturteilsstreit* that these essays were written. These disputes involved, in part, a conflict between Weber and both the Historical School and classical economists about the nature and possibility of generalization in social science, and they were also part of his attempt to reconcile the scientific demand for empirical verification with *Verstehen* or the process of understanding meaningful action. But, above all, they represented his position in a debate about the practical implications of empirical science for policy choices in politics. The later essays on the vocations of science and politics were, in many respects, an extension of this discussion, as was clearer to competing émigré commentators than to American readers. While some of the ideas of neo-Kantian epistemology were among the premises that informed Weber's work and perspective, he regarded epistemology, as a discourse and activity, with suspicion and as something that had in part initiated the *Methodenstreit* and inhibited progress in empirical research.

Weber entered this discussion with reluctance. He was neither recounting the ideas that had informed his research nor laying down foundational principles for the pursuit of further work. He designated 'epistemological investigations' as a form of 'dilettantism' and 'embellishment,' and even a 'methodological pestilence,' which led social scientists astray and as a realm in which they were poorly equipped to participate. Such discussions, he argued, tended to draw attention away from '*substantive* problems,' and while there might be some value in 'self-reflection on the means that have *proven* to be valuable in actual research,' it was 'no more a foundation for fruitful research than is knowledge of anatomy a condition for the ability to walk "correctly".'[8] Whatever his preferences, Weber could hardly avoid such discussion, since he moved in an intellectual universe where metatheory was becoming the province of philosophy, which in turn had fundamentally intruded into disputes about the identity and practice of social science and defined the terms of discourse about such matters. If he could be perceived (and received in the USA) as the paradigmatic methodologist, it was by default and simply a consequence of his ability to dominate any discussion. But the crucial issue is what he was about when he emphasized the heterogeneity of fact and value.

Weber did explicitly maintain that there was a 'logical distinction between "existential knowledge", i.e., knowledge of what "is", and "normative knowledge", i.e., knowledge of what "should be",' which rendered claims about these matters 'absolutely heterogeneous.' Unlike American political scientists who claimed that to be scientific entailed excluding all nonempirical language, Weber's basic claim was not about linguistics but about confusing two distinct forms of practice – that is, mixing science and politics when the issue was the relationship between them. Within the category of values, Weber subsumed some very different things – evaluative statements, judgments, interests, ideals, moral and cultural perspectives, and so on – but what was common to these was that there was no way in which differences between them could be definitively adjudicated by second-order practices. Their validity, he claimed, was a matter of faith, and 'there is no (rational or empirical) scientific procedure of any kind whatsoever which can provide us with a decision here.' In the case of empirically observed facts, in contrast, validity is a matter of empirical truth. It is only, however, when we discern the rhetorical character of Weber's argument that we can grasp what was involved.[9]

First of all, he was calling attention to what was becoming the case, that science and politics, and the institutions and practices that attended each, were becoming distinct realms. And he had reasons for arguing that these realms should be distinct: he insisted that if science were not distinct, it would lack credible authority. He wanted to combat the ideologues who spoke from the academic podium and made political claims under the guise of science. As much as he sought the independence of science from the political influences that had characterized the German university, he very much wanted, in turn, to free politics from certain philosophical influences. Second, while Weber recognized that there had been periods of history marked by considerable homogeneity in society and consensual standards of normative validity, this was not the case in contemporary plural society. At the same time, exceptionally, the practice of science was becoming a community in which normal standards of validity *were* possible. Third, there was the issue of *who* was the arbiter of validity? If science and politics were becoming heterogeneous practices, then there could be no effective standards of validity that second-order discourse could impose on political life. But only when these spheres were analytically and descriptively distinguished was it possible to confront seriously the issue of the actual and feasible relationship between them, a relationship which Weber believed was not clearly perceived and understood.

It was also clear to Weber that, while social science might be relatively separate from politics and capable of agreeing on certain norms of empirical judgment, it was not, and probably could not be, ideologically uniform. The validity of causal and descriptive claims could be assessed, but the logical and epistemological means did not extend to guaranteeing an 'absolutely "objective" scientific analysis of social phenomena.' There were always presuppositions, for example, in the choice of what was studied. Even the choice of science as a value and vocation was 'subjective.' The value orientation of science was endemic not only because one could not prevent all overlap bween politics and science, or values and facts, but because every science required that experience be conceptually rendered. Since concepts were culturally and historically contingent and since science involved a selection of facts in terms of interests, concerns, and problems, that is, 'knowledge from *particular points of view*,' the two realms were always intersecting.[10]

The ethical neutrality of science and the distinction between fact and value did not really seem to imply a great distance between science and politics by the time Weber was done, just as Voegelin suggested. Values informed scientific choices, and the logical and empirical claims of science could predict the intended and unintended consequences of value decisions, indicate the means to ends, describe existing values and the relationship between them, estimate which means and ends were viable, and provide reasons for choices. How, exactly, science could be brought to bear on politics and values, and how science could escape distortion or delegitimation by politics was, nevertheless, something for which Weber had no definite answer, apart from suggesting that it might happen in the course of effective pedagogy in the university. He insisted, however, that the problem was, in the end, a practical matter that admitted no theoretical or metatheoretical solution, and it became the task of individuals such as Mannheim to engage the pragmatics of this relational issue in more detail. What most agitated Weber's critics, who often attacked Mannheim as well, was that his position did not provide a cognitive authority to overcome the gap between scientific rationality and ideologically charged political calculation.

On a superficial level, the arguments of Strauss and Voegelin were representative of much of the general reaction to Weber's addresses on science and politics, but their probing critical encounters with Weber's discussion of values provides an opportunity to observe how a rhetoric of inquiry, that is, a third-order discourse devoted to legitimating a form of second-order practice, could become abstracted and transformed into a philosophical problem and argument which in turn became the basis of other rhetorics of inquiry, both defending and criticizing positivist notions of the separation of fact and value and of science and politics. Once abstracted from its context and motifs, Weber's methodological or epistemological claims were free to be debated, as they have been not only by those who argued that such a distinction between fact and value is impossible, but also by those who argued that it neglects the critical dimension of social science, and by philosophers such as Richard Rudner or Ernst Nagel who endorsed what they took to be the claim that a credible social science must be based on a divorce between science and values.[11] Strauss and Voegelin, in contrast, were close enough to the context of Weber's arguments to know that it was the practical efficacy of second-order discourse that was really at stake in these discussions; and this knowledge governed their own rhetoric in appropriating him as object lesson and partner in their own theoretical projects.

Notes

1 John G. Gunnell (1993) *The Descent of Political Theory: The Genealogy of an American Vocation.* Chicago, IL: University of Chicago Press.
2 For a recent overview of the extensive literature, see Colin Loader and David Kettler (2002) *Karl Mannheim's Sociology as Political Education.* New Brunswick, NJ, and London: Transaction.
3 For a fuller discussion of these issues, see John G. Gunnell (1998) *The Orders of Discourse: Philosophy, Social Science, and Politics.* Lanham, MD: Rowman & Littlefield.
4 For a discussion of these issues, see Thomas Burger (1976) *Max Weber's Theory of Concept Formation.* Durham, NC: Duke University Press. Toby E. Huff (1984) *Max Weber and the Methodology of the Social Sciences.* New Brunswick, NJ: Transaction. Jay A. Ciaffa (1998) *Max Weber and the Problem of Value Free Social Science.* London: Associated University Presses.
5 Leo Strauss (1953) *Natural Right and History.* Chicago, IL: University of Chicago Press.
6 Eric Voegelin (1953) *The New Science of Politics.* Chicago, IL: University of Chicago Press.

7 Sheldon S. Wolin (1981) 'Max Weber: Legitimation, Method, and the Politics of Theory', *Political Theory* 9: 401–442.

8 Max Weber (1975) *Rascher and Knies: The Logical Problems of Historical Economics*, ed. Guy Oakes, pp. 14–15. New York: Free Press.

9 Max Weber (1948) *The Methodology of the Social Sciences*, ed. Edward A. Shils and Henry A. Finch. Glencoe, IL: Free Press, pp. 19, 51, 53–60.

10 Ibid., pp. 72–80. Some of the relevant essays by Weber include 'Rocher's Historical Method' (1905), 'Knies on the Problem of Irrationality' (1905, 1906), 'The Logic of the Cultural Science' (1906), 'Critique of Stammler' (1907), and 'On Some Categories of Interpretive Sociology' (1913).

11 Richard Rudner (1966) *Philosophy of Social Science*. Englewood Cliffs, NJ: Prentice-Hall. Ernest Nagel (1961) *The Structure of Science*. New York: Harcourt Brace & World.

10 'Leaving everything as it is'

Political inquiry after Wittgenstein (2013)

In light of the fact that Ludwig Wittgenstein did not directly address the practices of social and political inquiry, one might reasonably claim that it would be a *tour de force* to discuss the implications of his work for these disciplines and that it would be even further afield to suggest that this work is relevant for a consideration of a concept such as justice. Despite the importance of Hanna Pitkin's *Wittgenstein and Justice* (1972) in pointing to various dimensions of the relevance of Wittgenstein's work for political theory, the book did not actually focus on Wittgenstein's limited reference to the concept of justice. Pitkin's discussion was constrained by issues that, during the 1960s, had defined the subfield of political theory in American political science. Wittgenstein addressed the concept of justice in terms of his demand for achieving 'clarity' in producing accounts of various linguistic regions. This required rendering interpretations that were faithful to the indigenous meaning of the social practices involved and that avoided describing and evaluating them in terms of the *Weltbild* of the interpreter. In his criticism of how James Frazer, in the *Golden Bough*, had distorted the meaning of the exotic social practices he studied, Wittgenstein stated that, as either philosophers or ethnologists, 'our only task is to be just' and 'not to set up new parties – or creeds' (2005: §309). This attitude in no way implied an uncritical approach to the subject matter but only that it should be fairly represented. Wittgenstein's admonition raises an issue that contemporary political philosophy and social science have been increasingly reluctant to confront directly but that nevertheless is at the heart of these enterprises and their historical development as well as generic to social inquiry as a whole. This is their *practical* and *cognitive* relationship to their subject matter.

Although today there is a considerable conceptual and methodological distance between political theory and empirical political science, a distance that often seems quite acceptable to practitioners in both spheres, this division is actually a quite recent phenomenon and affectation and is largely a consequence of the evolution of academic discourse during the last half of the twentieth century. Recent work in the history of the social sciences (for example, Ross, 1991; Gunnell, 2004) has made it very clear that the origins of these fields were in reform movements and moral philosophy and were particularly focused on issues relating to democracy and social justice. The embrace of scientism in social science was initially not a turn away from normative concerns but a consequence of seeking epistemic authority for practical judgments about social practices and policies. It is a grave mistake to conceive of political theory and political science as deriving from separate vocations and traditions, yet while much of political science seeks to identify itself with the lineage of scientific naturalism, there is a deeply embedded assumption that contemporary academic political philosophy is the continuation of a tradition that began with the Greeks and is in a special position to make normative claims about matters such as justice and rights. Each sphere of inquiry seems willing to accept the self-ascribed identity and genealogy of the other, but both are in danger of becoming self-referencing discourses that reside in limbo between philosophy and politics. More important, however, is the fact that their absorption with the problem of their particular intellectual identity has inhibited confronting issues that are definitive of the human sciences as a whole.

My purpose is not simply to bring Wittgenstein's conception of philosophy to bear on various issues in these fields but to argue that *his vision of philosophy is, in effect, a vision of social inquiry* and one that is particularly important at a time when an interpretive social science seems to remain more an idea than a practice and when so many theorists are turning, or returning, to various forms of naturalism, such as cognitive neuroscience, as a ground of explanation and judgment. This article is devoted neither to a discussion of the secondary philosophical literature on Wittgenstein nor to a critical analysts of the reception of his work among political and social theorists. It is sufficient to note that despite instances of astute readings and applications of his work, this reception has more typically involved either seeking support for a variety of prior agendas or characterizing him as a progenitor of modern relativism and as a danger to the search for truth in both science and morals. Both approaches distance us from understanding his work. There is, however, one book from which a statement of my particular argument cannot be detached, even though the book is in some respects dated and has often become a surrogate for a direct confrontation with Wittgenstein on matters relating to social inquiry.

Philosophy and social science

More than a half-century ago Peter Winch addressed the significance of the later Wittgenstein for thinking about *The Idea of a Social Science* (1958) and for challenging the positivist account of the methodological unity of science, which at that point dominated both social science and the philosophy of social science. What was unique about his book, however, but often neglected, was the fact that, as the subtitle (*and its Relation to Philosophy*) indicated, he based his argument on what he claimed to be the logical symmetry between philosophy and social science. He stated that:

to be clear about the nature of philosophy and to be clear about the nature of the social studies amount to the same thing. For any worthwhile study of society must be philosophical in character and any worthwhile philosophy must be concerned with the nature of human society.

(Winch, 1958: 3)

Although my purpose here is not to engage in a detailed discussion of Winch's work, I take it as what Wittgenstein referred to as a 'signpost,' even though, as he noted, a signpost does not tell one exactly how to proceed (2009, §§85, 87). Winch's principal point was that philosophy and social science are both devoted to providing accounts of conceptually pre-constituted and intrinsically meaningful phenomena. Part of the confusion that attended responses to his book stemmed from his use of the term 'philosophy' to refer both to the academic field and to what he spoke of, somewhat metaphorically, as 'metaphysics' and 'epistemology,' that is, constitutive theoretical assumptions about the nature of social phenomena and about the criteria for knowing such phenomena. Such assumptions, he argued, were internal to the practice of any science, but in the case of the social sciences, they were also elements of the phenomena that were the object of investigation. Winch, drawing on elements of Wittgenstein's later work, such as the emphasis on rule-following, wished to indicate its implications for challenging how philosophers had conceived of social science, but although he stressed the logical symmetry between philosophy and social science, he did not explicitly claim that the *Investigations* presented an image of philosophy as a form of social inquiry. This article is intended as a prolegomenon to a more extended defense of that claim. Wittgenstein noted that calling his kind of investigation 'philosophy' could be misleading, because it was really one of 'the heirs of the subject which used to be called philosophy.' Philosophy, as he viewed and pursued it, was the investigation of the concepts that informed human speech and action, and, as in the case of much social inquiry, the purpose was often critical and therapeutic, both with respect to various conceptions of inquiry as well as to the subject matter. Although he denied that 'philosophy is ethnology,' he stated that it was essential to 'look at things from an ethnological point of view,' which requires 'taking up a position outside, an interpretive position, so as to be able to see things more objectively' (Wittgenstein, 1958: 28; 2005: 37).

Leaving everything as it is

Winch also did not directly confront the problem of the practical relationship between social science and its subject matter, but, taking his cue from Wittgenstein, he stated that social science 'left everything as it was' (Winch, 1958: 103). What Winch meant by this phrase was far from clear, and this was in part because Wittgenstein's remark that 'philosophy leaves everything as it is' was already cryptic and controversial. The remark, however, is the axis of my argument. The spirit of the remark might seem to go against the grain of the past and present motives and motifs of much of the literature of political philosophy and social science as well as to conflict with what were often Wittgenstein's own therapeutic concerns. Consequently, it is important to explicate the remark, place it in the context of his later work, and elaborate on its significance for thinking about some general issues that are central to the identity of all forms of social inquiry that investigate discursive or conventional objects (Gunnell, 1998), These issues include: *the nature of social phenomena; the cognitive and practical relationship between social inquiry and its subject matter; the concepts of interpretation and representation; the problem of knowledge of other minds; and what is involved in making descriptive and normative judgments about the subject matter.* Many critics have focused on what they take to be the philosophically conservative and minimalist implications of Wittgenstein's remark, while others have suggested that the remark appears somewhat paradoxical in light of his persistently critical attitude, his dedication to combating dogmatism, and his claims that he was exposing nonsense; releasing us from a picture that held us captive; destroying houses of cards; and showing the fly the way out of the fly-bottle (2009: §§115, 118, 309), What, then, exactly, is the meaning of this remark, and what relevance does it have for thinking about the vocations of philosophy and social inquiry?

G.E.M. Anscombe translated the remark (Wittgenstein, 2009: §124) '*Die Philosophie darf der tatsächlichen Gebrauch der Sprache in keiner Weise antasten, sie kann ihn am Ende also nur beschrieben*' as 'Philosophy may in no way interfere with the actual use of language; it can in the end only describe it.' 'May' and 'actual' as translations are ambiguous, and although in the revised edition, Hacker and Schulte substituted 'must' for 'may,' the basic sense and spirit of the remark might be yet better conveyed by the somewhat freer rendering: 'Philosophy is in no position to interfere with the practical application of language; it therefore in the end can only describe it.' Wittgenstein then went on to say: 'For it cannot give it any foundation either. It leaves everything as it is.' Wittgenstein never denied a critical role for philosophy, and, despite attributions to the contrary, neither he nor Winch, nor Thomas Kuhn (1962), said that one view of the world was as valid as any other but only that there was no neutral transcendental philosophical basis for choice and that judgment is always situated in the discourse of some practice and the particularities that attend the contexts ranging from science to morals. For Winch, as for Wittgenstein, doing justice to the subject matter sometimes entailed giving even 'the devil his due' (Winch, 1996). Wittgenstein and Winch are still today used as poster-boys by philosophers and social theorists, across the ideological spectrum, who conjure up the specter of relativism, but fear of relativism in these instances is less the manifestation of a genuine worry about the loss of criteria of truth in various practices, ranging from science to politics, than the residue of a repressed fear that philosophy and social science will lose the putative authority to either underwrite or call into question those criteria (Gunnell, 1998). Once it is recognized that there is no philosophical answer to the issue of the relationship between these practices and their subject matter, it is necessary to confront directly the actual character of that relationship.

Wittgenstein and philosophy

Wittgenstein claimed that there was no second-order philosophy (2009: §121), that is, no meta-philosophy, because philosophy was itself a meta-practice devoted to investigating other practices. As such, it was an inherently self-reflective enterprise. Because in the course of confronting the issue of its relationship to the practices that it studied, it could not avoid thinking about its own identity. While natural science usually leaves questions about the basic nature of its activity to philosophers of science, philosophy, as conceived by Wittgenstein and including the philosophy of science itself, cannot do so and remain authentic. And the same can be said of social inquiry. The history of institutionalized forms of such inquiry has been marked by perennial crises of identity, and although these have often been directly a consequence of their insecurity about their status as a science or about some other form of epistemic privilege, this insecurity is also rooted in the fact that these fields have characteristically sought to achieve practical purchase. The history of social inquiry is replete with examples of these fields attempting to reform themselves in order to better relate, practically as well as cognitively, to their subject matter. Wittgenstein noted that the first task of philosophers is to cure many ills of their own and that philosophy is in large part a matter of 'working on oneself. On one's own interpretation. On one's way of seeing things' (1984: 16). When he sometimes talked about philosophical problems disappearing, about philosophy finding peace, and about being able to stop doing philosophy (for example, 2009: §§109, 133), he was not talking about philosophy stepping away from problems that it might encounter in the course of its exploration of various practical language regions. He was referring to the kinds of problems that philosophy had typically and historically set for itself, such as determining how it could demonstrate the existence of the external world and what was involved in knowledge about the world. Philosophy had, as Winch indicated, presented an image of itself as a kind of master-science. This image was often rooted in philosophy's wish either to vouchsafe practices such as science and morality or to claim a title to these practices. Wittgenstein argued that such metaphysical ventures obliterated the difference between what he referred to as 'empirical and conceptual investigations' (1967: §458), by which he meant differences between fields such as natural science and philosophy.

When Wittgenstein spoke about philosophy leaving everything as it is and when he sometimes insisted on eschewing explanation and rejecting theorizing in general in favor of description (for example, 2009: §§109, 126), he was almost always distinguishing his endeavor either from explanations in natural science or from philosophical theories such as realism. He explicitly counted interpreting meaning in language as a form of explanation (*Erklärung*). He certainly was propounding what can reasonably be labeled a theory of linguistic meaning and what was entailed in studying it, and because he claimed that such meaning was peculiar to creatures that have 'mastered a language' and embedded it in 'this complicated form of life [*Lebensform*],' he was, in effect, advancing an account of the nature of social phenomena (2009: *PPF*, §1). With respect to his therapeutic concerns, it is clear that he did not intend to leave philosophy as it was, and the change that he wished to produce was the recognition that the task was one of understanding and interpreting the meaning of concepts and the practices in which they were manifest and that this entailed first clarifying the concepts of 'meaning' and 'understanding' themselves (2009, §3). At times he agonized a great deal about whether his work could, would or should have an impact on its subject matter. Following his remark about leaving everything as it is, he referred, as an example, to the philosophical analysis of mathematics (2009, §125), and from his earliest to his latest work, Wittgenstein was involved in criticizing attempts to achieve a philosophical foundation for mathematics and in exposing the Platonic ideas that had infiltrated the practice of the field. But it was not mathematics alone that lacked any external philosophical or logical foundation of certainty and that was open to criticism. The same could be said of religion, politics and other practices. Much of Wittgenstein's last work was devoted to psychology, and he had already spoken about the 'barrenness of psychology' and about how the field's 'experimental methods' were infused with '*conceptual confusion*' (2009: *PPF*, §371). These remarks could very well have been, and today still can be, applied to much of social science as a whole. There was, however, still an obvious ambiguity in claiming that philosophy left everything as it is, but, at the same time, in making the kinds of critical judgments that characterized much of his work.

When he spoke of philosophy leaving everything as it is, Wittgenstein meant that the claims of philosophy and changes in the conceptual and theoretical repertoire of philosophy, do not, by virtue of their performance, either transform or ground the subject matter of philosophy. The implication of his remark was, in effect, to *problematize* the relationship between philosophy and its subject matter. He was resisting the imperialism of logic such as that manifested in the Vienna Circle and in his own earlier work, and this resistance was symbolized in his demand to leave the 'slippery ice' of abstract logic and return to the 'rough ground' of practical language where one could gain a footing (2009: §107). But if philosophy, in the sense he indicated, left everything as it is, it is necessary to grasp the differentiating criterion that distinguishes those fields that do *not* leave everything as it is. His answer to this question was also his basic answer to the difference between natural and social science, and it explains to a large extent what he meant when he so often distinguished his work from that of natural science.

When the basic concepts of natural science change, some dimension of its conception of its subject matter, that is, what is meant by the 'world' or 'nature,' changes; and the same can be said of religion and other, what I will refer to as, *first-order world-presenting* or *world-constructive* practices. This is neither a metaphysical claim nor a claim about the inevitability of perspectivity but rather simply a matter of recognizing that after natural science has given us an account, for example, of motion, or, alternatively, after religion has claimed to reveal the word of god, we cannot judge these accounts by comparing them with motion or the word of god but only, as Kuhn argued, with some prior or competing theoretically incommensurable account. The conceptual constitution of the subject matter of practices such as natural science and religion is internal to those practices, that is, we might say that there is no gap between theory and fact apart from that opened up within these discourses. Wittgenstein's work has been one of the principal impetuses behind the critique of various forms of what is typically designated as representational philosophy and its correspondence theory of truth, what Richard Rorty (1979) characterized as the traditional quest to specify how language and thought can mirror nature. This kind of philosophy was marked by a pretension to be able to speak about truth and reality above and beyond the criteria operative in any substantive form of inquiry. However, there is inevitably some potential confusion, or at least irony, in portraying Wittgenstein as rejecting representationalism, because he viewed the task of philosophy as one of representing.

Wittgenstein was certainly concerned with the issue of how language was applied to the world, and thereby gained meaning, but, in his view, not all linguistic uses, strictly speaking, were representational. 'Representation,' in all its typical contexts and uses, and in Wittgenstein's work, presupposes the conceptual autonomy of the object that is represented. One might be tempted to say that Michelangelo's depiction of god on the ceiling of the Sistine Chapel is a representation of god or that Einstein's special theory of relativity is a representation of the physical world, but this requires qualification. There are no external criteria for judging such representativeness. These are, respectively, actually *presentations* of god and the physical world. Representation is, however, at the core of the vocations of philosophy and social inquiry, just as it is for landscape and portrait painters, legislators, lawyers and so on, no matter how they construe, and how well they undertake, the business of representing. In the case of philosophy, as conceived by Wittgenstein, and in fields ranging from history and social science to literary criticism, *re-presentation* takes the form of *interpretation* directed toward discursive objects. Wittgenstein claimed that the basic task of philosophy was to achieve *clarity* (for example, 2009: §133) about such objects, and he likened his philosophical approach to the conduct of descriptive natural history, making sketches of a landscape, or composing an album (2009: 3, §§3, 25, 123, 415). The subject matter of philosophy and social inquiry, what Wittgenstein referred to as the 'language-games' associated with *'forms of life,'* is, as he noted, 'given' in the sense that their meaning is not, at least in the first instance, a product of interpretation (2009: *PPF,* §345).

Interpretation and the social sciences

Since at least the 1960s, but as far back as Max Weber, various versions of the idea of an interpretive social science, often advanced as an alternative or complement to naturalistic images of inquiry, have surfaced in the literature of both the social sciences and the philosophy of social science, but they have not, even in the case of Winch, been clearly explicated. And it would be difficult to point to cases in which these versions have actually, or convincingly, been put into practice. The problem has in part been a failure to recognize that interpretation is not a particular method of social inquiry. The current propensity in fields such as political science to parse empirical/quantitative and interpretive/qualitative forms of inquiry fails to recognize that *all* social inquiry is necessarily interpretive and representative, because its subject matter is conceptually autonomous. Consequently, both cognitive and practical tensions potentially arise between these practices and their subject matter. Wittgenstein, like Kuhn and Winch, recognized that the only resolution of such fundamental conflicts, either within or between practices, is ultimately through 'persuasion' (1969: §§83, 262). To speak of this as a problem of relativism, as a problem for which there is a philosophical solution, is to assume that there is some external order of discourse that possesses indefeasible criteria for adjudicating such conflicts, but relativism is simply the nightmare haunting the dream-world of representational philosophy as well as its post-modern shadow that suggests that interpretation, so to speak, 'goes all the way down.' In social inquiry today, we are, however, often faced with a choice between mentalism, the assumption that meaning in language and action is an expression of mental states such as intention, and interpretivism, the claim that meaning is an endowment of interpretation. Wittgenstein rejected both positions and situated meaning in language and action itself.

Although Wittgenstein's work has often been interpreted as a form of linguistic idealism, he actually maintained that both the world and language ('grammar') were autonomous. It was simply that the world, either physical or social, did not dictate the language applied to it, that is, the manner in which it is presented or represented, and that the world is only manifest in the medium of language (2009: §§371, 372). Wittgenstein used the word 'grammar' to refer to both the subject matter of philosophy and the practice of philosophical analysis, and this parallel can be extended to social inquiry and its subject matter. What is involved is language describing language and conceptualizing concepts. The autonomy of grammar signifies the autonomy of the conventions that are constitutive of social objects in general, which are the subject matter of social science, and, in two respects, it entails the autonomy of social inquiry. While the discursive character of social phenomena distinguishes them from those of natural science, it also follows that social inquiry and its subject matter are each conceptually distinct.

If the task of philosophy and social inquiry is to reconstruct or re-conceptualize, that is, interpret and represent, social phenomena, the inevitable question is that of how, in principle, this can be accomplished. Wittgenstein's theory of language and meaning entailed an epistemology that included a crucial distinction between what he referred to as understanding (*Verstehen*) and interpretation (*Deutung*), which in many ways paralleled his more pointed and extended discussion of 'aspect-seeing' and the difference between 'seeing' and 'seeing-as' (2009: *PPF*, §§121–222). Understanding is what takes place within a practice, and interpretation is a rendition of that understanding. This distinction is a significant factor in locating the difference between Wittgenstein and philosophers, ranging from W.V.O. Quine to postmodernists, who claim not only that meaning is a product of interpretation but that there is an essential indeterminacy in meaning that requires 'radical interpretation,' that is, supplying meaning. For Wittgenstein, meaning was no more essentially indeterminate, either within a practice or with respect to claims about a practice, than all claims to knowledge can be subject to doubt. While the language of natural science *does* go all the way down, the language of social science comes up abruptly, cognitively and practically, against the language and practices of its subject matter and against the problem of representing that subject matter. There are, indeed, similarities between, on the one hand, Wittgenstein's claim that any interpretation of a rule might be construed as in accord with the rule and, on the other hand, various contemporary claims about the 'undecidability' involved in interpretation, but there are also fundamental differences. Maybe the most frequently noted instance of Wittgenstein's discussion of interpretation involves his claim about the infinite regress in attempting to specify the meaning of a rule by an interpretation of the rule. This was made famous by Saul Kripke's commentary (1982) in which he claimed that Wittgenstein's account led to a skeptical paradox about when an action was in conformity with a rule, but Wittgenstein's ultimate point was that the meaning of a rule is not, in the first instance, a function of its interpretation but of the 'technique' involved in the practice of understanding and following it (2009: §§197–200). Meaning was not something that could be determined by an individual, but, despite Kripke's conclusion, it was also not something decided by a community. At one point, Wittgenstein spoke of a *contrat social*, but he meant this to be much like J-J. Rousseau's. It was not an actual agreement but rather what might be called a tacit consensus, or what Wittgenstein referred to as agreement in 'judgments' (2009: §242) arising from being initiated into, and participating in, a practice. Normativity was already embedded in the practices that were the object of inquiry or, as Winch put it with respect to the case of social science, there are two sets of rules – those of the social scientist and those of the social actor. The main point, which Wittgenstein repeatedly emphasized, was that interpretation is always a supervenient claim, which he described as 'hanging in the air' along with what it interprets and which also does not give it any foundation. It is a *reconstructive* rather than a *constructive* activity. This general epistemology, however, posed the more practical methodological issue of exactly how discursive phenomena were to be interpreted and represented.

Methods and therapies

The problem was that of how it is possible to describe in a manner that is, as Wittgenstein put it, 'just,' and that does not reify the interpreter's *Weltanschauung* and impose judgments that reflect the interpreter's own ontology. Although Wittgenstein maintained that 'language-games' were the subject matter of philosophy, language-game was a categorical, taxonomic or 'family-resemblance' concept rather than a natural-kind concept. But language-games were also what he advanced as the basic means of representation and of solving the paradox involved in describing and thereby conveying the meaning of concepts. In one sense, as Weber had emphasized in his famous essay on 'Objectivity,' the facts of social science are, of course, constituted, or at least construed, within the language of social science, but Weber also stressed the sense in which the facts of social science, unlike those of natural science, are also pre-constituted in the language of social actors. Weber's answer to the question of how social science could represent was to recommend the vehicle of the 'ideal-type' and the manner in which varieties of these types could be invented and adapted to particular interpretive problems and changing situations and how they inhibited tendencies toward reification in the language of inquiry. Wittgenstein's answer was strikingly similar.

Wittgenstein noted that in philosophy 'there is not a single method, though there are indeed methods, different therapies, as it were' (2009: §133). It is, however, very important to note that it was in the remarks preceding his statement about philosophy leaving everything as it is that he first introduced 'the concept of a perspicuous [or synoptic or surveyable] representation,' which he claimed was 'of fundamental significance for us. It earmarks the form of account we give, the way we look at things' (2009: §§122–126). He worried a great deal about the status of this concept. At one point, he wondered if it was a *Weltanschauung*, but although he finally concluded that it did fit this general category, he later took pains to distinguish his position from that of Oswald Spengler, as well as Goethe, who both sought to locate some essence underlying what an investigator might construe as similar phenomena. For Wittgenstein, the perspicuous representation was a constructed heuristic. It was a device for encouraging individuals to see something that had not been at first apparent to them, and, as in the case of his extended discussion of 'aspect-seeing,' it was part of a distinctly interpretive endeavor. For Wittgenstein, such ideal typifications might be something as specific as his parable of the 'builders' that he used to demonstrate how a primitive language might operate (2009: §2), or it might be as generically conceived as the concept of a language-game itself, but it was constructed for the purpose of achieving clarity about a discursive object and representing its meaning (2009: §§67, 122, 130, 131). What he consistently and emphatically warned against was the tendency to confuse the means of representation with the object of representation, to conflate the language-game as a perspicuous representation with the language-game that was being interpreted. This kind of confusion led to such things as asking if the meter stick in Paris was a meter long or whether the sample of red in the color chart was actually red (2009: §§50–53, 104). In the social sciences, a similar kind of common mistake, which had been recognized by Weber, is still sometimes evident in the application of approaches ranging from systems analysis to versions of rational choice theory, in which there has been a tendency to allow the framework of analysis to function as if it were a presentation of reality. A perspicuous representation was a basis of comparison, what Wittgenstein referred to as exaggerated 'paradigmata' created in response to, and directed toward solving, a particular interpretive and representational problem and finding a discursive tool for communicating the meaning to others. Kuhn's use of 'paradigm' was very similar. A paradigm was not an element of science but a tool for characterizing and representing elements of science.

What often seems to be the thorniest epistemological problem in the theory and practice of social inquiry, and particularly attending the idea of interpretive inquiry, is that of how to access and assess the meaning of human speech and action if meaning resides in the minds of actors. This problem of other minds or of how to account for what people are thinking has perennially plagued claims about what would constitute an interpretive social science. From St. Augustine, as Wittgenstein noted (2009: §1), to recent philosophers as diverse in some ways as John Searle and Jerry Fodor (1975), it has been assumed that language is a vehicle for the expression of ontologically prior thought. Consequently, much of social inquiry, including social science, intellectual history and political theory, has set for itself the problem of discerning or inferring the intentions, emotions, beliefs, preferences and attitudes that inform outward behavior and its textual and institutional artifacts. Mental phenomena are treated like hypothetical entities that cannot be directly perceived and must be extrapolated from observational evidence.

This dilemma has often ended in stark choices between positions such as intuitionism and behaviorism, but, at the same time, at least from Winch's work to more recent claims about interpretive social science, a basic answer to the problem has been consonant with Wittgenstein's argument about the public character of linguistic meaning. It is claimed that because intentionality and purpose are expressed in a public language, they are, at least in a secondary manner, manifest and accessible. This position, however, still tends often to assume the basic autonomy and priority of thought, and we are still left with the theoretical problem of knowing other minds, which is crucial both for the practice of inquiry and for specifying what is involved in social actors understanding one another and sharing meanings. This position also leads to practical problems in the conduct of inquiry. Historians of political thought, for example, as different in many respects as Leo Strauss and Quentin Skinner, continue to maintain that, in the end, interpretation is a matter of somehow divining the ideas behind textual expression. One might argue that whether meaning is viewed as in the mind or in language and action is not significant, but the mind-first view has the effect of distracting investigation from words and deeds and of encouraging claims – often shaky ones – about ideas as the source of meaning. Although the emphasis on the public character of language has been important, its full implications have not been sufficiently examined.

Mind, language and meaning

There is a common type of psychological experiment that is sometimes referred to as the Sally/Ann scenario. This often involves spectators watching a staged drama or puppet show in which a child is playing with a toy that the child hides before temporarily leaving the room. In the meanwhile, another child comes into the room, finds the toy, and, before leaving, hides it elsewhere. When the first child returns, spectators are asked where the child will look for the toy. The results seem to indicate that while adults will of course typically say that the child will look for the toy where it had been originally hidden, young children are likely to say that the returning child will look where the toy has actually been placed. There have been two basic psychological/philosophical explanations of this so-called 'mind-reading' ability on the part of adults. One is the 'theory/theory' account, which holds that humans have an innate ability for discerning the thoughts of others but that it is not fully developed until about the age of six. The primary alternative contenders are various forms of simulation theory, which claim that humans have an intrinsic capacity for empathy and 'walking in another's shoes' (shades of Adam Smith) as well as for introspection and extrapolating their own inclinations to others – or that maybe, like certain monkeys, human brains contain mirror neurons. So what would Ludwig say?

I suggest that a Wittgensteinian answer to this problem would be along the lines of his claims about how language acquisition is predicated on initiation into the language-game of naming, much like Helen Keller's epiphany at the water pump. In the case of the Sally/Ann experiment, what might explain the mistake of the young children is that they have not really learned the game of hiding. Despite what Wittgenstein noted as the many and diverse uses of mental concepts, which share only a family resemblance rather than a common referent such as a neurological process, what we typically mean by 'consciousness' and 'thinking,' despite all the functional similarities with other creatures, involves the possession of highly developed symbolic capacities and the sharing of a complex language. It is the participatory sharing of conventions that enables one to understand meaning and interpret it. In this sense, it is not only animals, as Wittgenstein specifically pointed out, that – we might be inclined to say – are not thinking subjects but maybe young children who are not yet full participants in the language-games of their culture. Anyone familiar with young children realizes, for example, that they have not learned the art of keeping their language and thoughts to themselves, and, as Wittgenstein pointed out, concealing one's thoughts presupposes that they once were not concealed. When asked what one is thinking, there is no alternative to language in making a reply, and no more than in the case of sensation is it a matter of describing, in a phenomenal language, some inner event or process. There is, as Wittgenstein stressed at great length, only a public language for talking about what is often assumed to be private, such as pain, and the same can be said of what we typically refer as thoughts.

Wittgenstein famously argued at length that 'it is a solecism to use the word "meaning" to signify the thing that "corresponds" to a word' and that 'for a *large* class of cases … the meaning of a word is its use in the language' (2009: §§40–43), but arguably his principal emphasis throughout the *Investigations* was on the application of this point to clarifying the status of psychological concepts such as intention. Although Wittgenstein conceived of language as a tool or instrument (for example, 2009: §§11, 17, 23) and sometimes suggested that language is 'arbitrary' (for example, 2009: §497), his point was that meaning is a function of what we are doing with words. It is not that our concepts are whimsical and have no relationship to how things are in the world. The task of philosophy, and by implication any attempt to explain social phenomena, is not to seek hidden causes and essences but to achieve clarity about the meanings, which are in principle open to view even if sometimes hidden in plain sight. He noted that '*essence* is expressed in grammar' (2009: §§92, 371), and he emphasized the discursive character of social phenomena – even in the case of something such as emotion (Gunnell, 2012b).

The persistence of the issue of other minds as it is typically posed in both philosophy and social science is largely the heritage of representational philosophy and the dualism of thought and action that Wittgenstein did so much to combat. At the center of representational philosophy was the problem of how language can represent or make contact with the world, to which Wittgenstein replied that you see it every day as language is used and applied to objects (2009: §435). There is no intermediary operation of the mind that gives 'life' and meaning to a sign (2009: §§432–435). But for representational philosophy, at least from Locke onward, there was also the problem of how language could represent and express thoughts. Wittgenstein's answer was far more radical than simply stressing the public character of language. Meaning was *in* language and action, and there was only, what might be called, a pragmatic, aspectual or logical distinction between thought and its expression.

For Wittgenstein, language-games were not narrowly linguistic but inextricably tied to forms of social action – in fact, he stated, repeating Goethe, that 'in the beginning was the deed' (1984: 31). This in part informed his claim that the language for expressing pain was rooted in more primitive behavioral expressions, but it was also the real significance of his claim that the meaning of language was located in its use, that is, the actions one performed with words (2009: §24). Meaning was not some mysterious accompaniment to language. To imagine a language-game was to imagine a *Lebensform* (2009: §19). Language itself had its beginning in human behavior, and this phylogeny was repeated in the ontogenic acquisition of language by children through 'training' and in the initiation of adults into various practices. This entailed a collapse of the traditional dualism of the images of the 'inner and outer' which Wittgenstein referred to as a curtain drawn in front of the actual, and logically different, uses of language (1992: 63). His extended attack on the idea of a private language (2009: §§243–315) was a significant step in the development of a post-Cartesian social theory of the mind, but in philosophy and social science, dualism and the account of language as representing and expressing thought die hard.

While Wittgenstein's work has inspired some psychologists and philosophers such as Harré and Gillett to propose a discursive theory of mind (1994), what, in recent years, has been much more evident in the academic world as well as in pop-science is the enthusiasm for cognitive neuroscience as the latest answer to the questions of how to operationalize mental concepts, how social science can be really scientific, and how to know other minds. The pity is that too often the response to these questions has been, on the one hand, to embrace some contemporary version of neo-Cartesian linguistics, or, on the other hand, to conceive of consciousness as an impenetrable mystery and assume that it is impossible to grasp fully the *qualia* that define the experiences of other minds. And cognitive science not only embraces a reductive argument but reverts to a new form of dualism that simply substitutes the brain for the mind. Wittgenstein did not say that thought and language are the same thing, but he viewed them as having the same conceptual content. He focused on dispelling what he had referred to in his preliminary work as 'a kind of general disease of thinking which always looks for (and finds) what would be called a mental state from which all our acts spring as from a reservoir' (1958: §§1–7, 32, 143). But if we do not assume the reservoir of mentalism, how is it possible to know what people mean by what they say and do? Part of the problem with this question is the manner in which it is posed. Meaning (*meinen*) something is not an auxiliary act that occurs in the theater of the mind, and the meaning (*Bedeutung*) of a word or action is not some 'aura' surrounding it. It is a function or property of a particular language game.

Linguistic theorists such as Noam Chomsky and philosophical followers such as Fodor argue, however, that thought precedes language and that instances of language are expressions of thought. They maintain that there must be an innate language of thought or 'mentalese' in order to acquire one's first natural language, just as it is necessary to possess one natural language in order to learn another. The *Investigations*, however, began with a challenge to St. Augustine's claim that, as a child, he had learned language in order to express his thoughts. Wittgenstein, however, argued that language is first gained by training and ostensive learning – and even by blind obedience, and that it does not emerge from 'ratiocination.' This was not simply a matter of acquiring a disposition or being 'trained' in the sense that we might assume an animal is trained. A great deal of conventional stage-setting is involved as well as what Wittgenstein referred to as 'shared human behavior,' which involves the capacity for speech and thinking conceptually (2009: §206).

Wittgenstein also confronted William James's argument that 'thought was possible without speech,' which James based on the reminiscences of a deaf-mute who claimed to have had thoughts about 'God and the world' before he learned language. Wittgenstein suggested that there was something about the notion that 'deaf-mutes had learned only a sign-language,' but somehow spoke inwardly in their own 'vocal language,' that distinctly smelled 'fishy' (2009: §§342, 348), and there may be some empirical evidence that would tend to support his suspicion and his alternative account.

In *A Man Without Words*, Susan Schaller (1991) tells the fascinating story of her work in Los Angeles with Ildefonso, a Mexican immigrant in his late twenties, who was totally deaf and who possessed neither a natural language nor sign-language. He was beyond the age when many assume that a person without language can ever actually acquire it, and her initial attempts to teach him sign-language failed. He would simply look at her in a puzzled manner and repeat the sign, because miming had been his basic, but torturous, manner of communication. Unlike, for example, someone playing charades, his gestures were not semantic symbols. After many intense days of contact with Schaller, however, he finally achieved a Helen Keller moment and grasped the game of naming and the connection between words and things, from which he eventually went on, through learning sign-language, to think and act conceptually. When asked to recall and describe his thoughts before he possessed language, he said it was only 'darkness,' although he later sometimes projected his new concepts backward onto memory pictures from his former life.

Equally significant was research (Senghas and Coppola, 2001) conducted in Nicaragua. In this case, a group of deaf adolescents, who were isolated from their hearing peers, had created a rudimentary 'language' based on gestures – maybe somewhat comparable to that of Wittgenstein's 'builders.' The children, however, were lacking any gestures for mental concepts such as belief, thought and so on. When presented with a puzzle similar to that in the Sally/Ann experiment, which was designed to test recognition of false beliefs, they failed the test. Subsequently, a later generation of deaf children was introduced to sign-language at a relatively early age, and this language included sophisticated signs for mental concepts such as 'I know that you know' or 'you do not know what I know.' These children all passed the Sally/Ann test. Wittgenstein noted that thinking is not always exactly isomorphic with 'silent' speech, but if, in many relevant respects, one cannot be said to think without language, maybe one cannot really think without mental concepts. Is it, for example, possible to believe without the concept of believing? Or why, as Wittgenstein asked, does it not really make sense to speak of a dog as hoping, simulating pain and so on (2009: §§250, 357). Taking an intentional stance in the description and explanation of non-linguistic and even inanimate objects may be useful, but it often leads to yet another conflation of the means of representation and what is represented. Anything but a pragmatic distinction between language and thought, and the inner and outer, fades away along with the classic dimensions of the puzzle about knowing other minds. If we do not understand what people mean by what they say and do in the context of saying and doing it, it is simply regressive to look for the answer in some indefinable and inaccessible placed called the 'mind.'

Part of the continuing debate, in both philosophy and the human sciences, about such matters as whether language determines thought or is an expression of thought, turns on definitional issues. Steven Pinker (for example, 2007), like Fodor, claims that there is 'mentalese' or a universal language of thought consisting of ideas in the form of abstract *a priori* Kantian-like categories including space, time, intention and so on that are manifest concretely in natural languages. Part of their concern is to support the notion of a universal human nature and combat what they claim are the dangers of relativism inherent in various forms of linguistic determinism. They base their argument in part on the existence of linguistic devices such as metaphor and indirect communication, which they claim imply meaning behind language. When Wittgenstein referred to thought, he was, on the contrary, largely specifying what later philosophers such as Donald Davidson (for example, 2001) labeled propositional attitudes. There are important differences between Wittgenstein and Davidson, but they both claimed, in effect, that there was no thought without language and that only those who possess language can be said to think. Propositional attitudes are expressed in mental verbs such as believe, desire, know, think, hope and so on, and Davidson claims that thought involves a mastery of these concepts and the connections among them, which in turn explains the inter-subjectivity of language and the normativity of rules and conventions. And in this respect also there is experimental evidence in developmental psychology that indicates that the acquisition of these mental concepts evolves in children and that it is not until at least age four that the concept of belief and attending concepts such as objective truth and misrepresentation are operative. What unites philosophy and social inquiry, however, is not only the problem of understanding and interpreting but a characteristic and maybe endemic urge to judge, and prescribe to, their subject matter – to speak to the issue of what is just, right and real.

Doing justice

This propensity may stem in part from the fact that most of these fields have historically emerged from practices that are now their subject matter (philosophy of science, moral philosophy and social science are all cases in point). Although originally distancing themselves for the purpose of acquiring cognitive authority, they always retain at least a latent wish to rejoin the world from which they have sprung. What has accounted for much of the negative reaction to Wittgenstein has been the worry that his work undermines this authority – and this worry is well-founded. Wittgenstein provides little basis for licensing critical theory, which must stand on its own feet. But as Winch stressed in his later essay 'Understanding a Primitive Society' (1964), the consequences of 'only describing' are almost inevitably critical, judgmental and challenging, and, as Wittgenstein acknowledged, potentially destructive. In the case of philosophy and social science, only describing is actually re-describing, and often nothing is as devastating as the 'clarity' that Wittgenstein advocated as the principal goal of philosophy. Doing justice to the subject matter was first of all a matter of understanding it on its own terms without imposing the framework and ontology of the interpreter, but there was still the question of whether it was possible to pass judgment on the intrinsic character of other practices. Within science, politics, moral life and so on there are judgments, and as Wittgenstein noted, practices are constituted not by agreement in opinions but agreement in judgments. But external judgments *about* such practices are a quite different matter. While the constitution and conduct of particular practices necessarily contain, and constrain, criteria of judgment, the most significant problem arises when one practice, or even culture, seeks to judge another. Retreating to notions of what is sometimes referred to as immanent critique does not resolve the problem, which almost always drives inquiry to seek some transcendent basis of judgment. Even Winch and Kuhn could never entirely exorcize the ghost of relativism when reflecting on their own work. Wittgenstein's answer was that although judging other practices and forms of action is possible, there is no philosophical ground to which to repair in doing so and no certainty that the judgment will be practically efficacious. Nothing was more inauthentic than vacuous moralizing.

There has been a great deal of controversy about whether or not there are theoretically neutral facts, and many contemporary forms of philosophical realism, despite their rejection of positivism, are in one way or another based on making a case for the existence of a transcendental reality in terms of which truth claims can be judged. Although philosophers such as Searle (1995) and Charles Taylor (1971) have singularly stressed the distinctiveness of social phenomena as consisting of conventional, constructed or institutional facts defined in terms of purpose and intentionality, they not only embrace mentalism, but in the end claim that such facts are nevertheless grounded on what they both refer to as 'brute facts.' They claim that the latter are somehow given to immediate experience and ultimately provide a basis of judgment in both science and morals. They, as much as the positivists and realists, perpetuate a form of what Wilfrid Sellars (1963) famously labeled 'the myth of the given.' But these arguments for realism are very similar to the genre of the claims of G.E. Moore, which Wittgenstein criticized in *On Certainty* (1969). They are primarily simply emphatic reiterations of one's own *Weltbild* or of what almost everyone already believes. But Wittgenstein also recognized that Moore had a point. Wittgenstein referred to these claims as, among other things, 'hinge propositions' that may take the form of empirical propositions but that function as *a priori* foundational assumptions, which, however, as Kuhn also emphasized, sometimes change.

One interesting example was Wittgenstein's own synthetic *a priori* claim that no person had ever been on the moon, but a few years after he used this example, it was no longer viable as a parallel to Moore's claim about how the observation of his hands confirmed the existence of the external world. What had happened was that what Wittgenstein had referred to as the conceptual 'riverbed' and 'bedrock' to which specific factual statements had to conform and by which justification was both enabled and constrained, had shifted. He claimed that it was necessary to recognize the ultimate 'groundlessness of our believing' (1969: §166). For Wittgenstein, there was, in the case of philosophy, indeed a 'given,' but, as he specifically noted, it is the 'forms of life.' It is actually with respect to philosophical and social inquiry that it makes sense to speak of 'brute facts,' that is, the conceptually autonomous facts that are the subject matter of inquiry.

Wittgenstein often related philosophy to anthropology, and here the tension between description and what is described, between the *Sprache*, *Weltbild*, *Lebensform* and *Weltanschauung* of the interpreter and those of the interpretee, is most often evident, but the potential cognitive and practical conflict is always present. For example, philosophical reconstructions of the logic of science are seldom consonant with the self-image of the scientist, and social scientific renditions of politics and other social practices, despite often being couched in a language too esoteric for public consumption, imply significant potential cognitive conflict. Philosophy and social science are inherently critical enterprises, even apart from the ideologies that often inform them. What lingers on in both of these enterprises, however, that is, in positions such as philosophical realism and related versions of critical social theory, is the search for some transcendental or empirical ground that will bypass the problem of the contingent and practical relationship between a meta-practice and its subject matter and provide an apodictic answer to the hoary problem of theory and practice. The theory/practice problem is itself a practical problem, and, again, the only answer is persuasion, or as Wittgenstein said in *On Certainty*, knowledge is only knowledge when it is acknowledged (1969: §378). We may feel, like Nietzsche, that when we look into the abyss and see no universal grounds of judgment, that the abyss reflects back on us and we lose our capacity to give reasons, but, as Wittgenstein pointed out, we should forget this 'transcendent certainty,' and recognize that 'we use judgements as principles of judgement' and that 'justification comes to an end' (1969: §§47, 124, 192).

Wittgenstein's point was not all that far removed from Marx's claim that philosophers have only interpreted the world, when the point is to change it. What separates Wittgenstein from Marx is in part the fact that Marx, like most philosophers before him, believed that interpretation could be made to go all the way down either through conscious action or through the unfolding of history. Wittgenstein was certainly not happy with modernity, and he may have been overwhelmed by the complexities he discerned in the contemporary relationship between philosophy and its subject matter and by hesitancies rooted in his own psyche. He did not offer any clear vision of how the vocation of philosophy might alter the social world. Maybe he believed, like Spengler, that it was too late, but it is clear that he believed that there was no particular formula for or explanation of social change and the manner in which theory could be brought to bear on practice. Subsequent attempts to posit general answers have not, in any obvious way, been compelling.

Today, in fields such as political philosophy, there are exhaustive conversations about what might be called public reason, about such matters as the nature of justice and the character of justice in the liberal state, the balance between individual and society, and the apportionment of rights. It is often assumed by major contemporary authors and the secondary academic cottage industry devoted to discussing their work, that there is a kind of basic continuity in this discussion reaching from Plato to authors such as John Rawls and beyond. To the extent that the current literature is devoted to achieving clarity about the underlying issues involved in the politics of justice, it is salutary, but often these discussions represent what Wittgenstein spoke of as the sublimation of logic, that is, the belief that behind the particularity of judgments in various practices there is some universal foundation. This is not at all to say that political philosophy should refrain from making judgments about its subject matter, but rather that its first task is not to talk about justice in the abstract but to *do* justice to the subject matter in the sense of understanding and clarifying the practices of justice.

Acknowledgements

I am pleased to acknowledge my appreciation for continuing conversations with Linda Zerilli and for her supportive and helpful comments with respect to my efforts to probe and apply Wittgenstein's work. My correspondence with Rupert Read and reading his work have done a great deal to sustain my confidence in my interpretations of Wittgenstein and Winch.

Note

I have previously (Gunnell, 2012a) undertaken a comprehensive critical discussion of the reception of Wittgenstein's work among social and political theorists as well as a more extended treatment of Peter Winch. Wittgenstein's view of the relationship between words and concepts and his analysis of interpretation are also more fully discussed.

References

Davidson, D. (2001) *Subjective, Intersubjective, and Objective*. Oxford: Oxford University Press.
Fodor, J. (1975) *The Language of Thought*. Cambridge, MA: Harvard University Press.

Gunnell, J.G. (1998) *The Orders of Discourse; Philosophy, Social Science, and Politics.* Lanham, MD: Rowman and Littlefield.

Gunnell, J.G. (2004) *Imagining the American Polity: Political Science and the Discourse of Democracy.* University Park: Pennsylvania State University Press.

Gunnell, J.G. (2012a) *Political Theory and Social Science: Cutting Against the Grain.* New York: Palgrave Macmillan.

Gunnell, J.G. (2012b) Unpacking Emotional Baggage in Political Inquiry. In F. Vander Valk (ed.), *Essays on Neuroscience and Political Theory: Thinking the Body Politic.* New York: Routledge.

Harré, R. and Gillett, G. (1994) *The Discursive Mind.* Thousand Oaks, CA: Sage.

Kripke, S.A. (1982) *Wittgenstein on Rules and Private Language.* Oxford: Blackwell.

Kuhn, T. (1962) *The Structure of Scientific Revolutions.* Chicago, IL: University of Chicago Press.

Pinker, S. (2007) *The Stuff of Thought: Language as a Window into Human Nature.* New York: Penguin.

Pitkin, H. (1972) *Wittgenstein and Justice: On the Significance of Ludwig Wittgenstein for Social and Political Thought.* Berkeley: University of California Press.

Rorty, R. (1979) *Philosophy and the Mirror of Nature.* Princeton, NJ: Princeton University Press.

Ross, D. (1991) *The Origins of American Social Science.* Cambridge: Cambridge University Press.

Schaller, S. (1991) *Man Without Words.* Berkeley: University of California Press.

Searle, J. (1995) *The Construction of Social Reality.* New York: Free Press.

Sellars, W. (1963) *Science, Perception, and Reality.* New York: Humanities Press.

Senghas, A. and Coppola, M. (2001) Children creating language: how Nicaraguan sign language acquired a spatial grammar. *Psychological Science* 12(4): 323–328.

Taylor, C. (1971) Interpretation and the sciences of man. *Review of Metaphysics* 25(1): 3–51.

Winch, P. (1958) *The Idea of a Social Science and its Relation to Philosophy.* London: Routledge and Kegan Paul.

Winch, P. (1964) Understanding a primitive society. *American Philosophical Quarterly* 1(4): 307–324.

Winch, P. (1996) Doing justice or giving the devil his due. In D.Z. Phillips (ed.), *Can Religion Be Explained Away?* Basingstoke: Palgrave Macmillan.

Wittgenstein, L. (1958) *The Blue and Brown Books.* New York: Harper.

Wittgenstein, L. (1967) *Zettel.* Berkeley: University of California Press.

Wittgenstein, L. (1969) *On Certainty.* Oxford: Blackwell.

Wittgenstein, L. (1984) *Culture and Value.* Chicago, IL: University of Chicago Press.

Wittgenstein, L. (1992) *Last Writings on the Philosophy of Psychology, Vol. 2. The Inner and the Outer.* Oxford: Blackwell.

Wittgenstein, L. (2005) *The Big Typescript.* Oxford: Blackwell.

Wittgenstein, L. (2009) *Philosophical Investigations*, 4th edn. Translated by G.E.M. Anscombe, P.M.S. Hacker and J. Schulte. Oxford: Blackwell. In this edition material that was formerly presented as Part II is designated as *Philosophy of Psychology – A Fragment*, which I have cited as *PPF.*

Appendix

Questions from Christopher C. Robinson

CCR: Did you set out to be an innovator? Can you give readers a sense of your start in the field of political theory?

JGG: I definitely did not set out to be an innovator in political theory, and the extent to which I have been an innovator is really a matter for others to judge. I have intervened in several substantive areas of the practice of political theory, and although I am not sure how much I have changed how people perform in those practices, I believe that I have had some influence on how people think about them. If there is anything generally distinctive about my work, it is the extent to which I have engaged in comprehensive critical philosophical and historical reflection on the sub-field as a whole and on its relationship to political science, what I have characterized as the "metapractical voice." To explain this point requires describing the circumstances of my graduate education at Berkeley, where I entered in the spring of 1959. In the early 1960s, the department was marked by distinct intellectual divisions. The most general split was between traditional institutional political studies and an emerging behavioral persuasion. Political theory was predominately associated with the former, but it was beginning to take on a distinct identity, often related to the work of Sheldon Wolin, who gained tenure in the same year (1960) that he published *Politics and Vision*. There really was no such thing as the Berkeley school as a consciously articulated position, but functionally it began to take on such an image in its opposition to behavioralism and in terms of Wolin's account of the history of political theory as well as John Schaar's work on political "authority" and "community." Norman Jacobson was closely allied to this image of theory, and particularly the critique of the behavioral image of science, but in some respects he was something of an outlier as far as adopting any distinct position on some of the emerging issues. The year that Wolin was hired, he was awarded a fellowship and replaced for the period by Hannah Arendt, who was just completing *The Human Condition*, which, I believe, left a lasting impression on Wolin and many political theory students in the department. Wolin clearly believed that his account of the history of political theory, despite how that account may have appeared to a general audience, was quite different from that of theorists such as Leo Strauss, Judith Shklar, and others. There was also a distinct split within political theory at Berkeley. Richard Cox was a student of Strauss who had been hired in the late 1950s, and in 1961, the department hired Harvey Mansfield, Jr., from Harvard without realizing he was a follower of Strauss. Both, however, were forced, with the collaboration of both the theorists and behavioralists, to leave the department before I finished in 1964.

My personal situation, married with two children and recently out of the Navy, was more pressured than most of those in my cohort, and I actually took very few courses and was even away for a year as a Ford Foundation legislative intern in Sacramento. I had opted for graduate education in political science for no other reason than the fact that I had to choose some career, and California, where I had been stationed, offered an affordable graduate education. And when it came time to choose between UCLA and Berkeley, a former teacher of mine at Tufts University, who had never been to California, said that he thought I might prefer Berkeley because he understood that, literally, the grass was greener in the north and that it might seem more like my native New England. I chose political theory because it was the only undergraduate course in government that I had enjoyed. As I began my studies at Berkeley, I began to realize that, compared to many other students, my background in both political science and political theory was quite disadvantaged, but, as a consequence, I did not have any very fixed opinions about the field. I had one seminar with each Wolin and Jacobson, and my first assignment as a graduate assistant was with Cox. I was somewhat put off by the Straussian approach, but I was also not particularly drawn to the Wolin/Schaar contingent that seemed to me was beginning to take on a somewhat doctrinal aura. I gravitated to Jacobson, who encouraged independence and creativity in all things and stressed this in his popular seminar on the history of natural science, in which I first became distinctly intellectually engaged. And I chose Jacobson as my adviser and dissertation director.

After pondering what appeared to be the various approaches to the study of the history of political theory, the question that struck me was why scholars such as Strauss, Arendt, and Wolin, who really wanted to critically address contemporary politics and political ideas, found it necessary to make their argument in terms of a long story of historical decline ending in the present degraded condition. It seemed to me that the shadow of Heidegger hovered over much of this work, and I learned German and began to formulate a dissertation on Heidegger. However, after following his path back to the Greeks, I finally diverted and focused on what appeared to be a congenital tension between history or time and politics, which was the subject of my dissertation prospectus. Despite some dire warnings from both faculty members and students that I might be caught in the cross-hairs of departmental disputes about theory, my oral defense of the prospectus went well. This may have been in part because much of the material I had engaged was not within the province of any of the theory faculty, with whose positions I was attempting to avoid becoming entangled. I began to trace the tension between political space and time backward to pre-Socratic times and finally ended up, except in an epilogue, not getting beyond Plato.

This became *Political Philosophy and Time* (1968). It was the beginning of several years of critical reflection on the idea of tradition, but already in the dissertation, I had decided to move away from the dominant genre and its story of decline and plea for redemption.

CCR: What were the problems that you were addressing in your dissertation and book on Plato? How has that study been received?

JGG: In my attempt to move beyond or outside the Berkeley perspectives on the history of political theory, I had turned to the work of Eric Voegelin. Although I would subsequently reject his narrative, it did lead me to Cassirer and to more general studies of language and symbolic forms, which played an important role in framing the dissertation, the initial draft of which was accepted by my committee (Jacobson, Wolin, and the Frankfurt school sociologist Leo Lowenthal) without any substantial revision. There are a number of people who have said, both to me and to others, they believe that the book on Plato was the best thing that I have written. I think that this assessment is in part a reaction to the fact that much of my subsequent work involved critiques of various dimensions of political theory, including my analyses of the image of theory in behavioral political science, the idea of the great tradition, and various forms of contemporary political theory. In the Plato book, I was doing the kind of thing that it was assumed political theorists should be doing. I however share some of that sentiment about the volume, which was very well received by both political theorists and philosophers. I do not believe that I could recapture the voice of that book, because at that point I was still enthralled by the romantic worldhistorical image of political theory. I felt truly inspired when I wrote it, but even the origins of the book anticipated issues that I would address later. As I have already noted, what originally prompted this study was the question I had posed in my dissertation prospectus about why historians of political theory, who clearly were concerned with the contemporary condition of political life and political thought, felt constrained to couch their analyses in a historical narrative that for many years had been a story of the progress but later of the declination, of politics and political thinking. This led me to consider the broader issue of political philosophy and time and the extent to which there was an internal tension between the idea of political space and its temporal and historical context. The central focus of the book was on the manner in which political philosophy was concerned with how political order could survive what seemed to be the mortality of all human institutions and conventions. I had begun to claim that this tension had reached a sort of culmination in the work of Heidegger and, derivatively, Arendt and Strauss, but while investigating this issue, it became clear to me that it had its origins in pre-Platonic thought and that it had become fully manifest in the work of Plato, which, in some respects, became the paradigm for thinkers as diverse as Machiavelli and Marx. When I wrote the book, however, I still believed in the reality of the "great tradition," and I assumed that modern politics was fundamentally shaped by that tradition. Today I believe that the classic canon is an edifying collection of a variety of works in diverse contexts that manifest how creative minds have encountered and directed their attention to political life and usually for a practical rhetorical purpose. The so-called tradition is the reification of a retrospective analytical construction. A significant problem that has haunted political theory is the assumption that academic political theory is the last vestige of the great tradition. I have been at pains to demonstrate that it is a very different thing with a different history.

CCR: What is the role of the political theorist today in relation to political science, political society, and the university?

JGG: I have consistently maintained that political theory is part of the same game as political science. Political theory had been, until the 1950s, the locus of specifying the identity of political science; it was the place where conceptual and critical reflection and change occurred. In this respect, I have been critical of the kinds of arguments put forward by Wolin, George Kateb, and others regarding an autonomous "vocation" of political theory that stands independently of political science. This image is a relatively recent development in the history of academic political theory.

The relationship between political theory and political science in the post-behavioral era became, in my view, one of, what I might call, log-rolling; "if you do not bother me, I will not bother you." To put it more formally, each acceded autonomy to the other and took the position that they were simply doing different things. This pushed under the rug crucial issues about the nature of social phenomena and what constituted a proper approach to social inquiry, which had animated debates about behavioralism and which were really central to both activities. In effect, both isolated themselves from criticism and debate, which, despite the problems of the behavioral era, had at least been a virtue of that era. Political theory and political science were each free to settle down to internal contentment and self-assurance of the righteousness of their own path. What this really meant was that the vulnerabilities of ideas such as the great tradition, which dominated the discourse of theorists, and scientism, which characterized behavioralism, could be pursued without interference or self-reflection. Both sides became increasingly doctrinal and created not only separate identities but even gave themselves different histories.

Individuals such as Wolin and Strauss both saw contemporary political theory as the besieged remnant of a covenant given by the Greeks, and mainstream political science saw itself as the modern vanguard of a search for scientific truth and maturity. And they accepted each other's self-serving vision of their own identity. As I noted, a more productive relationship would have been one of critical interaction but especially a recognition that they were ultimately faced with the same theoretical and epistemological issues and should recognize that genealogically they came from the same family tree.

Political theory has no more a special relation to political society than any other academic field. In my work, the criticism of any claim to "specialness" on the part of political theorists has led me to see that political science, political theory, sociology, social theory, and so on, are all dealing with the same sorts of problems, and I try to capture this unity of interests in the category of "social inquiry."

The relation of political theory to the university is actually primarily pedagogical. Here political theory does have a claim to uniqueness, because what it teaches is not found anywhere else. James Farr makes the interesting claim that pedagogy might offer both an answer to the problem of the relationship between political science and political theory and to their relationship to political society and that it reflects the foundational historical role that concern with civic education, despite problems with past formulations, has played in the formation of these activities.

As for my preferred job description for the contemporary political theorist, it would be someone who is doing serious scholarship – whether about the history of political thought, the interpretation of texts, the nature of social phenomena, conceptual analysis and clarification, or whatever. It would be easier to say what I would not include, which would comprise what Jacobson once spoke of as the tendency of political theory to revert to various forms of moralism and scientism and define itself in terms of a debate between these poles. I believe that the study of political thought should be in large measure about the thinking that has gone on, and goes on, in politics, and that it should be devoted to understanding and interpreting politics. I certainly have no problem with critical evaluations of political life or with the theorist as a political actor, but I am very wary of political theory becoming enthralled with the idea that it possesses some special authority to speak to public issues. My position reflects my reading of Wittgenstein's philosophy, which in some respects means seeing the political theorist as anthropologist seeking clarification of various domains of social life. Much of what I have had to say recently on this issue has been to the effect that there is an anti-democratic elitism present in much of political theory as well as the philosophical authorities on which much of political theory relies. I am distinctly an opponent of much of what would be characterized as critical theory with its metaphysical claims to truth – and even of the position of those who believe they see in Wittgenstein some kind of watered-down basis for judging from the outside. We can always judge from the outside but not on the basis of some form of epistemic privilege. I have no problem with a political theorist such as Wolin becoming, or trying to become, a public intellectual, and there are grounds for suggesting that there may be a capacity for doing so, but so many political theorists are engaged in attempting to lay down judgments about justice, rights, and all manner of things without actually engaging, or even investigating, the particulars of political life.

CCR: How has political theory changed over the course of your career? How has your own work changed?

JGG: When I began to study political theory the field was largely taken up with the history of political thought and with ventures devoted to the defense of liberal democracy as the culmination of that history. The important point to keep in mind is how integral this was to the discipline of political science as a whole.

A text such as that of George Sabine was in effect a vindication of political science and the values embedded in it. What was beginning to take place when I entered graduate school was a fundamental transformation that was being effected by émigré scholars such as Strauss, Arendt, Voegelin, Herbert Marcuse, and many others which despite the differences among them were unified in their rejection of the images of science and liberal democracy that had infused both political theory and the discipline of political science. Their new story of decline in politics and political thought was embraced by American scholars as ideologically diverse as Wolin and John Hallowell. It is necessary to remember that the founders of behavioralism were originally traditional political theorists, but they rebelled against the European incursion. The behavioral revolution was actually a counter-revolution, which introduced what they claimed to be "empirical" theory but which in the case of Dahl and others still clothed the basic values of liberal pluralist democracy. The debate about science was something of a red herring that concealed an underlying philosophical conflict about liberalism. By the 1970s, the work of John Rawls, Jürgen Habermas, and, later, individuals such as Michel Foucault and a variety of other scholars had given rise to what came to be categorized as "normative" theory – all of which largely stood outside the mainstream discipline of political science. And with the work of historians such as Quentin Skinner and J.G.A. Pocock, even the history of political theory began to take a different turn. This whole story about the evolution and speciation of political theory, which I detailed in *Descent*, is too long and complex to recount here, but the point is that in the two decades from 1950 to 1970, there was a fundamental transformation in the subfield and at the same time a growing alienation from the discipline of political science, as well as, I believe, from the realities of political life, and I believe that today we are living with many of the unfortunate aspects of that evolution.

In my own work, the changes were distinctly organic as I moved from one area of political theory to another. The summer after I finished at Berkeley, I was invited to return and participate in a six-week workshop on questions of time in comparative development studies. This work was what first led me into the literature of the philosophy of science and philosophy of social sciences – Peter Winch, Thomas Kuhn, Alfred Schutz, and others. This material had been totally foreign to the theory curriculum at Berkeley where, for example, I never heard a name such as Winch or Kuhn (even though Kuhn had already published his famous book and was teaching at Berkeley). My cognate field, however, was philosophy, and I had taken a seminar with the visiting Karl Popper who was assisted by Paul Feyerabend, so I had begun to have some sense of how issues in philosophy related to certain dimensions of political theory and political science. In the late sixties, I began raising questions about how images of scientific explanation in logical positivist philosophy had been imported to bolster the behavioral account of science, and I began to explore how in fact the positivist account was being challenged by philosophers such as Kuhn and what the implications might be for political inquiry. My 1968 article in the *APSR* and the controversy that it created initiated a program of study that I pursued in the ensuing decades. Although I had contemplated questions about what I later referred to as "the myth of the tradition" while still in graduate school, I began in the 1970s to take a more focused critical approach to this literature. As long as I was criticizing behavioralism, I was praised by the theorist fellowship, but when I looked critically at the tradition and other dimensions of political theory, Wolin and others worried that I was betraying the vocation. Although I had considerable sympathy and agreement with the work of Pocock, Skinner, and John Dunn, I also had reservations about various aspects of what they claimed was a proper historical method, and these issues led me yet deeper into issues in the history and philosophy of social science as well as to substantive work in the history of political science. A full account of how one issue led to another and to various forms of research is too long to recount in detail, but since the end of the 1990s, I have increasingly moved away from issues specific to the field of political theory. In my most recent book, I do not believe that I even referred specifically to "political theory." So maybe I have finally cast off the last vestige of the "vocation" of political theory and the idea of "the political" as some indefinable essence that lies behind the diversity of political life.

CCR: How do you respond to critics who regard your criticisms of the idea and myth of the tradition as an argument for eliminating the teaching of core texts like Plato's *Republic* or Machiavelli's *The Prince* from the curriculum? Were you seeking to found an alternative school of thought?

JGG: Teaching is central to what political theorists do. My own approach to these texts can be seen in the final chapter on my book, *Political Theory: Tradition and Interpretation*, which still represents my way of teaching this material. There I note that the texts can be taken as examples of creative thinkers confronting the problems of politics in their context, and although they share some definite family resemblances, we should not forget the rhetorical context in which they were written. This literature can be studied without reference to some philosophical argument about a conversation occurring between thinkers across history and certainly without any claim about a vocation that unites these endeavors.

I was personally very much opposed in my own endeavors to establishing anything like a school of thought in political theory. This was in part a consequence of my experience at Berkeley where I saw many talented people succumb to attempting to emulate and instantiate the ideas of their teachers, sometimes with personally tragic results. And early on I witnessed the same kind of conformity with people who studied with Strauss or Straussians. But in all fairness what was also involved in my reluctance to encourage students to become followers was the fact that early on I begun to focus on criticizing various things such as the positivist residue in behavioralism, the idea of the tradition, and so on. This critical approach was not an easy thing for many graduate students to deal with, because it did not offer them a truth to which they could cling and a program in which they could find intellectual security and identity. I have felt somewhat guilty for not providing an academic "religion," but I myself never settled down to basing my career on some such position.

CCR: Can we focus on the linguistic turn in your work? In particular, how did Austin and Wittgenstein influence your thinking?

JGG: In graduate school I had discovered some elements of ordinary language philosophy and phenomenology on my own, but the Berkeley theorists tended to treat this material as positivist and relativist. While in graduate school, I had not really known Hanna Pitkin, who was a few years ahead of me, but in later conversations, she recommended that I read Stanley Cavell's doctoral dissertation, "The Claim to Reason." The dissertation's focus was on Austin, and the principal sections on Wittgenstein came later when the dissertation became the book. My impression of Austin was that he was incorrectly interpreted, that is had been read by individuals such as Skinner as though illocutionary force was a·manifestation of psychological intentionality in the sense of H.P. Grice, but for both Austin and Wittgenstein, language was the source of mental predicates. By the late 1970s, I had begun to see the problem with that view of Austin and Wittgenstein, but I did not fully explore it until the 1990s. Through the seventies, I was convinced of interrelationships between linguistic philosophy and phenomenology, and I believed that Winch and Schutz were on the same page. Gradually, however, I left phenomenology behind, because it was too metaphysical, and turned to linguistic philosophy. Wittgenstein did not, however, become the primary focus of my work until the beginning of the 1990s. *Orders of Discourse* was my first book written from a fully Wittgensteinian perspective. Various claims about mind, intention, and purpose, which were still the concern of individuals such as Charles Taylor, were supplanted in my work by the claim that these were primarily a function of linguistic conventions and that conventionality was at the core of social phenomena. Whether manifest in individual or group action, these phenomena were instantiations of conventions.

Before *Orders*, my use of Wittgenstein had been very selective, but I began to approach his work more systematically. By the turn of the century, I found that I was very dissatisfied with the uses of Wittgenstein by political theorists, and (2004; 2011) I attempted to provide a detailed critique of those uses as I developed my own vision of his relevance for the field. It has become clear to me that Austin and Wittgenstein were more similar than often assumed, and I believe that Austin, Wittgenstein, and Ryle were actually very much engaged with one another's thinking. Ryle and Wittgenstein took walks together, and as early as 1931, Ryle was reflecting these conversations in his writing. Austin, Ryle, and Wittgenstein were in many ways not compatible personalities, but they agreed about the basic character and relationship between language, thought, and action. In the last few years I have continued to be involved in issues in the history and philosophy of political and social science, often from a Wittgensteinian perspective, but my general direction has been toward demonstrating how Wittgenstein's approach to philosophy, after 1930, increasingly became a vision of philosophy as a form of social inquiry and toward the implications of his work for all forms of such inquiry.

CCR: How does your thinking on the history of political thought overlap with and depart from Pocock and Skinner?

JGG: As I have already mentioned, there was a significant resemblance between my arguments and those of Skinner, Pocock, and Dunn, who came to be identified with the Cambridge School of Political Theory. They all argued for a more truly historical approach to the study of political theory rather than the imposition of some philosophical scheme, whether Whig or critical, on the classic canon. What they could not understand was why I seemed to agree with them but yet criticized what they claimed was an authentic historical method (see my *Tradition and Interpretation*, 1979, and particularly "Interpretation and History of Political Theory: Apology and Epistemology," *American Political Science Review*, 1982). This, however, raised an issue to which I had been devoting increased attention.

This issue involves the general relationship between philosophy and social science and is related to what I had referred to as the "alienation of political theory," which involved not simply the tension between political theory and political science and between political theory and politics but the manner in which theorists had become increasingly dependent on seeking their identity from philosophy, whatever the philosophical persuasion that might be chosen at any particular moment. This, I claimed, undermined the autonomy of the field. The Cambridge School drew upon much of the same philosophical literature that I first discussed in 1968, but I argued that what they took from that literature was less a theoretical claim about the nature of social phenomena than an epistemological claim that they advanced as a method of inquiry. This focus on epistemology was, I believed, not significantly different from the manner in which behaviorists had attempted to extract a scientific method of inquiry from the positivist philosophy of science. This syndrome seemed to me to be present in many varieties of political theory.

This issue had been a prominent focus of my work until I turned to putting some of my more positive arguments about historical research to work in the study of disciplinary history, as exemplified in *Descent* and *Imagining*. In between these two works, however, I attempted to not only present the core of my general critique of political theory, but, in *Orders* to delineate my claims about the nature of political inquiry. I was much in favor of a more historical study of the history of political thought, but I also did not think that the Cambridge School really overcame some of the problems that attended the myth of a tradition. Their brand of contextualism was, as I attempted to elaborate further in various books and articles, problematic, and they were still attached, as much as Strauss, to the assumption that interpretation was a matter of recovering of what Skinner referred to as the "mentalities" behind a text. I have had much to say about problems of various forms of contextualism as well as textualism, and this is why I gravitated toward the internalism of Kuhn, even though I have recently written some about why there is a significant difference between the history of natural science and that of social science.

CCR: After years of engaging critically the work of David Easton, you became his friend, collaborator, and biographer. How did all this come about?

JGG: David and I first met by accident in Finland in 1985. This was right after I had written the chapter on political theory for the initial volume of *Political Science: The State of the Discipline.* I was also working with Raymond Seidelman on his book on the history of political science, which was included in a series I edited for State University of New York Press. And I was beginning work on what would become *Descent.* It was helpful to talk with David about this work. I had been writing on and criticizing his arguments about science for twenty years, and I had imagined him as a somewhat personally formidable figure. Our wives had accompanied us to Finland, and it turned out that in a short period we became very good friends. We traveled around Helsinki together, and during the conference, David asked me to join him in forming a committee to study the comparative history of political science, which led to the organization of several conferences and panels as well as to two volumes. Since I had begun the research for *Descent,* I interviewed him at his home as part my research. At this point, the American Political Science Association was reviving its oral history project and had asked David if he would participate. He agreed on the condition that I conduct the interviews. These were extensive and wide-ranging conversations. I learned that he had been a leftist activist in Canada in his youth. He and his wife Sylvia decided that the best way to participate in achieving political change would be for him to become a political scientist. While he later admitted that he had become swept up in the methodological issues relating to behavioralism, the impulse to make political science more scientific was part of a larger project to gain the intellectual authority to make political science more relevant politically and democratically effective. Easton arrived at the University of Chicago, just as Charles Merriam was ending his career and shortly before Harold Lasswell departed for Yale. David basically inherited the vision of the Chicago School of social science, which by that point was in decline because of the reorientation in the university under Robert Hutchins, who was recruiting individuals such as Strauss. Easton became the principal spokesperson for behavioralism, which in his view was the successor to the program of Merriam and Lasswell and on which David's image of the political system was predicated.

David passed away this past year, but we had remained close friends for thirty years. In 2013, I wrote a long piece detailing his intellectual career ("The Reconstitution of Political Theory: David Easton and the Long Road to System," *Journal of the History of the Behavioral Sciences*).

CCR: Finally, can you talk about your sympathies for, and criticisms of, reform movements within political science, from the Caucus for a New Political Science to the more recent "perestroika" movement?

JGG: With respect to my analysis of the "perestroika" dust-up in political science, this was largely a footnote to my work on the history of social and political science and the center of a recent symposium in *Perspectives on Politics*. What had emerged from this was attention to the paradox that attended the origins of the social sciences, which was particularly manifest in the history of political science. These sciences were the emanation of both religion and various social reform movements. Social science did not begin as an academic enterprise but rather as an extension of arguments for social change that sought the emerging imprimatur of science. Science, however, was increasingly located in the academy, to which social science then gravitated in search of the epistemic authority that would achieve practical purchase. Once separated, the fundamental question, by the end of the nineteenth century, was how to get social science and society back together. This was particularly manifest in the case of political science, because while some social sciences studied a rather vaguely specified subject matter, such as in the case of sociology and society, politics was a specific and concrete practice in which matters of public policy were not only salient but where political actors could take umbrage at being studied and critically discussed.

No matter how much political science often seemed to forget why it wanted to be scientific, the practical concerns were endemic and continually resurfaced. Consequently, the discipline was always seeking to reform itself in order to connect more effectively with its subject matter, both cognitively and politically. While this was still very apparent in the 1960s, "perestroika," in my view, as distinguished from, for example, the foundation of the American Political Science Association in 1903 and the Caucus for a New Political Science in the 1960s, was to a large extent the manifestation of an attenuated memory of what was involved, which largely played out as a professional protest driven by concerns about diversity in research programs and employment opportunities. But even the Caucus did not really find a way to address the basic issue of the relationship between theory and practice, and it still seemed to assume that there was an epistemic answer to the practical problem. Underlying all this, however, was the problem of pluralism, which, from the beginning, had been the governing ethic in both politics and the study of politics. Professional political science originated as a holding company for some quite diverse fields of study, and it was continually faced with the paradox of how it could claim scientific authority if it was not, like economics for example, a scientifically and methodologically unified discipline, and, at the same, time it had to appeal to a variety of political constituencies. I am sympathetic to claims such as the demand to "make political science matter," and I believe it often can and should matter, but from the beginning the aspiration was always to make the discipline matter and not simply the efforts of particular political scientists. Much of political theory has continued to take on the image of nineteenth-century moral philosophy, but while the latter spoke to a somewhat unified image of the public, political theory today does not seem to have a clear idea of either to whom its claims are addressed or of how those claims are to be delivered. I have come to what I consider to be the somewhat Wittgensteinian answer that political theory "leaves everything as it is" in that the primary task, and what it is best suited for, is to interpret, represent, and to achieve clarity about its subject matter. The performance of political theory does not, simply by virtue of that performance, change anything, and it has no special authority to do so. This does not mean, however, that it cannot or should not have a practical effect, but such a result is both contingent and arguable. I believe that there is a deeply elitist and anti-democratic propensity that characterizes much of the medium of the discourse of political theory, no matter how democratic its message may often appear.

Index

new history of political theory 113, 115, 116, 118–19, 124, 127; post-modernism 163; Skinner, Quentin 224 (philosophy of interpretation 115, 116); social science 148, 221–2 (inter-pretive social science 205, 215, 221, 224); Weber, Max 150, 220; Wittgen-stein, Ludwig 142–4, 150, 214, 218, 220, 221–2, 224 (reconstructive rather than a constructive activity 222); *see also* hermeneutics

'Interpretation and History of Political Theory: Apology and Epistemology' 6, 111–28, 242; Conclusion 126–7; Epistemology, theory, norm, and method 114–16; History and herme-neutics: the case of Skinner 116–23; The new historians 112–14; Text and context in intellectual history 123–6; *see also* new history of political theory; Skinner, Quentin

intuitionism 224

Ionescu, Ghita 1

Isaac, Jeffrey 7, 185–7, 193

Jacobson, Norman 234, 235, 236, 238

Jacoby, Russell 189, 191; *Chronicle of Higher Education* 189–90, 191

James, William 228

Journal of Politics 70

Kant, Immanuel 174, 183, 185, 201; *see also* neo-Kantianism

Kaplan, Abraham 26, 39, 77, 81; auton-omy of inquiry 27

Kateb, George 237

Keller, Helen 225, 228

Kelsen, Hans 75, 76, 79

Kimball, Roger 191

Kissinger, Henry 192

Koselleck, Reinhart 6, 131

Kripke, Saul 135, 222

Kuhn, Thomas 2, 4, 6, 51, 90, 166, 183, 217, 220, 239, 240, 243; concepts 135–6, 137, 139, 141, 142; paradigm 135, 224; relativism 221, 230; *The Structure of Scientific Revolutions* 135

Laclau, Ernesto 167

language: concepts 134, 135, 136–7; interpretation 136; language-games 137, 138; language, thought, and action 241–2; lexicon 135, 136; logical empiricism 19; meaning 143, 144–5;

Wittgenstein, Ludwig 150, 156, 218, 220, 221–2, 225–9, 241 (language-games 134, 144, 145, 149–50, 220, 223, 225, 226; philosophy may not interfere with the use of language 147, 194, 217)

Lasswell, Harold 39, 48, 71, 75, 77, 80, 81, 243

laws 41, 71, 168, 201, 203; deductive model 18, 21, 22, 23–4, 25–6, 27, 28, 30, 32; natural law 58, 72, 73, 75, 76, 173, 208; scientific explanation 25

'Leaving Everything as It Is: Political Inquiry after Wittgenstein' 6, 8, 214–33; Doing justice 229–32; Inter-pretation and the social sciences 221–2; 'Leaving everything as it is' 216–18; Methods and therapies 223–5; Mind, language and meaning 225–9; Philosophy and social science 215–16; Wittgenstein and philosophy 218–20; *see also* Wittgen-stein, Ludwig

Lentricchia, Frank 176–7, 194

liberalism 3, 239; alienation of political theory 41, 48, 49, 70; American poli-tical science 38, 48, 49, 72, 73, 74, 77, 83; behavioralism 42, 70; crisis of modernity 70, 74, 79, 82; critique of 82; decline of 74; German émigrés 38, 69, 71, 82, 239; liberal relativism 204; political theory 77, 81–2; Strauss, Leo 77, 203; totalitarianism 70, 74, 82; Weber, Max 209; *see also* 'American Political Science, Liberalism, and the Invention of Political Theory'; democracy

Lindblom, Charles 189

linguistics 90; linguistic action 101, 102; linguistic philosophy 241; linguistic turn 116, 133, 241–2; neo-Cartesian linguistics 227; theory of action 5, 102; *see also* language; theory of action; Wittgenstein, Ludwig

Lippincott, Benjamin 71, 76, 78

literary criticism 116, 118, 176–7, 220

Locke, John 79, 185, 226

logic of explanation 15; deductive model 22, 24, 29; philosophy of science 14, 17; scientific logic 17, 19; symmetry/asymmetry between natural and social science 14, 15, 19, 52; *see also* expla-nation; scientific explanation; social scientific inquiry

For Product Safety Concerns and Information please contact our EU
representative GPSR@taylorandfrancis.com
Taylor & Francis Verlag GmbH, Kaufingerstraße 24, 80331 München, Germany

www.ingramcontent.com/pod-product-compliance
Lightning Source LLC
Chambersburg PA
CBHW071849270326
41929CB00013B/2164